PENGUIN BOOKS
The Living Village

Paul Jennings was born in 1918 and educated at King
Henry VIII School, Coventry, and Douai School. While
still a lieutenant in the Royal Signals he began doing
freelance work for *Punch* and the *Spectator*. After working
for the Central Office of Information for a year he became
a copywriter for an advertising agency. In 1949 he joined
the *Observer* and till 1966 wrote his 'Oddly' pieces, which
were decanted over the years into twelve books from
Oddly Enough to *It's an Odd Thing But*. He has also
written two children's books *The Hopping Basket* and
The Great Jelly of London. His recreations are listed as
madrigal singing and thinking about writing another vast
serious book. He lives in Suffolk and is married with five
children.

PAUL JENNINGS

The Living Village

A report on rural life in England and Wales,
based on actual village scrapbooks

PENGUIN BOOKS

Penguin Books Ltd, Harmondsworth,
Middlesex, England
Penguin Books Australia Ltd, Ringwood,
Victoria, Australia

First published by Hodder & Stoughton 1968
Published in Penguin Books 1972
Copyright © Paul Jennings, 1968

Made and printed in Great Britain by
Cox & Wyman Ltd,
London, Reading and Fakenham
Set in Linotype Pilgrim

Contents

For, the time
Had never been when throes of mighty Nations
And the world's tumult unto me could yield
How far soe'er transported and possessed,
Full measure of content; but still I craved
An intermingling of distinct regards
And truths of individual sympathy
Nearer ourselves. Such often might be gleaned
From the great City, else it must have proved
To me a heart-depressing wilderness;
But much was wanting: therefore did I turn
To you, ye pathways, and ye lonely roads;
Sought you enriched with everything I prized,
With human kindnesses and simple joys.

– from *The Prelude*, Wordsworth

Foreword

At the present time there are 9,000 Women's Institutes in England, Wales, the Channel Islands and the Isle of Man. 461,000 women belong to these Institutes and every month – in an old village hall or a brand new school – they meet to hear perhaps a talk from the County Planning Department or the local Historical Society or to watch a demonstration on lampshade-making or yeast cookery. They paint in WI art classes, sing in WI choirs, walk their local footpaths, run WIs in mental hospitals, qualify as producers and judges, and arrange tours for community development students from abroad. Three thousand WI students every year attend their residential college near Oxford to take courses on anything from How to run a WI Market, to conversational French, or Byzantium.

Despite all this useful activity and enjoyable learning, their greatest contribution to country living undoubtedly arises from the fact that the WI in any village or country town is representative of the *whole* of that community. If you have just retired to some remote rural area, or if you have just married and moved to a new housing estate on the edge of a fast expanding village, WI membership immediately offers you a chance to become part of that community.

It was of course to record life in these communities as it was in 1965 – the Golden Jubilee of the WI movement – that in that year WIs were invited to make scrapbooks, records of village life.

Many of these books are very beautiful and in every one of the 2,600 books there is information of great interest to the social historian. Since then of course the problem has been to persuade the WIs who made them to hand them over to the care of the local librarians or archivists. So much can disappear in a Secretary's suitcase or the President's attic.

For this reason alone, and for a great many others, we were delighted when a writer as distinguished as Mr Paul Jennings was asked by the publishers to write a book, based largely on these scrapbooks, about the quality and the facts of village life today. *The Living Village* is, of course, bound to be of immense interest to any country dweller, but personally I think it will be of equal interest to the urban reader. Strangely enough, as people's lives in town and country become more alike, so too illusions about countrymen seem to increase; for instance, the view that every countryman resists *any* change, or that all countrymen know all about the local flora and fauna. Mr Jennings is much nearer the truth when he concludes that in the countryside today 'There is a powerful sense of living in two times, in an old and a new Britain, with an awareness, an agility in effortlessly leaping from one to the other, that makes one realize how hopelessly wrong all those famous "media" are about ordinary people living in villages.' In other words there is room in the countryside today for 'the nightingale on the television aerial'.

SHIRLEY ANGLESEY

Acknowledgements

I am most grateful to all those Women's Institute branches, and the many writers (mostly unsigned) who have provided the extracts from the WI Village Scrapbooks, all having given their permission to reprint; and I wish particularly to thank Mrs Molly Millard, of the National Federation of Women's Institutes, for her invaluable help in coordinating the cooperation I received at all levels – village, county and national. I am also grateful to my friend Mr Norman Scarfe for some informed advice and corrections, and to Mr Malcolm Barker and the Dalesman Publishing Co. Ltd for permission to reprint Mr Barker's article on quoits.

Acknowledgements for verse quotations are as follows: The Oxford University Press, for extract from *The Windhover* in *The Poems of Gerard Manley Hopkins*; the Estate of Mr T. S. Eliot and Messrs Faber & Faber for extracts from *Burnt Norton* and *The Waste Land* in *Collected Poems 1909–1962*; Mr M. B. Yeats and Macmillan & Co. Ltd for extract from *Among School Children* in *Collected Poems of W. B. Yeats*; Laurence Pollinger Ltd, the Estate of Mrs Frieda Lawrence and Heinemann Ltd for extract from *End of Another Home Holiday* in *The Complete Poems of D. H. Lawrence*; Miss D. E. Collins for extract from *The Bridge-builders* in *The Collected Poems of G. K. Chesterton*.

Books from which prose has been quoted are acknowledged as *Progress and Religion* by Christopher Dawson (Sheed & Ward); *Suffolk Dialect of the Twentieth Century*, by A. O. D. Claxton (N. Adlard Ltd, Ipswich) and *Collins Guide to English Churches* by John Betjeman.

Introduction

This book is simultaneously random and objective. It is random because ten writers, let alone one, could not do full justice to the wealth of material available, and there must therefore be an element of personal choice, indeed even of mere chance, in what has been selected.

My own travels and observations, and discussions ranging from casual pub talk to formal interviews, must inevitably provide one of the connecting threads; but the main matter of the book is provided by the people of villages in England and Wales, writing about themselves and their lives. In 1965 the National Federation of Women's Institutes, to celebrate the Golden Jubilee of their movement, organized a national competition for village scrapbooks. At this time when country life, like everything else, is under immense pressures of change, they felt that what was wanted was, nevertheless, 'not a history, but a picture of your village and its life in 1965, which you can hand down to future generations'. In their brief they also suggested four main headings: *The Place, The People, What they Do,* and *The Future.*

I sometimes wonder if London knew what they were starting. It was the Domesday Book all over again, only on an infinitely greater scale (a reviewer in a Northern paper, surveying the scrapbooks for Northumberland, calculated that if Newcastle had been researched on the same scale *per capita* of population the result would have been a volume a hundred and eighty feet thick). Scrapbook Committees were formed, subjects were allocated ('Mrs X, Religion and Wild

Life', it says in one of the contents lists); quite often the entire community was involved, from young children (the majestic list of wild flowers on pp. 54–5, for instance, originated with a boy of *ten*) to nonagenarians and their memories. Nor was it by any means a women's effort; there were plenty of contributions from men. Over 2,600 villages responded, with scrapbooks anything up to six inches thick. The one for Llanilar, the Wales and West prizewinner, is two thick volumes each about the size of N to Z of the *Shorter Oxford Dictionary*

Judging them must have been an impossible task, since there could be so many criteria. Some were most beautiful objects visually; lettered throughout in marvellous script, bound in vellum, or in covers with expert *petit-point* local views. One book contained specific instructions that it must only be handled by persons wearing gloves. Several, as I found to my cost, had a plastic, tight-fitting envelope over each page, easy to slip off and hell to get on again. Some excelled with the photography, some with illustrations by professional artists living in their village; there would be a page or a margin filled with tiny delicate paintings of birds or flowers done with the same love and unself-conscious skill (and often as anonymously) as the pictures in mediaeval missals. Other books might be quite scruffy physically but would contain fascinating and well-written information.

I travelled nearly 10,000 miles, from Northumberland to Cornwall, Caernarvonshire to Kent. Even so, some counties did not get visited at all, although I can certainly claim that all regions were covered; and of the 127 scrapbooks I looked at most were the two or three best of their county. As may easily be imagined, outline programmes had to be modified *en route*. I began my research roughly six months after the results had been announced, and already it was clear that there was some uncertainty about the ultimate future of these books, of which the value as records is obviously going to increase as the years go by. Should they be kept in the house of the local WI President or Secretary? In some villages, reckoning a fortnight's stay in the house of everyone who wanted to see it (and they're not books to rush through, especially if you know all the people concerned) the book still had three or four years just travelling round the village to do, before any decision was made about pressures from local universities or county archives.

On the other hand, many scrapbooks were in the county archives already. Sometimes I would go to a village on my list and find the book had just recently gone to the archives in a town I had passed through twenty miles back. The library would be due to close in an hour and a quarter. Should I risk it (maybe it would be one of those merely beautiful books, not much use to me; and almost certainly there would be nowhere to park) or should I go on to the next place? People would be away on holiday, which they seem to do at the drop of a hat and at the most extraordinary times in the country, or they would feel unhappy about letting me see it without a committee meeting. I didn't actually miss a single book I wanted to see, but it will be evident that at some point a compromise had to be made between seeing *more* scrapbooks and starting this actual work.

Some people who received me very kindly may perhaps be disappointed not to see their scrapbook mentioned; others, barely aware from a telephone call that I was studying their book in some library, will be surprised to see themselves so frequently quoted. To all I can only plead that this was how the material fitted into the form I have chosen. I could easily make another book from what was left out (let alone whatever untapped treasures lie in the other, unseen 2,480-odd scrapbooks).

This brings me to the second quality of this book; its objectiveness. I am convinced that even if some godlike writer (or maybe just young, and with private means, able to devote twenty unhurried years to the task) who had gone through every single scrapbook were to do what I have done, he would find, as I did, long before he got even to this mere 120, that *all* the writers quoted, indeed all the writers in all the scrapbooks, have an extraordinary amount in common. This is not to say that there are not individual differences in style; there are bits, particularly perhaps in the nature writing, which I personally think would stand out anywhere. But here they don't stand out. What unites the writers is more important than what separates them.

What is this quality? I would say it is an immediate, unarguable sense of *reality*. This is real life being reported on. But it is not 'reported' in the usual sense of that word. The writers are not thinking of anonymous readers of their local or any other Press. There is very little attempt at Fine Writing. Yet it is more formal and organized than the kind of writing they would put in letters to friends. I hope the reader will become, as I did, progressively aware of this unique, shared tone of voice, cumulatively irresistible as a witness of something that *is*. It is as though, for a moment, the conflicting voices which assail us from every side were magically silenced and these writers, speaking across time, really had subordinated everything to carrying the living human voices of ordinary village people across the silent gulf to *The Future*. That's what they are addressing; they are telling The Future how it is, now, in our village.

Contrasts

Villages are facts. No doubt the distinction between urban and rural life which is as old as our civilization is becoming blurred. No doubt the tendency to equate the country with pastoral, ideal bliss and innocence and the town with complexity and sin, which runs from Virgil's *Eclogues*, through *As You Like It* to the English novel from *Pamela* onwards (to the great disgust of Mr Angus Wilson), is weakened in an age when the entire population sees the same kind of television. No doubt today, also, our vision of 'the country' is blurred, made relative and dreamlike, by the speed with which we move through it in our cars and trains. Indeed there is a perpetual tension between the mobile, quasi-tourist life now available to most people and the real, rooted life that goes on in a house. *Teach us to sit still*, wrote T. S. Eliot. The motorist is so seduced by horizons; the wooded bank across the river, hazed by distance and English mist, looks so mysterious that any actual place where he makes the effort to stop, to get out, to *be* again, is something of an anticlimax. Yet here people live and have their roots. *Teach us to sit still*. Here, greeting each other in those strange but familiar pubs, mowing those evening lawns outside new bungalows, seeing their fair-haired children off to that new comprehensive, are those who either by birth or by choice still live, in mid-twentieth-century Britain, a village life.

It is a crucial and extraordinary time for such life. It does not need a moment's reflection to realize that we have come to the end of that stability (in the sense of *stabilitas* – which is one of the vows taken by a Benedictine monk – to stay in the same place and way of life) which still seems, to the harried urban motorist, to be the main rural virtue. There are families in every village with names that can be found in parish registers going back hundreds of years. In Smarden, Kent, they are Butt, Cooper, Buss, Cornes, Gurr, Judge, Morris, Offen and Ottaway. In East Bergholt, Suffolk, one may read in the recently published correspondence of the painter Constable that the gardener of his crusty and unwilling grandfather-in-law, the rector, Dr Rhudde, was named Peck, or that Constable's mother in 1811 'this day paid Jos. Aldous 10/6 for cases and strainers for you'. When I went to live there Miss Peck was our next-door neighbour, Mr Peck worked for Mr Aldous the builder on our house.

In every village there is a dwindling nucleus of people who, even if their families have not been there for centuries, certainly share memories of a childhood where they all went to the village school till the age of fourteen; it is only since the last war that such schools, where they have not closed, have become primaries for children up to eleven, who after that are taken by buses to secondary schools covering wide 'catchment areas' (the official term).

Prize Day (1965) was also the closing-down of Longhurst School. The Chairman of the Managers presented Miss E. Robinson, retiring headmistress, 21 years' service, with a silver tea service, purchased from subscriptions from Managers, PTA, children, old pupils and friends. A similar presentation was made to Miss E. Jackson, infant teacher for 31 years and one of our WI members. July 25th will long be remembered as a sad day for our community. It is the closing day for our school. Not a few tears were shed and heart-aches felt, but the teachers were faithful to the last. When the bus called for the last time Miss Robinson watched the bus out of sight, then turned back to a building no longer a school now that it was empty of children and their chatter. Another page in our village history turns. Our children will now be conveyed by bus to Pegswood Primary School. The old school building – who knows what fate may hold in store? It will never cease to hold a special place in the hearts of those of us who spent many happy days there. The original, a church school, was at the extreme north end of the village. Curtains formed division between classes. Pupils were mostly drawn from surrounding farms, and as their help was needed on the farm attendance was greater during the winter months. Sandwiches were brought for lunch, and tin bottles filled with tea to be heated on the stove. The Vicar examined the children regularly in religious knowledge. A certain headmaster, a stern disciplinarian, invariably stood behind the Vicar, stick in hand, reminding the class of things to come if they failed to answer correctly. All work was done on slates. A treat of Christmas pudding was achieved by all contributing ingredients. Mrs Jackson of the forge boiled it in her clothes pan and it was carried in triumph down the village to be quickly demolished. The school closed in 1934, and the children and teacher, Miss Jackson, were transferred to the new school at Longhurst.

(Ulgham, Northumberland)

But we are coming to the end of such population-stability, of the village as a closed community. Except for the eldest sons of farmers or owners of beautiful old houses, of what child born in a village can it be predicted that he will die in it? In most villages now there are three distinct areas; the old village, the council estate, and the residential estate (very often post-war). There may be several of the latter two. There may be some small local industry, but the majority of the people will commute to the nearest town to work. Nevertheless, in spite of this blurring of distinction, the urge to live 'in the country' does not represent simply an urban invasion. It is not as simple as that.

In one sense it is a return. In past ages, possibly because a thousand years free of invasion left us free to get on with it in a slow, uninterrupted, organic way, we built up the most man-made rural landscape in the world. The unique English hedges, which any other country would have planted with an effect of arid geometry, followed illogical but natural shapes, and enclosed fields of all kinds of sizes – with, incidentally, all kinds of names

Fanny Field	Ninepenny Piece
Crabmills	Archers Close
Flagon Flats	Broad Dyke
Ruddings	Wind Cover
Crook Shaws	Fair Points
Wildermires	Jinhodgson
	Nutbins

(Crayke, Yorks.)

Burial Ground	Rushes	Itchy Field
Tavern Field	The Bogs	Sally Frost
Magpie	Top Hat	
Stripe	Axletree	

(Willoughby, Lincs.)

Shatter Oak	Good Water
Tainted	Crumpled Horns
Gallows	Beggar's Bridge
Rope	North America
Little Wild Carrots	Crooked Tom
Oyster Shell	Long John
Hawk's Eyes	Oven
Germany	Snug Horn
Snail Thorne	Fight Field

The last commemorates a prize fight which took place there in 1859 between the champion Tom Sayers and Bill Benjamin. A thousand spectators came from London by train to where the new Dover Railway ended at that time.

(Smarden, Kent)

The houses and churches of local material (limestone in the limestone belt that runs from Gloucestershire to the Wash, flint in stoneless East Anglia, sandstone in the west Midlands) *grew*, almost literally. No doubt it is irritating to those concerned with Britain's technological prestige for the country to be represented abroad, for tourist purposes, as a park full of milkmaids and old codgers outside thatched pubs. But this humanized countryside, so intricately partitioned into so many areas immediately, visually evoking a rich regional past, is the thing that first strikes the visitor – or the native too, if he keeps his eyes open.

Where, in France, or Germany, or anywhere else for that matter, would it be possible to see in a day's driving such sharply-defined and logical local cultures of architecture, materials and landscaping, in such diversity and proximity yet all somehow sharing a national quality? It is alleged that the drivers of coaches taking American tourists to areas such as the Vale of Evesham in Spring go up and down, doubling on their tracks, making them seem bigger than they are. But really there is no need for this. Who could believe, when actually in the Fens, that they do not go on for hundreds of miles? How impossible it is, at Chatsworth, where misty hills form a backdrop to the superb house in its wooded valley, to think of Sheffield fifteen miles away! How inviolate the Lake District is, even now!

This is partly due to geographical, sometimes to merely geological good fortune. All the same, you have only to look at a Cotswold stone village, a planted coppice on a Berkshire hill, the siting of Haworth Parsonage (or of Stonehenge, for

19

that matter), to see how deeply integrated the human co-operation has been.

Now, the main part of all this was of course achieved before the Industrial Revolution. When this began there was as clear-cut and traditional a distinction between town and country in this as in any other land. After it, our eyes were on wider horizons than those of our own shires; we knew palm and pine, as well as oak, we had a world-consciousness, and the beating heart of it was felt to be in the busy, grimy, roaring, new industrial cities. Of all European countries Britain became the one most removed from any lingering peasant tradition (even if it was also the one in which everyone, never mind land shortage, insisted on a house with garden both in front and behind, both of them attended with passionate care).

Now we are no longer the nerve-centre of an Empire. Although by our recent history we have acquired (what in any case all must have now that the world is McLuhan's electronic village) a world-consciousness, that certainly has not contracted with that Empire, the acreage that we can, as it were, take for granted *has* contracted. Suddenly millions of us look at our own countryside, from which the whole vast adventure began, and see it with a new and contemporary eye. What we see is a contrast very much more complex than the old urban-rural one. It is a contrast in simultaneities, a perpetual confrontation between the surprising amount of that unique man-made landscape that has survived (pylons and all) and the facts of modern, mobile, industrial civilization.

A lot of this country now has more population to the acre than India. Except in certain obviously remote or National-Park areas, therefore, there is something faintly surprising about finding what one might call pure villages, set in pure fields; indeed, throughout much of the country one may get a fleeting, generalized impression that nothing has changed except for a few television aerials. Driving to Kettering from Huntingdon, up one of those roads that sometimes are idyllically empty, sometimes have occurred to half the heavy lorry drivers in the country as a more interesting route than the motorways, one passes the village of Ellington; a spire above snug trees, a sharp edge of red brick falling like a small cliff into a froth of orchard – and then The Country (although no doubt there's a sprawling new bit there too, somewhere off the road). There are thousands such. All the same, the essential, first characteristic of our countryside, now that so many of us are living in it, is not the urban-rural contrast but the traditional-modern one.

Some villages are almost untouched, some have new commuter communities, some are almost swallowed up by neighbouring towns. But the new, increasingly mobile population shares with its ancestors an instinct for doing things empirically, one and one. It is only necessary to look out of the train window at the little strips of garden reaching to the bottom of the embankment to see, in the vast majority, living examples of an instinct for moulding and subdividing the land which has survived a century and a half of urbanization. Oblivious of the trains hurtling past, of the lack of space and of real privacy, the owners trim the edges of their tiny lawns, carefully tie bits of paper to miles of cotton to keep birds away from seedlings, burn neat bonfires, lay crazy paving in straight lines or in wild baroque sweeps curving through all of ten yards, build tiny fountains and ponds, lean-to conservatories for tomatoes and chrysanthemums, and everywhere trellis arches and pergolas for roses.

Modern mobility has made it possible for quite a lot of those with a buried desire to live in the country to disinter that desire and act on it. Inevitably, as more of them do it there is less country for them to go to. They have brought their cars and their industries with them; but perhaps in no other country is it so possible by subtle delimitations, sub-divisions, hedges, *culs-de-sac*, golf links, bits of common land, pubs, gardens, unadopted roads, preservation societies and a thousand customs grafted on to an already uniquely man-made landscape, still to observe a distinction some-times in quite un-rural looking areas, between a town and a country consciousness. The latter will speak for itself in this book; but first let us look at some examples of this con-tinuing shock of contrast between the ever-spreading, homo-geneous industrial culture and the highly particularized, thousand-year-old agrarian tradition of the countryside – a contrast which is at once the immediate first impression and the ever-present background.

It is only fifty-seven miles from Carlisle to Newcastle; how vulnerable it seems – as though a determined paratroop attack could quite easily seal off Scotland from England! As Churchill remarked, 'Some chicken! Some neck!' Never-theless to drive along this busy road, through this lonely country, is to experience the strange silence of the Fells, to forget the worldscapes of the twentieth century, to be re-minded by a name such as *Armstrong* over a shop of the border raiders – and to keep coming across Hadrian's Wall.

In the village of *Gilsland* the Wall actually goes through part of the rectory garden. On a calm, cold, cloudless April evening I was reading the Gilsland scrapbook. Out of the window I could see the Roman encampment in the flat even-ing sunlight. I had just got to this bit:

Gilsland Convalescent Home for Miners was once Gilsland Spa Hotel. Sir Walter Scott proposed to Miss Charpentier, a young French lady, in the grounds of the hotel, and the 'Pop-ping Stones', where he popped the question, are the favourite attraction of the Home. Tradition still lingers, for in recent years many ardent Romeos have followed Sir Walter's example and popped the question while they have been on holiday. 'Mostly they are middle-aged, elderly widowers, spinsters and widows,' says warden of the Home, Mr Whitehead. Mr Whitehead believes in encouraging romance. What Sir Walter did at Gilsland in the eighteenth century is today being repeated in the lives of many lonely middle-aged people. Mr Whitehead tries to mix the sexes together as much as possible and says he would never dream of putting six women together at the same table. Last week he had three widows and three retired miners sharing the same table. It is perhaps the only convalescent home in the country to have a licensed bar. Each year the Home takes 400 Northumberland miners and convalescents recommended by cooperative societies, some of whom go to the home on free or aided holiday. Foreign girls often go to work at the Home, and recently a Finnish girl met her husband there.

Suddenly there was a most extraordinary belching, reverberating roar, like a continuous but somehow controlled clap of thunder. Just northwards, over that cold purple-green fellside, haunted not merely by Scott but by the Romans, they had been test-firing the Blue Streak rocket engine. Or test-firing *something*, at the Spadeadam Rocket Research Establishment. On my map the area, coloured as for 1–2,000 feet, is known by the chilly title of Spadeadam *Waste*. And in red print, DANGER ZONE.

Practically the next item in the Gilsland scrapbook is a letter from a girl married to a rocket technician now in Woomera, Australia:

Woomera being a closed town means that only people employed by WRE (Weapons Research Establishment) are permitted to live in this town. We are a very modern town with a very new theatre, Olympic-size swimming pool and a second in

23

construction. We have three lovely churches; St Barbara's Church of England, St Michael's Catholic, and the United, which embraces all the other faiths in existence in Woomera. We have a very mixed background; predominating are the English, Italians and Scots coming a close second, and a good sprinkling of many other races, not forgetting the 'dinkum Aussies'. There are lots of people here from Carlisle, or near Carlisle, all directly connected with ELDO. These men have been sent out by their firms to take part in certain projects all closely connected with the launching. I saw each stage of the Blue Streak launching. A more wonderful sight one couldn't see. That breathless silence as the count-down starts until blast-off, then the slow rising of the great rocket, looking like gold as it soars into the sun. We all breathe a sigh of pride and relief when we see another successful launching. We feel greatly privileged to be able to see at first hand the results of the work and brains of all these clever workmen. Many of us have a nostalgic feeling when we hear a letter from England being read. We miss terribly the lovely leafy lanes and the sweet-smelling wild flowers, the songs of the birds or the feeling of snow on our faces, especially when the temperature is over 100 degrees, which it very often is when the snow is falling in England. Woomera has been likened to an oasis in the desert. I think it is just that, more especially when we get a hot north wind blowing at about 40 m.p.h. bringing all the sands from the Simpson Desert.

Bransgore is one of those villages on the edge of the New Forest where long strips of housing, 1930s-style, the windows seeming to have a lot of woodwork, have sprung up on the narrow roads skirting meadows at the edge of the forest; as its book says it has

a great variety of dwellings, from old cottages to modern bungalows, houses of all shapes and sizes and styles, and the village of today shows only too clearly the result of haphazard or completely lacking planning. The gardens of the newer dwellings are smaller, reflecting the increasing scarcity of good building land, the difficulty of obtaining labour, and the larger proportion of retired people who do not want the hard work entailed in a large garden.

There is a sense of furious building going on behind long hedges, and of a spectrum that runs from Victorian mansions (now subdivided) to caravans and Calor Gas cooking. There is an RAF estate, with its own sewage and drainage system. There was a petition from the residents of Furzey Whistlers, a *cul-de-sac* off the Burleigh Road, against a change of name to Cuckoo Close. One lady lives in

a permanent residential caravan 34 feet long. Sitting-room, well-fitted kitchen and bedroom, ten windows and three skylights. Separate electric supply, water from main by underground pipe, electric fire and radiators, water heater, Calor gas cooker. 'I find caravan life very pleasant. The advantages are many; not much housework, compact comfort, plenty of light and ample cupboards, enabling one to keep tidy in essential and limited space, and leaving time for the pleasures of life, in my case gardening, motoring, wine-making, embroidery, reading etc. and even knitting the odd blanket.'

There is, on the fringe of the forest, a holiday caravan site to which come people

from all parts of the British Isles. We even had a Dutch dermatologist last year. The solitude attracts people to this site, and the surrounding trees are much appreciated. The caravanners come from all walks of life; Harwell scientists, doctors, national newspaper editors, photographers, ornithologists, international opera stars with Rolls-Royces, dustmen, coal miners, etc.

(Surely there was only one international opera star with a Rolls-Royce at any one time?)

A blacksmith comes round, with a portable forge (mostly

25

for the ponies of little girls). One large farm disposes of the following equipment:

7 Fordson tractors, 2 three-furrow reversible Ransome ploughs, 1 two-furrow Bamford plough, 1 four-furrow conventional Ransome plough, 1 three-furrow conventional Ransome plough, 2 Ransome trailed cultivators, 2 Ransome mounted cultivators, 1 spring tine cultivator, 2 New Holland balers, 2 Ransome combines, 1 potato planter, 2 potato diggers, 1 dung spreader, 2 elevators, 2 forage harvesters (one used for chopping up potato tops), 1 flail mower, 2 conventional mowers, 1 corn drill, 1 drill, 2 sets of discs, 2 sets of Cambridge ring rollers, 1 sprayer, 2 granular fertilizer spreaders, 2 tedders, 2 side rakes, 1 grass broadcaster, 4 two-wheel tip-up trailers with corn and silage sides, 4 four-wheel trailers, 4 two-wheel trailers, 2 lorries (one tip-up), 1 continuous drier, 1 cleaner, 5 irrigation pumps, 150 irrigation pipes, 1 mill/mixer (1 ton capacity), 1 roller mill, 4 grain augers, 2 mounted weeders, 2 toppers to cut off grazed grass to an even height, 1 rotavator, 1 front-loader (grain and ordinary buckets), 3 buck rakes, 1 steerage hoe, 2 sets zig-zag drags, 2 chain harrows.

One 5-acre field on this farm has 14 land-drains dating from the eighteenth century and all working perfectly.

The only important common right nowadays is *Common of Pasture*, which is attached to a considerable amount of land in Bransgore. People who occupy these lands are New Forest Commoners. They have the right to pasture ponies, horses, cattle and donkeys on the Forest throughout the year, on payment of a small fee, collected by the Agisters, who mark the animals by clipping their tails by way of a receipt. As the beauty of the Forest is largely maintained by the grazing of cattle and ponies, and it tends, in the opinion of the Verderers and the Forestry Commissioners, to be under-grazed, non-commoners may put out animals on payment of a slightly larger fee. Although the 'marking fees' are low, there are offsetting drawbacks to running animals on the Forest. They are liable to injuries from tins and broken glass left by picnickers, they may wander miles from where they are put out and take weeks or even months to find, and they may be killed by cars. If not enough pigs are put out at 'pannage' time ponies may be poisoned by eating too many acorns. Each of the Agisters has his own tail mark. Ray Stickland of Lynwood is responsible for animals in our part of the forest. His tail mark is 'one cut out of the offside' (of the tail).

Holly and old gorse give food and snug quarters for ponies in bad weather. In snowstorms they go to bed in such a larder and wait for milder days, warm and well fed in their 'mares' nests'.

No doubt Verderers and Agisters were among those who looked up at the maiden flight of the BAC 111 from Hurn Airport nearby, where some Bransgore people go to work.

*

It is impossible to drive over the North Yorkshire moors without seeing, from some horizon, the globes of the Fylingdales Early Warning Radar system; dangerously innocent, like giants' golf balls, mysterious shapes from the next century, looming through a pearly mist. As a matter of fact they are on Lockton High Moor, in the next parish to *Fylingdales*, which does not care to give them its name. A scrapbook poet writes

> The world is under a misapprehension
> And grave may be the outcome if it fails
> To be informed by timely intervention
> That Lockton High Moor isn't Fylingdales.
>
> Who knows what cataclysmic emanation
> May strike the world, and all that it entails
> Because some Early Warning radiation
> Was misdirected into Fylingdales?
>
> Therefore I beg you, sir, to raise the matter
> And rouse the countryside to agitate

27

And Fylingdales, especially, should natter
With Lockton Moor before it is too late.

And as for us, although we're not si clever
And maybe haven't travelled varry far
And dean't set up to knaw a vast – however,
At t'varry least we do knaw where we are!

A technical account by an American officer (who has now retired to Robin Hood's Bay) is immediately preceded by a note about deep ploughing and its ability to pierce the hitherto impermeable top layer, the 'moor pan', so that experimental patches of barley and corn may now be seen. Then:

Fylingdales is strictly a Royal Air Force station. While Radio Corporation of America GB personnel outnumber those of the Royal Air Force by about six to one, RCA (GB) is responsible for operation and maintenance by contract to Air Ministry, working under the auspices of the Royal Air Force. A small contingent of less than 40 US Air Force personnel is stationed at Fylingdales to respond to inquiries by the North America Air Defence Command in the United States, to operate communications strictly peculiar to USAF requirements, and to assist in the acquisition of technical spare parts supplied from the United States. Fylingdales has digital communication with Royal Air Force Fighter Command, Bomber Command and Air Ministry. In these locations as well as similar ones in the United States displays are automatically activated by the computer and communications converters to show alarm or threat levels. Automaticity is so complete that human intervention is necessary only for those rare incidents for which the computer is not programmed.

We have come a long way, although in what direction is not quite certain, since radar was invented in these islands, and indeed saved them. But here is the contrast – the strange brooding shapes, the communications converters clicking (or whatever they do) God knows what messages, within sight of a church with a three-decker pulpit and containing many faded garlands hanging from the ceiling of the chancel, because of a custom from 1760 to 1869 of carrying garlands at the funeral of a maiden. Within sight, too, of this:

The Court Leet of the Manor of Fyling, a survival of the Manor Courts which dispensed justice long before our present judiciary system came into being, has been held at least once every year since probably before Norman times. In the past it had criminal jurisdiction, with power to hang, but it meets today only 'to receive rents and fines in respect of encroachments in the Manor of Fyling'. As long as anyone can remember its venue has been the Robin Hood's Bay Hotel, but this year the new landlord refused to entertain the Court, and on December 7th 1965 it assembled at the Victoria Hotel. The Court consists of 17 officials, namely the Seneschal or Steward, Mr Peter M. White, who represents the Lady of the Manor and acts as judge; the Bailiff, who collects the fines; a Moorsman Pinder, who rounds up straying animals, 12 jurors and 2 Affearers, whose job it is to 'well and truly tax, assess and affear such presentments as shall be made to the Court without fear or favour, affection, hatred or malice'. A Foreman is selected by the jurors, and all are sworn in by the Seneschal, different oaths being taken by different officers.

The office of Moorsman Pinder, which has been vacant this year, has been in the same family for over a hundred years. The Moorsman, who retired at the end of 1964, Mr F. M. Tindall, succeeded his father, Mr S. O. Tindall, who followed *his* father, Mr R. F. Tindall, and before him Mr John Tunstall, his father-in-law, held the office. Mr John Tunstall was the last Moorsman to impound straying sheep in the pinfold at Raw. The total revenue from rents and fines imposed by the Court increases as more encroachments take place, but many fines are very small indeed. The Old School at Thorpe pays a penny a year for a small strip of land in the playground. This year Mr Ernest Atkinson delivered on foot the notices of fines due. The year before, the notices came by post, in some cases costing a 3d stamp for a 1d or 2d fine. Fines may be sent by post, but most people like to attend the Court and present their fines personally. Some of the money collected provides a dinner for the members of the Court Leet on the day the Court is held.

There follow three documents.

Dinner Menu, Court Leet 1965.
Vegetable Soup
Fillet of Plaice and Lemon
Roast Pork, Apple Sauce and Stuffing
Roast and Mashed Potatoes, Sliced Beans and Carrots
Christmas Pudding, Rum Sauce
Cheese and Biscuits
Coffee.

Manor in the County of York, to wit, Fyling. You are hereby summoned and required personally to be and appear at the Victoria Hotel, of Fyling, on Tuesday, on the seventh day of December by Twelve O'clock in the Forenoon of the same day, then and there to serve as a juror at the Court Leet with a view of Frank Pledge and Court Baron of Miss Monica Lucy Ann Strickland, Lady of the said Manor, and this you are in no wise to omit, as you will answer the same at your peril. Dated this nineteenth day of November in the Year of Our Lord 1965, by Warrant from the Steward, Ernest Atkinson, Bailiff of the said Manor.

Manor of Fyling

Sir,

I shall attend at the Victoria Hotel, Robin Hood's Bay, on Tuesday December 7th 1965 at 10 o'clock in the morning to receive the rents and fines payable in respect of encroachments in the Manor of Fyling. The undermentioned sums appear to be payable by you, and if not paid at the time above named your

encroachments will be abated. By Order of Miss M. A. Strickland Lady of the Manor, her Agent, P. M. White.

Rent or Fine 3d
Arrears .... —
Total 3d
Bring this notice with you.

*

St Erth is a village near enough to Penzance for you to feel
sea on both sides, England coming to a point (after Penzance,
a village called Drift; lots of Edwardian woodwork porches,
a lacy domestic look. JACKSON, GROCER, BUTCHER. THE
LAST STORE IN ENGLAND. *The Last Inn, 100 Yards.* Sea
light, distant buildings profiled on open landscape. *Sea View,
Vacancies. Caravans to Let.* A lot of aerials. Turf, wind,
gulls, breakers far below. Land's End. A car park facing America). St Erth was a Celtic saint, said to have come from
Ireland on a floating millstone. In the scrapbook his feast in
October is thus remembered:

I remember the days when our Feast was something to look
forward to, not just like today with only the Pigeon Shoot.
There used to be Pigeon Shoot, Sheaf Pitching, Donkey-shay
Riding, also Bareback Donkey Riding, Slow Push-bike Riding,
also Walk, Run and Ride with Pushbikes. In those days we had a
brass band in the village, which was used on festive occasions,
especially with musical chairs. As daybreak came on the
Monday morning stallholders would come from many places
around and put up their stalls in the streets to sell their sweets
and wares, which would go on till midnight. People used to
come from miles round to join in all the fun. There would be
two concerts on that evening, one in the chapel school and one
in the church hall. If you weren't early you didn't get a seat, the
room would be full to capacity. There would be as many as
three or four policemen on duty in the village on this festive
occasion to keep law and order, and they were respected in

31

those days. All this has died away since the Second World War.

The St Erth book begins thus:

Our village today is passing through a transitory stage in its history, brought about by the process of modernization ... many old cottages and properties standing derelict and decaying are among the last links with the old village. They stand as witnesses to generations who were acquainted with hardship, struggles, poverty and disease, large families and small incomes. They experienced, of course, times of happiness of a type, and they had their own peculiar interests and amusements. Miners and farm labourers chiefly inhabited these cottages, and many found their way into the far corners of the world when the mining activities diminished. Perhaps it is only fitting that with the advent of better days these memorials to the past should pass away, for they await the hammer of the demolition gang. Several of the last inhabitants of these cottages are now accommodated in the two council estates.

Some diversions at St Erth owe nothing to the twentieth century:

Something really exciting happened this month, when my son, and his friend, both keen bird-watchers and members of the Cornwall Naturalist Trust, spotted an unfamiliar bird in a flooded field near the river. The identification showed it could be only one thing – a STILT!

Others owe quite a lot:

The helicopters from Culdrose Naval Station come once a month and practise landing in a clearing in the woods near the railway station. They use it because the trees and the various buildings in the locality make it tricky and they have to learn to handle these conditions. Lots of people come and watch these fascinating machines manoeuvring in the confined space between the trees. They have rescued so many people from the cliffs and sea that although the noise is very distracting we willingly put up with it for a few hours each month. They usually come in flights of three and hover about the station. Every now and then they will circle over the village at rooftop level, which is a bit disturbing when one is doing a bit of sunbathing.

*

Obviously a great deal less 'country life' in the conventional sense is possible in a village like *Bramcote*. Today if you drive along the five miles of dual carriageway from Nottingham, with houses everywhere the eye can see (although there is a vague vestigial sense of a climbing, wooded hill on your right) you would not at first think you were in a village at all; merely a suburb.

With its population of 6,000, for all practical purposes it now *is* a suburb. It *is* true that

in the past ten or twelve years rapid housing development in and around Bramcote has swallowed up the hills and fields which were formerly covered with couch-grass, wild flowers, gorse and the lovely yellow broom which thrived on the sandy soil of the district, and gave it its name. Most of the existing trees have been cleared, but a few oaks, sycamores and hawthorns still remain, and some residents have carefully preserved the native wild broom in their now well-ordered gardens. In the early days of development the scurrying rabbit could still be seen on the unmade roads, and one could watch the white mist creeping over the rough grass on the hills. Many early residents must have watched the numerous wild birds and wondered how long the wild life would be able to survive amongst the new red brick buildings, and when they would leave for pastures new. Did the soaring skylark leave first, or was it the old owl? Did the swallow and the house-martin go elsewhere to find the mud so badly needed to build their nests? Did the willow-warbler and the chiff-chaff become afraid, and the strutting wagtail panic?

Why didn't the little wren, the blue-tit, the robin and the hovering sparrow-hawk remain, why were the finch and the linnet so anxious to leave, and even the blackbird and thrush prepare to visit us only in the depths of winter, driven by unbearable hunger? Gone were the fieldfare, the magpie and the jackdaw from the new house, the bleak garden. It was sad to see the birds go, but this was progress. More houses were built, and with the passing of the years even mellowed a little. Gardens were cultivated and hedges were grown. Silver birch and other ornamental trees flourished. Miniature orchards sprang up and flowering shrubs graced the gardens. Soon the ever-present house-sparrows joined with the tree sparrow in the new, almost instant greenery. The dainty hedge-sparrow ventured back to pick the insects from the cushions of rockery plants, and back came the blackbird to claim the worms turned up by the spade and to build his nest in the cover provided by the new-grown hedge or tree.

Although the recent demolition of the blacksmith's cottage could not be prevented,

old cottages still remaining are being snapped up by people who have revolted against the uniformity of modern estates and have chosen to live in these less convenient but more individual homes. Gradually Town Street and the top of Cow Lane are taking on a more cared-for appearance as the new owners modernize the interiors of their homes and refurbish the exteriors with whitewash, paint and wrought iron. The large houses of the eighteenth and nineteenth centuries are in general (in 1965) in good order, but in most cases their functions have changed, and only one or two are still private homes. The village was built compactly on its hill, and has preserved the nucleus of the old village, together with its charm.

Because the churches, chapel, memorial hall and church schools are here, newcomers on the estates have been drawn to the centre of village life and have become an extension of village life rather than isolated communities.

The Grange, a well cared-for Georgian house, once the home of Henry Enfield, a prosperous solicitor of 1864, in 1965 was used by the British Sugar Corporation as a research laboratory in conjunction with the sugar-beet factory at Colwick. *The White House* at the top of Town Street, the Victorian home of the Pearson family until 1958, when Colonel Pearson died and the house was sold to the University of Nottingham, is now a hostel for the male students and has been renamed *Bramcote House*. *Broomhill Terrace* is the last example of a terrace of weavers' houses left in the village. The three-storied cottages housed the framework knitters of the early nineteenth century. The knitters worked on the top storey of the cottage, where the windows had been made as large as possible to admit the maximum light. But the stockeners, seamers, setters-up and other allied craftsmen and women had either to follow their trade in the new factories which were starting up in the neighbouring towns or turn to coal mining in the Trowell pits.

Bramcote Hills Park is the site for a school campus of a particularly comprehensive and spacious kind

... modern post-war buildings which have had a considerable impact on village life quite apart from day-school activities. The scope for adult education has been widened, particularly with the woodwork and metalwork facilities available. The excellent halls and stage equipment have enriched the social life of Bramcote. The grammar school, opened in September 1957, [by 1965 had] some 85 former pupils following degree courses at 18 universities.

It may of course be questioned whether this is rural life at all. Certainly it is at the far urban end of the spectrum of non-city life in Britain today. But even the dual-carriageway road (which now carries heavy traffic to the nearby M1 motorway), looking just like any other road out of a large city, with its anti-pedestrian railings, mud-sprayed verges, concrete lamp-standards dispensing orange light at night, can be looked at as from a village, still:

A link with Bramcote's agricultural past disappeared when the blacksmith's cottage was bulldozed to make way for the traffic island. Less than ten years ago the blacksmith was shoeing horses, mainly for riding schools, at his forge. Day and night a continuous stream of heavy traffic passes through Bramcote along the road we know as the A52. As long ago as 1759 this stretch of road was important enough to be made into a turnpike road . . . we are used to our own little bit of it, but although we see the daily two-way flow of traffic we seldom visualize the whole road, stretching almost due east to west across England. It can be traced westwards as far as Nantwich in Cheshire, and eastwards to Boston, where it then follows the coastline northwards to Skegness and Mablethorpe. Before the days of refrigeration was this a necessary link between the salt mines of Cheshire and the east coast fishing industry? Certainly, timber seen on the dockside at Boston is often seen on lorries lying on their side by the great roundabout in Bramcote.

In fact, it is only necessary to look just beneath the surface to see that all the taken-for-granted motoring in the world cannot quite destroy the mystery of roads, connecting far-off, one and one places; in our own familiar country but sounding as strange as Vladivostok. *Nantwich, Boston*, even *Skegness* . . .

Forges may be bulldozed and Georgian houses become sugar laboratories and well-lit schools grow among trees, but a village can preserve not only a historical identity but a prehistoric, indeed a geological one:

Standing high and dry on our Bunter Sandstone foundations we have beneath our feet tangible evidence that great seas once engulfed our land. Wherever weathering has eroded a hilltop down to its sandstone backbone, water draining down the slope after heavy rainfall will wash cleanly over a sandy bed, and where drainage pipes carry storm water through the new wall surrounding Bramcote Hills Park mounds of pure sand are deposited on the pavements beneath, recognizable to any child as the stuff he builds castles with on the Lincolnshire beaches 75 miles away. Tons of sand are quarried in Bramcote, and much of it goes to the foundries to mould the tools of industrial Britain. The evidence of the Bunter Pebble Beds lies very clearly over everyone's gardens. Every planting time finds loads of sea-smooth pebbles removed from the seed-beds, and the first heavy rainfall exposes another layer to view.

It is perhaps not surprising, therefore, that Bramcote objected fiercely when the Boundaries Commission recommended that four such districts be incorporated in the city of Nottingham. Its scrapbook ends with press cuttings of protest –

Young men from Arnold and Stapleford are to take part in a twenty-four hours' 'freedom run' to Whitehall . . .

There was an inquiry, and they won. The cutting bears the splendid headline MINISTER THROWS OUT CITY.

*

. . . both doctors also have Ansaphones. It will also take a message from the caller, should he wish to leave one. The first time this machine was in use the message recorded was 'O my gor, whatever next!', and on another occasion the voice said 'but doctor, how can you be out, I can hear you speaking to me right now!'

(*Grampound, Cornwall*)

*

From the scrapbook of *Dunsop Bridge*, a perfect, grey stone, unspoiled village set where road meets clear stream under great sweeping fells and moors, and to open a window in the evening is to hear sheep and rushing water:

Discussion on results of major exercise. Exhibition of plots of very successful triangulation of simulated nuclear burst and progress of radioactive fallout. Announcement that ROC considered so important that Corps would hardly be affected by Government defence cuts. Demonstration of contamination meter and detection of mild radioactive samples distributed amongst members. Meeting followed by hot-pot supper and social evening.

*

Perhaps it is not necessary to have Celtic blood to have an obscure sense of homecoming, of something lost being found again, when one finds oneself, in western river valleys or far Atlantic hills, among the unmechanical courtesies of the Welsh or the Irish. Successive invaders into the fat lowlands of western Europe have coalesced into conglomerations with urban centres that have long since overlaid earlier simplicities. But paradoxical though it may sound at first, there is a sense in which Wales is more English than England – or, if that is too much for them to take, although it is meant as a compliment, more western than the West.

Christopher Dawson, in *Progress and Religion*, says 'his [Le Play's in *Les Ouvriers Européens*] attention was especially directed to the primary nature-occupations which are the foundations of all material culture. These fundamental types are six in number; first the hunters and food-gatherers, secondly the pastoral peoples, thirdly the fishermen of the sea coasts, fourthly the agriculturalists, fifthly the foresters, and sixthly the miners. Not only does each of these types possess its appropriate geographical environment, so that we have in Europe the Samoyede hunters of the Northern tundras, the Tartar nomads of the Eastern steppes, and the fishermen of the Western sea coast, but each of them is also represented in any typical civilized natural region. As has been shown by Professor Geddes and Mr Victor Branford, who have done so much to introduce and extend the methods of Le Play in this country, every river valley contains, at least potentially and as it were in section, every type of natural occupation, from the shepherd and the miner in the hills, through the woodmen of the uplands to the lowland farmers and the fishermen of the coast.'

Wales is *all* river valleys, and in an afternoon's driving one can see all these cultures, more sharply differentiated and closely juxtaposed than in England. And in addition there is a curiously symbolic quality about everything – a house seems more a house, a village seems more a village, under the shadow of those mountains. (Soon after one enters Wales by the road from Whitchurch a signpost offers the wonderful, eternal choice: HOPE or MOLD. Or, in the village of Kilcain, set in a wide valley, a hundred cars outside a chapel for a Sunday evening *cymanfa ganu*, a sort of hymn-and-music convention, one may opt either for PANT-WYNMYR, whatever that is, or LOGGERHEADS).

In a day one may pass from the North Wales familiar to the tourist, through the slate valleys and down to the rich farmlands of Pembrokeshire (early flowers and potatoes, sunniest area of Britain) and Carmarthenshire. The road from Aberystwyth to Carmarthen seems to run through one long private valley. The roughcast or concrete-looking houses all along it, with their square stone door and window-frames, have almost a French appearance – and yet there is something of Ireland here too. You have the feeling that they know each other for miles up and down the road. There are couples strolling about, two or three miles from a village, people sitting on bridge parapets and chatting in the evening. There seem to be a lot of piles of logs. Yet in an hour or so one can be whizzing along the motorway that curves at chimney level round Port Talbot, aware of tank farms and new-looking installations along the coastline which serves the old mining and industrial valleys now so intricately interwoven with farming country, so that the scene changes from ridge to ridge:

Twice a day, morning and evening, there is a decrease in the rate at which the traffic is moving, and it is especially noticeable in the evening when motorists travelling homeward after their day's work, plus a considerable number of passengers who are likewise longing to get home gradually come to a standstill. There is no policeman on duty, no traffic signals, and no road-man signalling his orders because road-works are ahead. What is it that brings about this subtle change? Ah, the cows! A herd of Friesians are ambling their way along from their pasture ground at one end of the village, near the East Glamorgan Hospital, to the farm near the electricity Central Control Station in the middle of the village. The cows are guided by the farmer, trapped and guarded by his dog, but they show no concern for the impatient motorist. They move from one side of the road to the other as it suits them. They come to the crossroads. They know where to turn. Haven't they done so for many a year? Now the traffic coming towards them must wait until the last cow has gone. Are they conscious of the busy highway along which they tread? I think not. The modern houses, the Old Folks' Home, the post office, the supermarket, the hotel, the adjoining betting shop, the spacious car park of the Control Station – they are no different from the allotments, the fields and the hedgerows. There is one way to the farm and they know it. Once they have gone through the gate the traffic moves again. The march of progress demands that the traffic must be kept moving, but the cows, bless them, are steadfastly maintaining the last vestige of life in a rural community.

(*Church Village, Glam.*)

The same sort of distance westwards instead of eastwards would have brought one to the end of the Pembrokeshire peninsula – an English-speaking region where their dialect words look as much Norman or Norse as Welsh (*drang*, narrow passage; *burgage*, a small field; *skaddly*, grasping; *stivvle*, to freeze; *crut*, boy; *mitchin'*, absent; *kift*, awkward), and where placid agriculture meets the oil age:

Dale has one of the most picturesque settings of any school in the county. Set back from the approach road to Dale at the top of a hill, it commands a view of Dale beach and up the Haven to Milford. In term time sailing activities in Dale Roads and the passage of many ocean-going tankers must cause many an eye to stray from the printed text.

(*Uzmaston, Pembs.*)

As it happened I did not go east, or very far west, from Carmarthen. I went on down to the coast, to a village on an estuary. Colour-washed houses in a soft evening light. Many steps and raised pavements, solid handsome front doors. Outside one, a blaze of flowers:

Mrs Griffiths, Platform House, gives us a gratuitous flower show nearly all the year in pots and boxes, on the platform instead of a front garden.

My contact was a Miss Griffiths. A lady was leaning meditatively out of a bedroom window, so I asked.
'You see that house with the white railings? Then it's the vicarage, then it's another house, then it's Miss Griffiths.'
Before I knocked on Miss Griffiths' door a milk float came by. I bought a half-pint from a milkman with a scholarly face. 'Would you return the half-pint bottle? They are not making them any more. I would be very pleased if you would do that.' A quiet, lilting voice.

41

The milkman was a student at Aberystwyth University where he secured his Bachelor of Laws degree and was destined for the law. His mother's illness prevented him from following this career and he returned home to the farm. Possessed of a very kindly nature and keen sense of humour, his kind deeds and words of advice have helped many.

The scrapbook was not in the possession of Miss Griffiths, the WI Secretary (they hardly ever were). Down a steep side road, in among houses just set on the land wherever there was room. No pavements. One might have been on a Greek island. I found the house where they had the scrapbook, and took it down to read by the estuary. The church, I read, had over 250 communicants, and there was now only one chapel. I was, in fact in

linguistically . . . part of the South Pembrokeshire English-speaking area, and it is a fact that it has a dialect of its own, especially amongst the older people. Many old words and customs of speech still remain in current use, such as *thee* and *thou*, *maid* instead of *girl*, to *key* instead of to *lock*, and many others.

The community of a thousand or so had become very closely knit over the years:

The shops of the district are all family concerns, as are the eight public houses. It is said that every other house used to sell beer, and from the house names such as *Rose and Crown* and *Butchers' Arms* this would seem to be only a slight exaggeration. We have seven grocers' shops, two drapers, two butchers, one post office, one newsagent, one chemist, one baker, one sweetshop and one betting shop, with some doubling up – and what is more, for our convenience we can buy tomatoes at the bakery, fresh lettuce at the chemist, pork chops at the grocer's and bananas at the butcher's, and even antiques at the newsagents.

. . . always divided itself, although only in conversation, as

'Up Street', from the end of Wogan Street up to the church, which comprises the larger houses, and 'Down Street' where the smaller cottages are, which runs from the end of Wogan Street, around The Grist and out to sea. In the previous year the inhabitants of this part of the town rejected an RDC proposal to pull down part of Frogmore Street and erect council bungalows. Whilst these renovations were being undertaken interesting scraps of local history came to light. For instance, when the recently deceased Mr James J. Roberts was discussing the future renovation of Devonshire House he remarked how the piles of old papers in the upper storey would have to be disposed of. They were Bills of Loading and Unloading the boat called *Lively*, captained by his father and grandfather, plying between Bristol and ...

Mr H. R. Pearse, more often called 'Dicky', converted a disused carpenter's shop over an old brewery beside the new 'Three Mariners' into a modern flat for Mrs Nancy Morris. The ruined slaughterhouse at the 'Old Pound' owned by Mr Jack Edmonds was converted into two garages. Evans and Edmonds altered the interior of the butcher's shop at Abercorran House to convert it into a betting office, run by Mr Howard Lewis ... it is an interesting comment on house ownership and family ramifications to note that when Mrs Morgan of 'New Shop' died this year, thirty-two houses in that area changed hands as a consequence.

When the new Secondary Modern was opened and the children were transferred the Parent-Teachers Association strongly objected to the dismissal of Mrs M. P. Thomas from her temporary post. After representations to the Director, Mrs Thomas was reinstated as a permanent member of the staff, which was very suitable, as she is the only resident teacher, apart from Mr Bradshaw, and has been very satisfactory for many years with the infants.

The late Mr E. V. Williams, ex-schoolmaster at the Carmarthen Grammar School, and organist and choirmaster at St Martin's, was a figure so loved and respected that when he died in 1964 a gloom settled over the whole town. Mr Bradshaw, the headmaster [of the village school], said how the morning after Mr Williams' death a little boy of seven came into his office and said 'Sir, E.V. is dead. I am very sorry, sir, because I loves him.'

When I was parking, later on, someone else leaning out over a windowsill said, 'It is better to leave the lights on, the policeman here is a bit sharp.' It was unbelievably in character. I was in a place where we had all been before, a place bursting with life and idiosyncrasy:

Percy and Tom are real people ... Percy is an old sailor and Tom an old soldier. When they are not quarrelling over the merits and demerits of the Army and the Navy they score off each other by playing practical jokes. The loser pays for pints at the local. At the moment Tom is one down. A hale and hearty 82-year-old verger, he was finishing off a deep family grave when Percy paid him a visit. Without any preliminary chit-chat Percy looked down on Tom and said 'Tell me, Tom, how old art thee?' Without thought of mischief Tom replied 'I'm 82, boy.' 'Ah well,' said Percy, with an air of resignation, 'It's not worth thee going home again, is it?'

Dicky Pearse, the Milkman B.A., Up Street and Down Street, E.V. the Beloved Organist, Howard Lewis's Betting Shop, Miss Thomas for whom the people fought the bureaucrats, Percy and Tom, the Old Jokers, Grandfather the Captain of the *Lively* – do not such characters remind us of another Welsh community, a murmur of life among the murmur of the sea? Well they might, for this was the scrapbook of *Laugharne*.

Forty-odd years ago, when the writer was a child, many a happy summer hour was spent on the cliff walk watching the ferrymen, brothers, repairing their net, which was always spread out along the wall above the Boat House. To her the Boat

House below was just another house, hardly ever given a second thought, but being rowed across the ferry, at a charge of six-pence, was always a source of delight. Today the ferry no longer plies. The ferrymen are all gone, and it is the Boat House that people now come from all over the world to see, drawn by the magic name of Dylan Thomas, whose home it once was. Laugharne, which in those far-off days hardly ever saw a stranger – indeed, a strange face was always a cause of much speculation – has now become tourist attraction. They come to see the Boat House and Dylan's grave, and stay on to enjoy Laugharne's wonderful natural beauty and to delve into its his-torical background. A few of the large private houses have now been turned into guest houses, and many of the smaller ones find themselves besieged with requests for accommodation throughout the summer. True, the tourists no longer see the cockle gatherers coming home with their heavily-laden donkeys, or the small fishing smacks returning with their catches. When the WI movement was born fishing and cock-ling were two of the main industries of the township. Cockles were sent as far away as the Black Country. Through the years these industries steadily declined as the cockle beds moved and the fishing was no longer an economic proposition, and at the outbreak of the Second World War many of the local men were out of work. The opening of the Proof and Experimental Estab-lishment by the Ministry of Defence in 1940 gave work to many, and it is still one of the major sources of employment in the district. At the present time 91 men and 17 women are em-ployed there from Laugharne.

Laugharne is snugly set in a cleft where a river drops through high land down to the sea, and one can sit by the silver, wood-banked estuary and hear the imagined voices of *Under Milk Wood*, the reverie of Captain Cat as one reads of the *Lively*, the prattling of Polly Garter's babies as the family in the next car get out their picnic stuff. But there are explosions from time to time from over the next hill, presumably from the Proof and Experimental Establishment, and the baby in the car next to mine burst into tears when a jet screamed over very low indeed.

They have, as well as a Parish Council, a Corporation founded in 1307, whose Portreeve wears a gold cockle-shell.

The other exception to the general dairy-farming pattern is the system of land tenure still practised by the burgesses of the Corporation of Laugharne. The Corporation had its lands and charter granted in the year 1307, and senior burgesses of the town have ever since inherited strips of unfenced farm land of from about 8 acres to just under one acre on the open fields of the Leys (39 acres) and the Moor (98 acres) or on Hugdon (167 acres). These strips have hay or corn in season and are afterwards opened to stock for grazing from about early November to late January every year. Some burgesses, if they are not themselves farmers, let their strip to a neighbour, but the system carries on the land usage practised under the feudal system, and it is interesting to all lovers of history, if not of agriculture! However, this custom does provide an extra income, albeit a small one, to some of our inhabitants. It is a strange anomaly to see a combine harvester doing a three-acre strip in a feudal open field, and a unique sight, too.

A poet's dream could flourish in such a place, even though its unity be achieved by leaving out the Proof and Experimental Establishment or Mr W. T. Cole:

The Parish Council. A letter from Mr W. T. Cole of Glan-y-mor was received, requesting support for his application for permission to erect a further 25 cedarwood chalet bungalows on the estuary. He stated that in the event of permission being granted the development would take several years, during which time more trees would be planted to ensure adequate screening.

England and Wales are full of such places; they are pretty close to one end of the spectrum of rural life (although there are of course many very much smaller communities – Laugharne is in fact a 'township' – with fewer articulate middle-class historians, whether newcomers or resident). The other end is represented by places like Bramcote, where to find so much true village feeling behind a façade at first sight so uncompromisingly suburban is to be surprised, as though one's bank cashier had suddenly started reciting poetry to one across the counter.

It is not a bit of good pretending that modern civilization is not *hard*. It is based on hard things – metal, concrete, plastic. The stage and screen are filled with cold-hearted little 'black comedies', music is a dry jerky crackling, everything is short and hard and dry, no one attempts a work of art like a river, something flowing, warm, irresistible, broadening out from living human springs. The television brings horror and violence, whether documentary or synthetic, into warm soft homes full of babies and carpet and slippers; in such private domestic surroundings it might seem like news from another planet if we were not so insulated from it by familiarity that it isn't news or reality at all. As one moves across the country, the actual motion somehow becomes more real than what is moved through, the countryside becomes a mental background for an endless traffic of hard metal and rubber. Between one village and the next, one or a hundred lorries; high, square-sided lorries with coke or gravel, huge oblong lorries in Lincolnshire with the names of unlikely West-country firms, vast car transporters, big red lorries full of crates, lorries with mysterious green tarpaulins that give nothing away, lorries from Glasgow, Nottingham, Coventry, Yeovil, and, surprisingly often, Beccles; lorries with Brussels sprouts, cigarettes, iron rods, cement mixers, cornflakes, refrigerators, biscuits,

47

trousers, sugar-beet, bricks, timber, chemicals, toffee, furniture; immense, powerful, hard, resolutely passing one another with a speed difference of three miles an hour. The serious commerce and traffic of the country, a massive reality to daunt and chasten the frivolous private motorist. Yet at any lay-by companionable men, often very young, may be observed in the high cabins, eating sandwiches, listening to the radio, snoozing, obliging you with a match.

In much the same way the urban twentieth century is a cover or carapace for a carefully, not to say artfully preserved rural life. In spite of the lorries, the factories, the pylons, the new estates, the television and the cars, in this longest-industrialized and most park-like country of ours the ancient broad distinction still remains; either you want to live in a town or you don't. If you do there will be, as we have already seen, plenty of contrasts and paradoxes; but somewhere in your consciousness – possibly inarticulate, possibly highly developed through observations or study, but in any case a deep personal preference – will be a feeling for nature.

Nature We Loved

There was once an article in the *New Yorker* which suggested that Constable was not a pure painter, not like those Frenchmen so single-mindedly concerned with the quality of light; he tried to paint a summer's day itself, he wanted you to hear the leaves rustling and the birds singing. This is not what painters are *for*, said the article rather coldly, and anyway it's not possible. Nevertheless we go on trying, not entirely without success, when one thinks of *A Midsummer Night's Dream*, or *As You Like It*, or poets from Chaucer to Herrick to Clare to Wordsworth (all unimaginable in continental literature) to celebrate nature with art.

Possibly, indeed, we have had a surfeit of it; so much has been so well said that there's no point in trying any more. Mr Salter, in Waugh's *Scoop*, voiced the notion of many sophisticated persons that nature writing now is always something along the lines of '*feather-footed through the plashy fen passes the questing vole . . .*'

That's the kind of writing that might happen when the writer is thinking of his style. But if he is absorbed by nature, thrilled by his observations, and able to communicate the thrill, there is no need for the reader's heart to sink when he gets to the section on *Nature*. There is still some pretty direct writing.

At dusk on the 2nd of November my son identified the distinctive note of redwings flying overhead, although he was unable to see them . . .

The heron was seen on the 3rd of August flying up-dale against a strong west wind. In spite of its size and powerful wings it appeared to be blown about and to have some difficulty in flying against the wind. The same day we heard a snipe drumming in the East Lotment. This sound is produced by the widely-spread tail feathers as the snipe dives during its display flight . . .

Shortly before sunrise on a cold winter's morning I set off down the beck-side to fodder the cows in our lowground barn. Treading noiselessly on the thin layer of overnight snow, passing the old blighted ash which stands by a clear, willow-lined dub, I heard a strange noise in all the stillness, and turned towards the beck-side wall to discover its source. Within arm's-length of the wall I paused, and at that moment, not six feet from me, a gaunt grey Heron rose from the other side of the wall, soared vertically through the dead branches of the ash tree and with slow and effortless wing-beat made away over the river and towards Crow Wood. I had time to see his quick gold-rimmed eye in detail. For the rest, he was a rush of grey and white, around a yard long from that long bright bill to his trailing feet, and his wing-beat as broad as the span of a man with his arms outstretched. On looking down to the beck-side where he had been standing I saw a big trout gasping in the snow and the grass. An eight-ounce, twelve-inch fish, as I measured him later. He was marked across the centre of his body by the swift bill which had plucked him from the water, and a bloody froth bubbled from the wound just above the gill opening, inflicted by the same weapon and resulting in the sound which had first caught my attention. It was this sound which also lost the heron his breakfast, for crows were around in his absence, and rather than leave so fine a trout to them I slipped it into my pocket to be eaten afterwards, with all thanks to the grey fisherman.

(*Askrigg, Yorks.*)

At its most organized and, as it were, self-conscious, the study and conservation of nature obviously involves societies, committees, authorities, trusts:

Some roadsides with wide verges have a good rich flora, and by agreement with the County Trust the County Council has marked certain outstanding examples with white posts marked 'N.R.' (Nature Reserve) primarily to draw the attention of workers on the highway to the agreement that there should be no dumping of road materials etc. without previous consultation. One stretch of Dauber Lane is so marked, and its flowers include cowslips and primroses, adder's tongue, early purple spotted and butterfly orchids.

In autumn large groups of Shaggy Ink-cap appeared in the potato field by the chapel. It is a kind of mushroom; it is edible, but no one cared to try it.

Hoplands Wood was purchased in 1964 by the Lincolnshire Trust for Nature Conservation from Mrs S. Rawnsley of Wellvale, Alford. The purchase was greatly assisted by generous grants of £500 from the World Wild Life Fund, £250 from the Society for the Promotion of Nature Reserves, from its Pilgrim Fund, and an interest-free loan from the SPNR's Nuffield Loan Fund. Hoplands is a typical East Lincolnshire Boulder Clay woodland, which is more fortunate than most in having escaped wholesale wartime felling, so that many fine mature stands of trees are one of its main attractions.

The Willoughby to Claxby road bounds the northern edge, and to east and west lie the fields of Cottage Farm, Claxby. The southern edge of the wood slopes gently into the valley of the Burlands Beck, a little chalk stream which rises half a mile away in Claxby village where it forms a clear shallow pool by the roadside. Hoplands was long managed in the traditional method of an oak wood with coppice, the coppice being cut for local requirements – fencing, hurdles, beanpoles and peasticks. By 1965 this method had proved unprofitable for years, and in consequence the once-coppiced ash, hazel, alder and sallow had now grown into clumps of tall spindly growth cutting out so much light that our much-loved spring flowers – primroses, violets, anemones and many more – struggled to exist in many areas. Overgrown woodland rides, badly drained, were too shaded and wet to be the flowery glades that they once were,

51

attractive to butterflies and other woodland insects.

With the cooperation of the Nature Conservancy and the Forestry Commission, the Lincolnshire Trust has prepared a management plan for the Hoplands Wood. Much of the eastern part of the wood is now high forest. The big oaks, ashes and wych-elms give such close canopy that there is little undergrowth. This forest will be maintained. Other parts of the wood will be managed in the traditional method of coppice, with standards, the coppice being mostly hazel and ash, and the standards ash and oak. The old coppice must be felled back to its old 'stools' and new coppice and standards must be planted where there are gaps. The rides must be widened, the drains re-opened and the overgrown paths re-cut.

Early 1965 saw progress in the immediate tasks of clearing rides and paths, thanks to the efforts of Conservation Corps teams who worked at week-ends from mid-January till the nesting season began and the birds were left undisturbed. These teams were made up of Trust members and teenage pupils, both boys and girls, from the Alford Secondary Modern and Grammar Schools and Skegness Lumley SM and Grammar Schools. Felling the larger overgrown coppice, often nine inches in diameter, presented a problem to the inexperienced, until the Trust purchased a power saw, which was used by the Warden from Gibraltar Point Field Research Station or the Nature Conservancy's Warden Naturalist for Lincolnshire, and provided much material for the younger ones to trim and stack. Roaring fires of 'brash' cheered the company on winter days and gave an attractive backwoods atmosphere to the scene. Everyone enjoyed this fine outlet for their energies. There are always as many or more young volunteers as there are available adults to lead and supervise them, and they are always encouraged to understand just why each particular task is undertaken, and its place in the pattern of conservation. Some of the most enthusiastic workers in 1965 were Willoughby boys who already knew the wood ...

There is a heronry in the wood ... there are about 2,100 pairs of herons in Britain. Research was carried out to see if there was organo-chlorine insecticide residue in herons or their eggs. Although a few nests were sited in ash trees the majority were in oaks and were upwards of 25 feet from the ground. The investigators were able to examine the contents of the nests with the minimum of disturbance to the birds by seeing them in a mirror set at an angle and hoisted into position on a telescopic pole. 39 nests occupied. Average number of young fledged per nest, 2.66.

(*Willoughby, Lincs.*)

From the membership card of the Lincolnshire Trust for Nature Conservation Ltd.:

This card should be carried whenever a visit is made to a reserve. At the Saltfleetby-Theddlethorpe Dunes Reserve it is important for their own safety that visitors should comply with the RAF safety regulations. Members are strongly recommended not to visit the Reserve when the bombing ranges on the foreshore are in use. Visitors are warned that adders may be present in several of the Reserves.

(*Willoughby*)

Heron: Many fewer than some years ago, but this autumn, when they disperse, we have seen them several times. One came to fish the farm pond, and was chased by a crow and an autumn lamb. Though harried, the heron stayed round the pond and went on fishing till crow and lamb got tired.

(*Smarden, Kent*)

It is true that not all villages could produce a list as scholarly as that of *Kilcain* (*Flint*):

The area known as the Fron is also on acid soil above glacial drift and shale. At the west end of the Fron is a patch of wet ground on which grow two very interesting plants. These are the Round-leafed Sundew (*Drosera Rotundifolia*) and the Butter-wort (*Pinguicola Vulgaris*), which belong to the group of carnivorous plants able to catch insects and digest their bodies.

Some of the commoner species found on walls include Herb Robert, Shining Cranesbill, Pellitory-of-the-wall, Ivy-leaved Toadflax, Maidenhair Spleenwort and Wall Rue.

In agricultural fields and waste places are frequently found Meadow Buttercup (*Ranunculus Acris*), Bulbous Buttercup (*R. Bulbosus*), Creeping Buttercup (*R. Repens*), Silverweed (*Potentilla Anserina*), Sun-spurge (*Euphorbia Helioscopia*), Knot Grass (*Polygonum Aviculare*), Red Shank (*P. Persicaria*), Broad-leaved Dock (*Rumex Obtusifolius*), Scarlet Pimpernel (*Anagallis Arvensis*), Germander Speedwell (*Veronica Chamaedrys*), Common Hemp Nettle (*Galeopsis Tetrahit*), Field Madder (*Sherardia Arvensis*), Spear Thistle (*Cirsium Vulgare*), Creeping Thistle (*C. Arvense*), Ragwort (*Senecio Jacobaea*), Coltsfoot (*Tussilago Farfara*), Good King Henry (*Chenopodium Bonus Henricus*), Mullein (*Verbascum Thapsus*), Toadflax (*Linnaria Vulgaris*), Rosebay Willowherb (*Chamaenerion Angustifolium*).

But then not every village can include among its residents a lecturer in botany at Leeds University. In any case the excitement of knowing things and naming them – the god-like excitement of the first task entrusted to Adam – is only a part of the pleasure to be got from nature; it is primarily a matter of *seeing*, of living with. In the scrapbook for *Goosnargh*, a village five miles outside Preston with a curious frontier feeling (all that industrial clamour so recently left, and here one looks from the churchyard across level meadows and lifts one's eyes to hills and moors merely five miles away), a ten-year-old boy collected, even if he did not know all the names of, the following:

Arrowhead, Bilberry, Birdsfoot Trefoil, Bistort, Bladder Campion, Bluebell, Blue Scabious, Bracken, Branched Burr Reed,

Bramble, Broom, Bugle, Butterburr, Buttercup, Butterwort, Carline Thistle, Cathartic Flax, Cat's Ear, Chestnut, Chickweed, Coltsfoot, Comfrey, Common Agrimony, Common Fern, Common Hawkweed, Common Hemp Nettle, Common Ling, Common Mouse Ear, Common Nettle, Common Orache, Common Rush, Common Thistle, Common Vetch, Common Yarrow, Corn Fever-few, Cornflower, Cow Parsnip, Cowslip, Creeping Buttercup, Creeping Cinquefoil, Creeping Thistle, Cross-leaved Heather, Cuckoo-pint, Daisy, Dandelion, Deadly Nightshade, Dog-daisy, Dog-rose, Dog's-mercury, Dyer's Rocket, Elder Flower, Enchanter's Nightshade, Fat Hen, Field Convolvulus, Forget-me-not, Foxglove, Fumitory, Garlic, Garlic Mustard, Germander Speedwell, Goldilocks, Goose-grass, Gorse, Greater Bindweed, Greater Celandine, Greater Knapweed, Greater Salad Burnet, Greater Stitchwort, Great Mullein, Ground Ivy, Groundsel, Guelder Rose, Hawthorn, Harebell, Hazel Catkin, Heather, Heath Milkwort, Hedge Woundwort, Herb Bennett, Herb Robert, Honeysuckle, Iris, Ivy-leaved Toadflax, Knotted Figwort, Knotweed, Lady's Bedstraw, Lamb's Lettuce, Lesser Celandine, Marsh Marigold, Mayflower, Meadowsweet, Meadow Vetchling, Monkey Flower, Mountain Ash, Orange Poppy, Oxslip, Periwinkle, Pink Wild Geranium, Plantain, Primrose, Purple Cromwell, Purple Orchis (Early), Ragged Robin, Ramson, Rosebay Willowherb, Scarlet Pimpernel, Sea Pink, Self Heal, Sheep's Sorrel, Shepherd's Purse, Silverweed, Sloe, Small Plantain, Sorrel, Spear Plume Thistle, Spotted Orchis, St John's Wort, Sun Spurge, Tufted Vetch, Valerian, Violet, Water Crowfoot, White Campion, White Clover, White Deadly Nightshade, White Dead Nettle, Wild Carrot, Wild Hop, Wild Pansy, Wild Parsley, Wild Radish, Wild Red Poppy, Wild Rose, Wild Strawberry, Wild Thyme, Willow Catkin, Wood Anemone, Wood Horsetail, Wood Sorrel, Yellow or Biting Stonecrop, Yellow Rattle, Yellow Toadflax, Yellow Water Lily.

The Elizabethan names scattered among this noble and resounding list suggest a look at the scrapbook for *Charlcote*

(*Warwicks.*) – one of the most beautiful books to smell and to touch, since it is bound with skin from a deer in the famous park of the Lucys where Shakespeare is said to have poached:

Two factors have caused changes in the natural life of our countryside. Firstly the removal of some hedges containing large elm trees which gave Warwickshire the title 'leafy', accompanied by the mechanical cutting of the remaining hedges and verges, and in some cases the spraying of the verges and hedge bottoms, resulting in lack of herbage for food and also lack of cover for the shelter, of wild animals such as rabbits, weasels, stoats or even mice and rats.

Moles are still helpful to the would-be gardener, who needs extra fine soil for her garden; but the lady who found several mole-heaps – 'oonty-tumps' – on her lawn thought they were very much a blessing in disguise . . .

Our local countryside offers a wide variety of flora, although there are two outstanding absentees; one, the Marsh Marigolds, 'Polly-blobs' or 'May-blobs', and the other, the Goat Willow. During the latter years the sprays used by the County Council or farmers and the mechanical cutters used on the grass verges have decimated the numbers and varieties of the wild flowers. *Kex* and *paigles*, beloved of Shakespeare, have suffered so much that is is almost impossible to make many cowslip balls or to implement the wild bouquet with the cow parsley, so resembling *Gypsophila*. However, any country child can still gather Wild Yellow Toadflax, nicknamed Eggs-and-bacon.

The sandy brow of the fields along the Scar is covered in July with Large Purple Scabious, Yellow Agrimony and Bedstraw, Mauve and White Yarrow, Pink Rest Harrow and the beautifully-striped pink flowers of the Bindweed . . .

Our new addition to the flora is the Orange Balsam. This was found three years ago by the weir at Luddington and has gradually made its way along the Avon. Last year it set its *pied-à-terre* in the little ditch by the bridge in Hampton Lane, in company with Purple Loosestrife and Meadowsweet. We hope that it has found itself in congenial surroundings and has decided to stay and multiply.

The river offers rushes and reeds, with a few marsh-loving flowers such as Burr, Marigold and Water Mint, if one does not mind if one's feet become wet and muddy. The rushes need to be cut off from a canoe, but are good quality for the making of mats, baskets and flower containers such as those made by a WI member which adorn the window ledges of our church at festival time.

Along the Scar, especially in the coppices, there are many clumps of Teazles, if the seeker for Christmas decorations is prepared to wait until the goldfinches have helped themselves to the banquet of Teazle seeds.

When one of the fields was excavated for drainage the plants which grew on the new topsoil were most interesting. The 'pennies' of the Penny Cress were extra large and soon turned yellow. Orache leaves and flowers were extra red. Corn Camomile was extra aromatic, with the flowers fine and white, while the Goosefoot lived up to its name of Fat Hen and looked full of therapy for the old ploughman's rheumatism.

When Shakespeare wrote 'I know a bank whereon the wild thyme grows' it is said that he referred to a bank at Hatton Rock. Unfortunately the thyme is not in evidence now because progress demands other crops for cattle food . . .

There is always documentary, and quite often drama, to be seen simply by looking out of the kitchen window:

One morning I tied the rind of a leg of pork on to our rowan tree. A short time after a young rat strolled along the lawn towards the tree. He sniffed round alertly as he got nearer, until he was right under the rind. How to reach it? He sat back on his hind legs viewing it. He raised himself higher, like a dog begging . . . no good. He tried to climb the tree, slipped and fell, tried again and again, positively dancing with rage in his efforts. In the end he had to give up, and I swear as he stumped off he was saying to himself, like the fox in the fable, 'I bet it did not taste very good'.

'The wind that blows on March 21st will blow on June 21st.'

More pork rind on the rowan today has enticed a new bird into the garden. I saw it while washing up. Could not place it, so had to get out my bird book. I found it was a Pied Woodpecker and was so thrilled I could not settle down to ordinary house-work for a long time. It has visited my garden quite a few times after this, and each time when leaving landed on the same tree by the stream, so I shall visit it later in the year to see if there is any sign of a nest.

The end of the month saw the start of the annual March of the Frogs. Where they come from and where they go to I don't know. The first signs are squashed bodies that have been run over halfway down the hill at Station Road. After that life becomes very dodgy, in the true sense of the word. Walking in the dark one shies away from every object in the road. Why? Have you ever trod on a big fat frog? Things are nearly as bad in a car. One can see the petrified amphibians in the headlights, so one tries not to run over them. The army advances as the days go on, till they finally disappear, just before they reach the level crossing in Mill Lane.

(Little Houghton, Northants.)

June 20th. Hedgehog enjoying himself tucking into a bar of striped Cleethorpes rock by the railway line, obviously thrown out of a passing train.

July 19th. Glorious lark songs to cheer up washday.

September. A Pied Wagtail seen frequently around the station gardens.

August 3rd onwards. A plague of very small and exasperating harvest flies, inside and outside house. 13th, 14th, 15th; forest fires in miniature. Great crackling. Mr Watson burning the stubble in his fields.

October 4th. Kestrel hawk seen hovering many times over the Carrs. These birds often seen in our flat areas.

October 8th. Beautiful sight of harvest bonfires, stubble burning along the Worlaby and Elsham Tops.

(*Wrawby, Lincs.*)

Children still tell each other that if you pick dandelions you
will want to pee.

Most of the grasses you would expect to find by the wayside
occur there; Cocksfoot and Catstail, Yorkshire Fog and Wood
Pea, Blue Grass, False Oat and Common Bent. Where it is wetter
there is sometimes Reed Canary Grass. On the heaths grow
Purple Moor Grass, which is particularly susceptible to fire in
the early months of the year, and Bristle Bent, which is very
plentiful in Hampshire and Dorset, though not conspicuous elsewhere.

(*Bransgore, Hants.*)

It would be interesting to stop a hundred motorists in the
New Forest and see how many 'would expect to find by the
wayside Cocksfoot and Catstail, Yorkshire Fog and Wood
Pea' and the rest, or indeed had heard of them. Nevertheless,
there is something undaunting and democratic about this
kind of specialized knowledge, a feeling that the books in
the running brooks are there for *anyone* to read. Plenty of
sharp observation can be made in suburbanized villages
(which some of those quoted above certainly are); but
perhaps it is not surprising that the nature writing that rises
above observation, however acute and well conveyed, into a
form of its own, linking us with White or Mitford or the
great diarists, should come from really 'traditional' villages.
In the scrapbook for *Bradford Abbas*, (*Dorset*), nature observation is clearly so much a way of life that another con-
tributor can toss off these casual paragraphs before they
come to their main diarist at all:

A Spotted Flycatcher tried to nest at Orchard Close in May,

but was ousted three times. First a cat climbed up the rambler rose and ate all the babies. The hen then tried to build a nest in a clematis, but sparrows chased her. She finally built a nest in the climbing rose on the wall of Chantry Cottage, but once more the sparrows attacked her. She gave up and flew away.

On May 20th swans left the moat at Wyke. Walking with the two cygnets on their backs they went down to the River Yeo half a mile away. The male swallow built a nest in Orchard Close but had no mate. In late August he found a female. In October swans returned from the river to Wyke, walking in line, father in front, then the two young ones, nearly full grown, mother bringing up the rear. Young swans take flying lessons and land in bushes on October 3rd. This month sees the arrival of the fieldfares and redwings in their thousands, and with the first frost one can hear the wildfowl flighting over the village at night, on the way from the saltings to the Somerset moors.

There follow these *Nature Notes: by a Nurse on night duty*:

Wednesday, March 3rd. The great eastern blizzard. Wales covered. Awoke for night duty at 5 p.m. to find a carpet of snow and howling blizzard. No taxi, so had to walk to work in Sherborne. It took nearly two hours against blinding, drifting snow. How I missed the hedges, where they had been replaced by wire fencing! A car which got up the hill by Red Lane Farm after three tries must have been one of the last to get through. As I couldn't carry a heavy spade I took a wooden spoon and cookery strainer in case I had to dig myself out, but managed not to fall into snowdrifts.

Sunday, the 28th of the same month. The first real days of Spring. Pruned roses. A small, old moon in golden sky over Sherborne Abbey. First blossoms of blackthorn on bushes left above the closely trimmed hedge. Arab Spears are broader, more like shields now. Tortoiseshell butterflies about. Celandines in bloom. Green plants of young cleavers are now quite high.

29th. Frost in the early morning, followed by bright sunshine. Oak and ash still in very tight bud. Beech buds coppery, with old husks still on boughs.

Drama by the second elm below the Combe crossroads. Female cyclist found unconscious about 9.20 a.m. Two rescuers, Mr Courtney and Mr Benny Cleal, suspected of knocking her off until evidence investigated. Front lamp had slid down narrowing fork, become looser, swung round and caught in wheel, throwing cyclist over handlebars on to head. Prompt action of said rescuers probably saved her sight, if not her life, as severe lacerations to face and left eyelid needed immediate hospital attention. Unfortunately for this diary, said cyclist happened to be the WI member who has been keeping in touch with the wild life and weather along the Bradford road while travelling to and from Sherborne, where she works on night duty. Henceforth entries are interrupted by the diarist's long spell in hospital until she is fit for work. The diary must become rather a series of brief impressions.

(At this point the handwriting is noticeably altered.)

The rest of April was spent in my own hospital, pleasantly enough, as all my colleagues and friends spoil me. The flowers that turn my private ward into a florist's shop keep me in touch with the rapid development of Spring, from daffodil time, with primroses and violets from the lanes to the opening of the tulips and the first pinks. My hospital window overlooks fields and gardens where, without my smashed glasses, I see a fog of changing colours, and guess at forsythia, sycamore and red may.

Monday, May 3rd. Home after just 28 days in hospital. Still no glasses, but as the car takes me along the familiar road I gasp to see how much greener and denser the hedges are. All the leaves are unfurled, and I don't know whether the oak or the ash came first. I am amazed at my own dense forest of American currant, green forsythia, green plum-leaves, green arbutus and green rambler roses. The overgrown Honesty and forget-me-nots hide the shrivelled early bulb flowers with a sea of mauve and blue.

Suddenly the trees, bushes and windows are alive. Appearing from nowhere, my eight cats swoop on me with cries of joy and give me a wonderful welcome with velvet paws, prickly tongues and ever-nibbling teeth which fasten gently over my fingers.

July. After the first few pickings of blackcurrants I am Sent For to have my eyelid straightened by minor plastic surgery, so good-bye once again to the Bradford road. Am greeted by the best thunderstorm Wiltshire can demonstrate. This wakes me with a nearby crash at 5 a.m. A bright start to Op Day.

When I return home, wet and cold July is nearly over. As one of my eyes is still out of focus it is easier to remember former sights than to squint at today's details of the familiar road. The thunder reminds me of the gossamer tents of the brown-tipped moth caterpillars, which I watched last summer every time I pushed my bicycle up the third hill from home. The tiny wriggling caterpillars grew fatter and fatter in their hedgerow camp, until I looked forward to the final exciting cycle in their lives – but alas, a thunderstorm wrecked the tents and washed away their lousy builders!

Wednesday, August 11th. Brilliant sunshine, rare this year. Commotion in garden. Found my black cat, Peter, chasing an angry flying mouse – a pipistrelle bat with a ferocious little face like a wild boar going into battle. Only his lower squawks audible to human ear. As he went up the scale his fierce red mouthings were silent to us. Rescued him, and hooked him on the Wayfaring Tree to continue his daytime sleep. Huge full moon tonight, ideal for night flyers.

Tuesday, 17th. Seen along the Bradford road: mallow, yellow toadflax, stinging nettles, common sorrel, bindweed, hemlock, persicaria, spear plume thistle, white bedstraw, dovesfoot cranesbill, common agrimony, scentless mayweed, yarrow, corn marigold, mouse-ear, ribwort plantain, scabious, rest harrow, lady's slipper, red clover, Dutch clover, traveller's joy, red poppy, hop trefoil, liverwort, scarlet pimpernel, common comfrey, common burdock, mugwort, honeysuckle, deadly night-shade, red campion, grass pea, white dead-nettle, ragwort and teazle.

Wednesday, September 22nd. A 'misty moisty morning'. Golden pippins, flavourless after the wet summer, lie thick on the lawn. A second crop of red and white campion brightens the grassy lane.

Thursday, 23rd. A bronze young slow-worm basks in the sun, motionless as I pass in the lane.

Friday, October 8th. A clear night, with an almost full moon. Sirius and Orion shine brilliantly through children's ward window.

Thursday, 14th. First foggy morning. On the way home, along the hill bordered by beech trees, I found a moth, held down by sticky particles of road grit, like a medieval prisoner with ball and chain. It took me quite a time to free it, but at last it was able to flutter away, no longer weighed down by tiny lumps of grit.

Saturday, 16th. The weather could not have been more perfect for Jennifer Cox's wedding. As we watched the photographers outside the church the white and golden harmony of bride and bridesmaids matched the white clouds and golden autumn sunshine.

Monday, November 1st. Boisterous gales.

Friday, November 5th. A clear cold night with bright gibbous moon, to the delight of the firework parties.

Monday, 15th. A snow wave was forecast and hit the country hard but just missed this part of the world. All we had to remind us of Siberia was a vile east wind hitting me in the face as I struggled against it on my bicycle.

Tuesday, 16th. The horrible east wind is less vigorous.

Wednesday, 17th. A wet and warm night, followed by a misty moisty morning.

Friday, 19th. Still warm and wet underfoot. Winter violets flourishing in the garden. Wrens very active.

Sunday, 21st. Venus huge and brilliant, sinking in the west after church, while Jupiter rises in the east.

Friday, December 10th. Cold and damp, the kind of weather one associates with November rather than December.

Saturday, 11th. Today the bleak brightness looks more like December. Nearly all the leaves have fallen and lie wet and dark. The berries are nearly over, and the cows rush eagerly to their ration of hay. The wintry glow of sunset enhances the blackness of the ragged clouds.

Friday, 24th. Christmas Eve was wet. Winter violets in full bloom.

Saturday, 25th. Christmas Day, a warm damp morning. No birds shivering in the hedges, so I saved their Christmas treat. A starry night; Jupiter and Venus very brilliant in the east and west. Orion shone in through the corridor window at 3 a.m.

Sunday, 26th. Christmas Sunday. A morning like a Japanese print! Hills swathed in mist, with sun breaking through. A thick white frost, so the birds had their Christmas treat of 'Swoop', which I scattered as I cycled home. As the year goes out, bright with the berries of holly, cotoneaster and rose, the bulbs are already showing green swords to greet the spring. The first snowdrop in my garden is in bloom for the New Year. Already the violets, polyanthus and wanda primroses have joined the winter jasmine to brighten the greyness of winter and to remind us that, come snow or hail in January or February, we are half-way through the winter and less than three months from the Spring equinox.

Nature, in fact, is very much too big for anyone to 'specialize' in it, from the vast processions of the planets to the life of moths. Some, however, can become very much more aware than others; starting as children:

The Rintoul children had great success with their tadpoles this year. They had all stages from the egg to the tadpole, then some with front legs and a tail, then some with four legs and a tail, and finally a complete frog sitting on a stone in the centre of the dish. Unfortunately before they could be returned to the pond one committed suicide by jumping on to the floor, where it remained unseen and was later found dead.

The greatest success of these budding naturalists was the Elephant Hawk Moth. Last autumn they found a caterpillar, a large green fellow with four spots behind his head and a curious spike on his tailpiece. He was duly put into a jar with lots of willowherb to eat and some damp moss for him to crawl under. He was, of course taken to school, and having survived that adventure he settled down to eat, and eat, and finally one day they found he had become a hard brown pupa. Again he went to school, and afterwards he retired in his jar to the woodshed, which had the right kind of atmosphere. On Wednesday, 16th June the excitement reached fever pitch when he emerged as a beautiful pink Elephant Hawk Moth. At this point the doctors were called in and the moth was duly anaesthetized, so that they had a perfect specimen. Once again he went to school to be admired, and then for a week he remained in his box, awaiting advice as to mounting. On the evening of the 24th of June there was a funny whirring noise in the drawing-room, and to their amazement the supposedly dead Moth had come out of the anaesthetic and was ready to fly. Naturally he was escorted with great ceremony into the garden, and with joy they watched him fly off to the greatest adventure of all – a free life.

(Grampound, Cornwall)

That could happen in any semi-detached; but it is still more likely to happen in the country. (As a matter of fact, also in Grampound,

One of our members, Miss Dawe, can imitate bird calls so accurately that they come to her when she whistles.)

Nature, like classical music, is something of which the true devotee cannot have too much; familiarity breeds wonder. It is interesting to see the reactions of those who live in places where there is, so to speak, *more* Nature than in less favoured parts; places that are famous for their Nature:

> Our surrounding countryside may not be beautiful, but Hickling Broad, the largest and wildest of them all, more than compensates for this. From the sparkling brilliance of a Spring morning, alive with excited twitterings, over the twinkling waves of the sun-warmed water whipped by a summer breeze, to the misty stillness of an autumn evening, or the complete silence of a vast expanse of ice under a frosty moon, the gorgeous sunsets, the flying spray of gale-lashed water and driving rain – the scene is always changing, and the whole area is rich in the great variety of its flora and fauna. Together with the normal bird life may be found the more unusual species; the Bittern, the Montagu Harrier and the Grebe. Four hundred swans share the Broad with the winter population of between two and three thousand coot and almost all species of wild duck, moorhens, dabchicks, as well as the reed warblers, water-rails, bearded tits, reed buntings, kingfishers and 'the Fisherman of Norfolk', the motionless herons.
>
> All these and many more may be seen in the cover of the great reed beds . . . some believe there is a huge five-foot monster pike lurking in some deep hole underneath the dark waters, too crafty to be caught . . .
>
> (*Hickling, Norfolk*)

It may seem illogical to deal first with nature-watching, which could be seen as a twentieth-century spectator sport born of modern man's alienation from nature. In a book about rural life should not the actual players, the farmers, come first?

No. Farmers are modern men too. Some, of course, are more modern than others:

> Mick Vernon . . . has scores of Jersey cows, hundreds of battery hens and thousands of broiler chicks. A sordid sideline, some would say? Mick smiled patiently. 'No, I don't think so.

The chicks are housed in a large, luxurious, well-insulated, well-ventilated, well-lighted, superb dwelling. The chicks are plunged into darkness for thirty minutes every day so that they won't be alarmed when there is a power failure. All equipment in their building 'hangs from the ceiling. No floor space is wasted. I am quite satisfied there is no cruelty. The broiler chicken enjoys its life. It wouldn't grow if it didn't,' Vernon said seriously.

(*Northern Echo* cutting from scrapbook of *Riding Mill*, *Northumberland*)

As farming becomes more of an industry (for in every village the tale is the same; the elderly shepherds, cowmen and labourers dying off or retiring, the impossibility of finding young replacements, the resort to mechanization, the consortia and cooperatives) the distinction between farmer and townsman – the old urban-rural distinction – is going to become less and less marked. It will be increasingly this informed observation of and joy in nature which is the distinguishing mark of the modern rural consciousness.

Obviously we must beware of generalization; urban or suburban infiltration of the countryside has a number of causes nothing whatever to do with nature, as we have already seen – the decentralization of industry, the affluent society with more people able to choose house sites, mobility. Yet when a family is making the decisive choice about a move – perhaps a company move, perhaps on its own initiative – from town life, the determining factor, sometimes perhaps not even consciously felt or expressed, may well be whether or not the wife or the husband are the kind of people who can drop everything when they see a new bird from the kitchen window and are excited for the rest of the day when they find it is a Pied Woodpecker. For an increasing number of people in Britain today it is possible to turn Dr Johnson's saying upside-down. The man who is tired of the country is tired of life.

The Farmers

If there were such a thing as a rusticity meter, on the lines of a geiger counter, it would obviously give its highest reading in areas, apart from actual mountains, where the only occupation was farming. It is still the *raison d'être* of the countryside and its shaper, it is both cause and effect. It has only recently ceased to be one of the largest industries in Britain, and obviously it is the industry occupying the most space.

Farming fluctuates wildly both in the public estimation of its importance to the nation and in the relative profitability of its various departments (not to mention the new Common Market uncertainty, gloomy for horticulture, promising for stock farmers). During wars we return to naked, basic truths such as that if we don't eat, we die. Girls in workmanlike green jerseys are drafted to the land, inefficient farmers are ruthlessly weeded out by strong regional committees, there is wild talk of ploughing up golf links. In peace time we return to the dream, unfortunately now shared (and often better realized) by more and more other nations, of being the world's workshop and top exporter. Let them grow their cheap corn and we'll give them switchgear, nylons and colour television (if only they wouldn't use that German system). Sooner or later the very Polynesians will be trying to export switchgear. It's all very well for economists to point out the obvious truth that a nation of merely primary producers could not possibly enjoy a high modern standard of living; but in most people there is a little, atavistic, non-economist voice which whispers that in an unpleasant and menacing world to live on a thickly-populated island extremely vulnerable to blockade is chancing our arm. How comfortable if we could have an industrial export surplus *and* be agriculturally self-sufficient!

Between these two hypothetical extremes – total mobilization, ploughing-up of parks and golf-links, wheat on mountains, plankton soup, the lot, and the turning of Britain into one huge mere factory – farming, to the superficial observer, looks very much as it has always done. He may notice the odd concrete Dutch barn or gleaming futuristic silo, he may miss a hedge here and there, and he certainly cannot fail to notice the extreme mechanization. But surely the field patterns, the farmhouses sited in folds of the land with that wonderfully instinctive eye for right positioning that now seems to have deserted us, the bare winter skylines, the men with pipes and battered hats leaning over pen rails in market towns, the rhythm of farming, remain unchanged?

To some extent. There are still vast areas of custom, atmosphere and tradition where to talk of the farming 'industry' at all seems out of place; it is still a way of life:

At the end of the harvest each year it is the custom of Wyke, a farm which lies to the south-east of the road leading from Bradford Abbas to Sherborne, to hold a Thanksgiving Service in the great Tithe Barn. For how many years this custom has been in existence is not known, but according to Mr Ronnie Loxton, who has farmed at Wyke for the past thirty years, the custom has been maintained throughout his occupancy and was already established when he first came to Wyke.

The Tithe Barn has stood for more than 600 years and is a well-known local feature. Built of local ham stone and 282 feet long, it stands proudly amongst the farm buildings, buttressed at regular intervals along its entire length like the nave of an ancient church.

The service is chiefly for those who work on the farm, but it is also attended by friends of the Farmer, who are of course delighted to be able to take part in this traditional act of thanksgiving, set in so natural a background.

This year the service began at 7.30 on a September evening. A section of the Barn had been cleared, and bales of straw, covered by sacks, were neatly arranged across the width of the Barn in the manner of the pews of a church, with a centre aisle. The men from Wyke, with their wives and children, took up their places at the rear of the Barn, in much the same way as the well-proved members of a congregation claim the rear pews of their local church. The guests, like new and self-conscious members of the congregation, sat further forward.

In the space left clear in front of the bale, and a little to the left, sat the women, boys and girls of the Bradford Abbas church choir, duly robed in cassocks and surplices. Beyond this space and behind wooden railings, in full view of the congregation, a number of calves drowsed, some standing, some lying, too sleepy to object to the violation of their evening peace, or perhaps awed into silence by the solemnity of the occasion.

Mr Loxton closed the huge wooden doors, whispered conversation died away, and the Vicar, the Rev. G. R. Buchanan, stepped forward to start the service. The choir rose with studied confidence, and the boys stiffened in soldierly fashion as the Vicar turned to them. The first hymn began with a little uncertainty, there being no piano or other musical instrument to pitch the key. Then the choir, picking up the Vicar's opening note (which had been offered with an air of open-mindedness), consolidated their efforts, and by the end of the first verse the congregation had overcome their diffidence at singing without the moral support of the church organ and were joining in, each man to his vocal capacity.

The service proceeded with prayers and hymns and finished

with a short address by the Vicar, and after the final hymn the gathering dispersed, the guests making their way to Mr Loxton's house for refreshment, whilst the men from Wyke and their families stayed in the Barn to enjoy beer, cider and cheese, also a well-established and well-deserved part of this Wyke tradition.

Whilst giving thanks to God for our daily bread is due from all men, and not merely from those who sow and reap, the atmosphere of a barn for those so fortunate to attend such a service is without doubt the natural aid to the expression of their gratitude.

(Bradford Abbas, Dorset)

As a matter of fact Bradford Abbas is the very last village in Dorset before you come to Somerset; but in such a scene as the above there are surely echoes of Hardy's church musicians? ('Joseph,' I said says I, 'depend upon't, if so be you have them tooting clar'nets you'll spoil the whole set-out. Clar'nets were not made for the service of the Lard; you can see it by looking at 'em,' I said. 'And what came o't? Why, souls, the parson set up a barrel-organ on his own account within two years of the time I spoke, and the old choir went to nothing.') But Wyke Farm, 574 acres, is typical of the larger units which result from the inexorable rationalizing trend of today. In his case the ownership is traditional enough, for Mr Loxton is described as the manager for those famous landlords, Winchester College (and if it isn't them, half the time the owners of large farms turn out to be one of the Oxbridge colleges). Another farm referred to in the same scrapbook is owned by Cow and Gate Foods, a branch of the Unigate organization:

It consists of 300 acres of mainly sandy and light loam soil and is very intensively farmed, mainly as a pig production unit. The main stock consists of a herd of 600 breeding sows and gilts and some 4,200 other pigs in various stages up to bacon weight.

Another exhibit in the same book is a photograph of Khrushchev and a lot of other burly smiling men:

British Certified Aberystwyth Perennial Rye Grass, S. 321, intermediate hay/grazing strain, grown on our Silverlake Farm, Sherborne, Dorset. Mr Khrushchev showed great interest in this variety at the British Agricultural Exhibition in Moscow during May 1964, where it appeared on the stand of Allied Seed Producers (Great Britain) Ltd an associate company formed by four prominent British seed firms, including T. B. Lock and Sons Ltd, for the purpose of trading in Eastern European countries.

The average farm, run by a family with possibly a helper or two, now seems somewhat uneasily poised between such large and highly specialized ventures, and the gradually disappearing smallholder. No one seems to be quite sure what the 'ideal' acreage is. As Professor Joad would have said, it depends what you mean by ideal. In the book of *Wrawby* (*Lincs.*) this is discussed (on the page after these splendid local words):

throng: busy. '*Throng as Throp's wife*', busy as can be.
stitherum: a yarn or tale.
moffry: a convertible cart or wagon (from *hermaphrodite*).
fell: savage.
goosen: to act silly.
bluther: to cry or weep.
gallibaulk: chimney.
put wood i'th' wal: close the door.

In the past twenty years the average acreage farmed by one man in Lindsey has about doubled. This means that the number of individual farms has halved. Some say 350 acres is an ideal holding. Others plump for about 600, and then there are those who want to creep into the four-figure bracket, either on their own or as a limited company. Very often the progressive farmer who just wants the one to make the right size is pushed out by an empire-builder.

From *Smarden* (*Kent*):

Changes we now expect. Farming no longer a job for a dull boy. Training at an agricultural college now practically essential. Few families will be able to afford it. Small farmers will be less and less able to survive competition, and will be forced to join combines ...

Major and Mrs Sothern, after a lifetime in the Army, then 16 years farming in Smarden, decided to retire. The house goes to a commuter, the oast-house to a speculator, and the land is bought by a large farmer living seven miles away. The new owner at once grubs the hedges and turns three little fields into one. He drains and ploughs it, and gets in a contracting firm to lime it. The contractor's driver, who nowadays is asked to spread the lime after ploughing instead of before, stands wondering how he will get his lorry though the deep mud in the gateway, let alone on to the land ...

Nevertheless, the basic picture of life on the farm is still very much a family one. Here is the year on a farm in *Crayke* (*Yorks.*), run by a family with five children and three helpers:

Of the population of just over 400 there are 72 engaged in full-time agricultural work. Very few of them are under 25 years of age ... The stock consists of 14 milking cows, 24 bullocks and 11 heifers which vary from the new calf stage to 2 years old, 2 sows, and an assortment of piglets, which they breed so successfully, and about 130 poultry. All the milking and calf-rearing is carried on at home by the boss himself, who is very fond of his cattle – a very fortunate point, considering that the cows must be milked twice, and the calves fed regularly, even on Sundays. He uses a Gascoyne Milking Unit, which soon makes short work of milking 14 cows, and of course he is able to do other small jobs while the machines are at work, as well as being able to milk three cows at once.

Calf feeding has a charm all of its own, at the very new calf stage at any rate. This is where the young sons of the family take over and feed the calves out of buckets. I think the attraction must be that a new calf has to be taught to drink by putting one's hand in the milk and allowing the calf to suck the fingers and draw in milk at the same time. It is very noticeable that when the calf can drink well and the finger-sucking business is over, the job is usually handed back to Dad.

Poultry-keeping is not carried on to the extent of a few years ago. Foodstuffs are very expensive, and the prices of eggs to the producer very low indeed. Gone are the days when the Missus had to run the house on the poultry money. Nowadays I imagine if there is any profit to be made in the odd hundred or so of poultry it will hardly keep the Missus in nylons. Day-old chicks are quite expensive, usually about £17 a hundred, and they have to be fed for 6 months before the first egg appears. After that the so-called reward is egg prices ranging from 2/6 to 4/3 per dozen over the year.

On the crop side of farming, the 164 acres produce 34 acres of barley, 22 of wheat, 15 of oats, 4 of sugar-beet, 8 of potatoes, 6 of mangolds, 5½ of turnips, 14 of clover and pasture for the cattle. Work in the months of January and February is generally confined to stock management and selling the previous year's crops, bringing turnips, mangolds, hay and straw. Feeding and bedding the cattle takes a lot of time, as they are indoors the whole time and so need attention three times a day and a final bedding down last thing at night.

Weather permitting, potato pies are opened and the potatoes sold to the merchants. Larger potatoes are sorted and packed into paper sacks each holding 4 stones of potatoes. This is a new idea. Prior to this year potatoes were sold in hessian sacks holding 8 stones of potatoes. All cracked, scabby or small potatoes are put on one side for home use or for feeding to the pigs. The farmer is supposed to get a guaranteed price of £14 a ton, but the retail price was about £25 a ton, which meant that somewhere between the farmer and the consumer an easy profit of £11 a ton was made by the middleman.

Quite a lot of threshing is done too in the early months of the year, when the farmer cannot get on the land, and of course extra straw is needed for bedding the cattle. Many farmers own their own combine harvester and use it for threshing. There is still a threshing-machine proprietor in the village, who threshes when there is not a combine harvester available. Cattle bedded indoors make continual mucking-out a necessity, and the farmer hopes for some good heavy frosts so that the manure can be led out on to the fields. This task is not the back-breaking job it used to be. No more 'muck-plugging' on to the trailer by the men. The manure is lifted by a hydraulic digger fork on the front of the tractor on to the trailer or manure-spreader. The trailer is more widely used on small farms, and the manure forked on to the land by the men. . . .

As soon as the land dries after the wintry weather the farm becomes a real hive of industry, the tractors buzzing all the hours of daylight, ploughing, discing, harrowing, drilling in the acres of spring wheat, barley and oats which have to be sown. After the corn has been sown the rest of the land has to be prepared and the sugar-beet and mangolds drilled and the potatoes set. This year, this again is an easier task than it was a few years ago. Instead of walking along the row planting a potato every few inches the man sits at a tractor-drawn machine and pops a potato into a hole down which it falls and is planted in the row – a very easy but very monotonous task.

At the beginning of May the bullocks are turned out into the fields for summer pasturing and the cows out to grass in the home fields, brought in to milk twice a day. The turnips are the last crop to be drilled, and when this has been done, the task of hoeing the previously-sown crops is started. Hoeing sugar-beet, mangolds and turnips can be a thankless task in damp weather if the rubbish doesn't 'kill', but instead re-sets itself and is still growing at the second time over. Corn is sprayed to get rid of the rubbish; a much quicker and more effective system than 'looking and hoeing' the rubbish out.

July is the month for hay-making. Once again it is very noticeable how machinery has simplified a once-hard task. After the hay is cut and dried it is baled – a much quicker process than the old fashioned cocking. Only one man is needed to drive the tractor and baler, which means that other work can go on at the same time. The bales are stacked in the same way as loose hay, but the task of carrying in the hay in winter is much easier in tied bales than cutting packed hay with a hay-spade.

In the interval between hay-time and harvest the farmer finishes the last of the hoeing and gets on with slashing the hedges. According to the weather harvest time varies a good deal, and this year owing to the very wet weather it was well into September before harvest got under way. Combining the corn is the obvious answer to a quick harvest, but the small farmer is handicapped by not having enough storage space. To overcome this difficulty most farmers combine the barley but cut oats, wheat and rye by binder and lead it into Dutch barns to be threshed later. A lot of corn was lost in bad weather, either by over-ripe corn spilling in the fields before the combine could get on to the wet land or by rotting in wet stooks. Harvesting went on well into October and joined up with potato-picking time. Here again the farmers had quite heavy losses through the wet weather, but on the whole reasonably good crops were gathered. Sugar-beet crops were not too badly hit by the wet weather, but lifting the crops was a slow, heavy and sticky business.

On the best days of this very wet autumn ploughing had to be done, and most farmers managed to get some if not all of their winter wheat drilled. Mangolds were lifted and pied ready for winter feeding for the stock. In November all the stock came back indoors for the winter. I should imagine that even animals would be pleased to get out of the rain this year! So the farming year ended as it began, the emphasis being on stock management, the hours of daylight being so short that there doesn't seem to be much time for anything else. On the whole I think most farmers were glad to see 1965 come to an end. It was one of the most difficult, disappointing years within living memory, but they had the consoling thought that at any rate 1966 cannot be worse.

The basic wage of the worker is £10/2/0.

The scrapbooks contain many such pictures of life on the basic mixed farm. To quote the list of local words which immediately follows this account in the Crayke book, life for the small farmer is a *maffled* (breathless) round of activity. From the moment he gets up and ties his *shibbons* (shoelaces) he must be *agate* (going). He has a lot to *thole* (put up with) but there's no point in *chuntering* (grumbling), even if a disappointing Farm Prices Review makes his position somewhat *cockly* (insecure); and he has no time to be ill, so it's no good feeling *whemells* (wobbly). Anyway, there are always the consolations of home life; *dowly* (tired) at the end of the long day, he may none the less relax by his hearth in the evening, watching the *kitlins* (kittens) *laik* (play) on the hearthrug. He may even doze off, and find the fire has sunk low; in that case he may poke it, causing a *lillilow* (bright flame) to spring up, reflected in the china and brass on the dresser.

A vivid account of one day in such a year comes from *Llanbedr* (*Denbighshire*):

The farmer has, of necessity, to be an early riser, between 6 and 6.30 a.m. If he is a dairy farmer the first job must be to do the milking. This is usually completed and the churns of milk taken to the milk-stands at the farm gate before breakfast. After breakfast the milking machine has to be washed out, and then the farmer is ready to go to work in the fields.

Today there is a ten-acre field of barley to be harvested and the local agricultural contractor will be arriving about noon with his combine harvester. It is not possible to start harvesting until the dew has risen and the sun has dried the ground. The first setback of the day occurs when it is discovered that there is a puncture in the wheel of one of the tractors. This means removing the wheel and putting it into the car trailer and bribing the long-suffering wife to run it into the garage to be repaired immediately. Following this hindrance the farmer gets on with the job of preparing his sacks for the grain, when his wife, who has returned from the garage, hurries into the shed to say that their neighbour has telephoned asking for help with a difficult calving. Having dispatched his workmen to cut hedges there is nothing else for it but for the farmer to go to his neighbour's aid. It is 10 a.m. when he gets back to his sacks, having done his good deed for the day. Shortly after this a car is driven into the yard; it is the representative of a firm of feeding-stuffs. An order has to be given to him, and this takes up another half-hour of the farmer's precious time. Representatives are never pushed for time, and will talk indefinitely if they think they can persuade the farmer to give them an order. Without further interruption the task of sorting the sacks is completed and the tractors and trailers are prepared for carrying home the sacks of grain. Fortunately the garage proprietor has kindly brought the tractor wheel back again.

At 12 o'clock the farmer and his men go off for their dinner which must be ready for them to swallow before they set off for the barley field. While he eats the farmer scans the morning mail. A Parish Council meeting tonight. 'They'll be lucky,' he mutters. He must also ring up and postpone that delivery of fertilizer due in the afternoon.

The contractor is, as usual, late, finally arrives at 2 o'clock and at last the drone of the harvester can be heard. One man rides on the harvester, two attend to the sacks as they slowly fill with the golden grain. The other two men are employed on lifting the heavy sacks of corn on to the trailers, and when they have a full load taking it to the farm for storage. It is a slow job, and a stop is made at 4 o'clock for tea, brought to the field by the farmer's wife. Now one man must go back to the farm to do the milking, and the others must push on if they are to complete the combining before dark. At about 6 o'clock the farmer's wife is again hurrying into the field, with the cheerful information that the bull has got out of its pen and is rampaging round the yard trying to get into the field which the milking cows have just been turned into. Everything stops for half an hour while the men return to the farm, and eventually succeed in getting the bull back into its pen.

Completion of the job of combining the barley is done by the headlights of the tractors, and it is 11 o'clock when a very weary farmer returns home for his supper, and nearly midnight before he gets to bed. Tomorrow the straw must be baled and carried in, and the corn will probably have to be dried, and as he climbs into bed the farmer suddenly remembers that the vet is due in the morning to carry out his annual tuberculin test of the dairy herd. But then 'tomorrow is another day'.

Sometimes the farmer's wife has even more urgent and unexpected tasks:

My husband was going to the Lonk Sheep Breeders' Annual Dinner. This year it was held at Todmorden. This happened to be on a very cold night. My last-minute instructions were to 'keep a look-in at that sow', which I did, but with several interruptions of several incoming phone calls, a neighbour to use the phone, and the grocer calling to deliver the weekly order, and getting the children to bed. It was two and a half hours or so between one look-in and the next. By this time there were nine little pigs, five of which were laid out as if dead, and quite cold, as they had not been under the infra-red lamp. I gathered them up in my apron, dashed indoors, gave them a hot bath and put them in the Rayburn warming oven. In a very short time they had completely recovered, and they were all back with the sow when my husband returned. What a night!

(Dunsop Bridge, Lancs.)

The sheep know by instinct when the weather is going to be bad, and make their way down from the fells. . . . On February 16th 13 store bullocks were sent to Hawes market, their average age being nine months, and they made an average price of £50. These beasts were sold before they were gradable because we were having difficulty in buying imported feeding-stuffs owing to the strike of New York dockers, which was holding up the boats in New York, so preventing maize etc. from coming to Britain. Although April has been a cold month sheep and lambs have lived reasonably well. When it is wet and cold in lambing time the sheep and lambs need constant attention. This is very hard work because it means walking round them from dawn to dusk and often during the night. When it is cold the lambs need to drink their mothers' milk as soon as they are on their feet. If they do not they will die of starvation, so it is necessary for the shepherd to be always there giving assistance. The latter part of the month, the land has been covered with fertilizer to make the grass grow for the hay crop, the sheep having eaten the first growth of grass.

Every year we have a lamb with some abnormality. This year we had a lamb which lost its wool when only a few days old, so we made a woollen jacket to keep it warm.

(*Askrigg, Yorks.*)

Since 1954 the prices you pay for food have gone up by 6/8 in the £. During the same period the prices we, as farmers, receive have actually gone down by 4d in the £. The farmer's wife had much to contend with – rising prices, in spite of the Chancellor's attempt to curb them, the seemingly never-ending trail of wet clothes, and power cuts. In 1965 the farmer's wife had to be prepared to milk cows, herd cattle, feed and dose calves, rescue sick and straying animals in torrential rain, feed hens, sell eggs, drive tractors, balers and combines, provide instant meals, keep meals hot, act as secretary and buyer of spare parts.

(*Long Wittenham, Berks.*)

*

Mobberley (*Cheshire*) is within jet-scream of Manchester's Ringway Airport.

Old Hall, built in 1612, a beautiful old house with six stair-cases, panelled rooms and wide oak stairs, a beautiful garden with lawns, yew hedges and a moat, was left to Manchester University by Miss Bishop.

No longer an isolated village . . . up till ten to fifteen years ago 'the village' was the area from the Old Hall, Roebuck Inn and the Bull's Head Inn, where the old Crêpe Mill used to stand till 1887 and the houses were built nearby for the mill workers. Now 'the village' is the area near the Ilford Works in Town Lane, where most of the shops and the new Post Office are.

Lanes across commons begin to be dotted with modern houses, town and country eye each other uneasily, the wind blows in over slopes, gravel pits, fields, housing estates, farms, sodium lights. Although it is only a few miles from Manchester there is enough farmland still for there to be

bullfinch, reed bunting, carrion crows, jackdaws and rooks, chaffinch, cuckoo, chiff-chaff and curlew, wild duck, widgeon and mallard, fieldfare and flycatcher, lots of gulls and grey lag geese, also the green finch; the heron, house-martin and yellow-hammer, jays and jack-snipe, kingfishers, lapwings or plovers, moorhen and magpies, nuthatch, owls both tawny and barn, partridge and pheasant.

And always there is the trend to rationalization:

Farms vary from 60 to 150 acres. More barley, and less wheat and oats, because this can be ground and used as cattle food and fed to fattening pigs and poultry. Quite a number of farmers keep a Hereford bull with a view to producing beef cattle. Two farmers have installed bulk mixing, whereby the milk is taken direct from cow to tank, and is collected by a milk tanker.

81

As we shall see, 'rationalization' does not necessarily mean specialization, doing only one thing; rather is it a matter of spotting profitability, of amalgamation or cooperation, of transport and marketing. Nothing could be more 'rationalized', in the sense of specialized use of a unique terrain, than sheep-farming in the Dales. But

... Even farming, which though of a Spartan nature has long been an important feature of our area, and which was put on a prosperous footing in the Middle Ages by those excellent farmers, the Cistercian monks, is now in danger of disappearing. Many Dales farms have been sold as uneconomic, the land parcelled out to various uses and the buildings converted into homes for retired people or as week-end dwellings for the townsman. The National Trust itself, which was originally intended to preserve the traditional life of the Dales, is unable to curb this tendency, and many of its own farms and buildings now house forestry workers or estate men.

(*Outgate, Westmorland*)

Wrawby may inform us that 'the sheep population is one tenth what it was at the turn of the century', but in *Bransgore*

Gravelly, well-drained soil is suited to sheep. Roughly five ewes to each acre, as he uses a breed which does best with plenty of room. He predicts an increase in sheep farming as sheep are easier to tend than cows, which is a great consideration in these days of rising labour costs. Also milk production is less profitable than it was, whereas the price paid for wool is better – 4/6 a lb. One ram and 34 Scots half-bred ewes. The ram was put in with all the ewes at once, ensuring that the lambs would all be born at about the same time. This method allows for a new-born 'orphan' lamb to be adopted and reared by another ewe. A ewe will not adopt a lamb which is more than a day old, as a general rule. 19 ewes had twin lambs, 13 had single lambs, and 2 ewes aborted. Total, 51 lambs in February ... lambs are kept until they are about 16 weeks old and their average live weight is 80 lb., which gives about 40 lb. carcass weight. Top price is 3/6 a lb. Lambs are tailed at 4 weeks, to prevent maggots, and dosed for worms at 8 weeks. The male lambs are castrated (wethers). Coats have to be trimmed and cleaned before the lambs are sold ... monthly spraying with DDT for maggot protection, instead of dipping. Foot-baths of formaldehyde are also used to combat foot-rot. Gross income per ewe, approximately £9 on lambs and £1/7/– on wool.

Some forms of agriculture, particularly those on its frontier with horticulture, have of course always been specialized; but even here there is change.

Amherst Hill is the only farm in the village using its oasts for their original purpose of drying the hops. Here there are 28 well-maintained hopper huts. Only one family came down from London this year, as the hops are machine-picked, and together with local labour 14 women did the final checking for quality and freedom from leaves. . . .

Although cherries and plums were fairly prevalent up to about 1960 – and what a wonderful sight in Spring, with sheep and lambs beneath! – they were subject to so many forms of canker that much has been grubbed and has been, or is being replanted with apples. There has been much planting recently of dessert apples, mainly Cox, with Worcesters as the prevailing pollinators. The sale of culinary apples, Bramley mostly, had decreased somewhat with the lack of enthusiasm on the part of the housewives to prepare them for cooking, so many are now sold to canneries, or sold locally to hospitals, canteens and other institutions. Spraying; as many as 13 or 14 washes in the growing season (see chart over).

The vision of frantic mixing up of chemicals for warfare

SPRAYING PROGRAMME

When	What against	What with	Per 100 gallons
1. Bud-burst to mouse-ear	Scab, aphids, caterpillars, canker	Spersol, DDT 50%, Lig. mercury	6 lb., 2 lb., 8 fl. oz.
2. Full green cluster	Scab, aphids, red spider	Spersol, DDT 50%, Rogor 40	5 lb., 2 lb., 10 fl. oz.
3. Early pink bud	Scab, mildew	Spersol, DDT 50%,	5 lb., 2 lb.
4. Late pink bud to early blossom	Scab, mildew	Spersol, Captan	4 lb., 2 lb.
5. Immediate petal-fall, 7–9 days after (4)	Scab, mildew	Spersol, Captan	4 lb., 2 lb.
6. Total petal fall, 7 days after (5)	Scab, mildew	Spersol, Captan	4 lb., 2 lb.
7. 7 days after (6)	Sawfly, aphids, red spider, scab, mildew	Rogor 40 and Spersol, Captan	16 fl. oz., 4 lb., 2 lb.

against the vast army of pests, conjured up by that account from *Pembury* (*Kent*), reflects a modern intensification of a specialization that has always existed; but a broader example of the rationalizing trend as it affects the actual life of a traditional family mixed farm comes from *Llanedwen* (*Anglesey*).

We changed our farming policy last September. After nearly thirty years keeping milking cows and selling milk we decided to rear beef calves and produce beef, carrying on as previously with the production of fat lambs. Consequently there were between 30 and 40 in-calf cows and heifers to sell off. It is fortunate that this type of stock are making good prices at the moment, and our well-bred Friesians, averaging 1,000 to 1,200 gallons of milk a year, have made between £100 and £132 each.

There were several reasons for making this drastic change – the price of milk tending to go down every year, and the cost (which included labour, feeding and rent) going up. Labour had become very difficult; and being a seven-day week job, both early and late, husband and wife had to carry on over the weekends.

... cattle at about £9 a cwt, live. They averaged about 11 cwt ... 106 lambs from 57 ewes in 3 weeks, only 12 ewes left to lamb ... estate agent calls as arranged; a relief to have been able to come to terms over farm rent. This again is a problem causing anxiety and insecurity to tenant farmers brought about by Government legislation during the past ten years.

27th February. Vet testing all cattle (76), Ministry's routine annual tubercular test. Test read in 72 hours; a relief – all are clean.

Bought 17 heifers for fattening from Dublin. Our calves have a virus disease of the eyes called New Forest Disease. It needs very regular and thorough treatment with an antibiotic.

April 3rd. Week starts sunny and warm and continues. Turn out 10 bullocks first time, brought in at night. Nitrogen potash fertilizer on 6½ acre field, for hay. 24 lambs weighed. Average 66½ lb. live; expect to receive 4/10 per lb. if not over 30 lb. deadweight, or 4/9 under 35 lb. Meanwhile it is surprising how many people have visited the Ancient Monument on the farm. It is a burial chamber of the Bronze Age, about 1500 B.C.

Turn out the 16 Irish heifers to fresh young ley. End of April, 2nd lot of lambs. May 1st, 2nd lot of lambs weighed. 36 go to FMC Caernarfon. Those remaining are injected for Pulpy Kidney, as a very good lamb has died suddenly. Also dose for worms. Collect all big stones brought up by plough and cultivator. Ewes whose lambs have been sold are to be confined to one field; save their food for those with lambs and get them ready for mating again.

Sow 18 cwt. Scotch 'forward' oats, with 12 lb. per acre of three varieties of rye grass. The oats will be cut by self-binder and fed to cattle on the sheaf, and the rye grass will grow on for grazing. Harrow and roll.

We have one helper.

29th May. The 16 Irish heifers to FMC Caernarfon. Excellent weight but killing-out weight disappointing.

400 yds. trench for water main has been opened with the new tractor-ditcher. Would have been out of the question without it.

July, cut hay two weeks late. Meanwhile 8 more Irish heifers sold ... 400 bales that were baled yesterday (23rd July) are stored in the barn. The second field is now clear. This has been done on Sunday. Owing to a shortage of labour and bad weather we have been forced to work Sundays these last two years ... tonight find a good yearling steer dead on the field, so the vet injects 33 yearling cattle with a vaccine against Blackleg as a precaution.

More trouble getting hay in, but fortunately son is here.

September 4th. Unsettled weather. 49 young cattle have been dosed against Husk. Some fat cattle have been sold and store cattle purchased. Store lambs have arrived from South Wales ... 54 Welsh ewes purchased at Dolgelly ... separate wet oat stooks by hand.

November 26th. Gales and some heavy rain, very cold. But kept dry long enough for contractor to spread 8 tons basic slag on 16 acres grassland. 16 lambs, the last for this year, and 1 in-calf heifer sold.

Obviously the problems of labour shortage are to some extent cancelled out by mechanization; but an extract such as the above gives an impression of a fight on several fronts at once.

We are accustomed to think of our internal communications as long since perfected and taken for granted. It is always faintly surprising to the townsman to be reminded that transport and marketing, for the farmer, are by no means the routine operations that they are for the commuter or even the industrial producer. There are wide enough divergencies in climate, in types of animal stock and crop, in fact in agricultural rhythm, for long-distance transactions as well as local market journeys to be necessary (and after all, it's 10 miles from Llanedwen just to Caernarvon, and 40 to Dolgelly). And it is in this sort of field that very British, empirical forms of farming cooperative are coming into existence:

The continuing economic pressure has forced farmers to look for methods of reducing their costs and improving their marketing techniques. In 1958 farmers in Loddiswell and adjoining parishes formed Avon Farmers Ltd as a non-profit-making company for this purpose. For 2½ years the company was administered from Lilwell Farm, but as membership increased the office was moved to Kingsbridge. The Company now provides the requisites for 800 farmers throughout South Devon, and last year had a turnover of £600,000. The commodities handled range from feed, fertilizer, seed, sprays etc. to any farm or domestic equipment the farmer or his family may need. Although some of the reared calves are sent to the local fattening farmers many of them travel by special lorries overnight to as far as Lincolnshire, Norfolk and Kent. Weaner pigs, too, often travel to the Midlands. One of the advantages of this system of marketing is that better farm prices can be obtained by sending the right type, quality and quantity of stock to where they are required. This is particularly true of fat beef cattle, and pork and cutter pigs. The volume of trade has also increased in this section to as high as 19 lorry-loads of stock despatched the 2nd week in December. The Buildings Department now employs 20 craftsmen and labourers.

To summarize, agriculture in Loddiswell Parish, as in other areas, is becoming more mechanized, and farmers must have some knowledge of engineering as well as stock and crop husbandry. Tighter economic circumstances are changing farming to an industrial business rather than a way of life. The farm

labourer of the past is almost redundant, and staff with specialist knowledge is becoming essential.

(*Loddiswell, Devon*)

'Rather than a way of life'? It will of course be a long
time, if ever, before this is literally and gloomily true. The
overwhelming majority of those who earn their living (as
opposed to their tax rebates) from farming do so because it
is a way of life.

In 1851 there were 1,788,000 farm workers, in 1901 there
were 1,399,000, and now there are 220,000. The National
Economic Development Plan of 1965 expects farming 'to be
able to meet a major part of the additional demand for food
expected by 1970' (estimates differ about how much of our
own food we could produce if this were given total priority:
at present we grow about 50 per cent, and produce two
thirds of the maximum possible temperate climate foods).
But at the same time manpower is expected to decrease
further. 'By continuing to improve its productivity, agriculture would continue to release substantial manpower resources to other industries.'

As we have already seen, as far as individual ownership of
farms is concerned, this must also decrease as the economic
units become larger. Such is the background against which
entry into farming has to be considered. For obvious reasons
the main way of entering it is to be a farmer's or farm
worker's son; but before we come to the flourishing Young
Farmers Club movement to which many of these belong,
there is the interesting story of the other way of entry, that
of the smallholder.

The figures above are from the Report of the Depart-
mental Committee of Inquiry into Statutory Smallholdings
(1966), otherwise and more happily known as the Wise
Report, after its Chairman, Professor M. J. Wise. I was im-

pelled to get it after a visit to a Midland farm of 100 acres,
(big bread-smelling kitchen, two brown-faced, fair-haired
children rushing in from school, 'Mum can I have four shil-
lings?') which was let by the county council. The farmer had
actually started on a two-acre holding of the Land Settle-
ment Association, which originally developed from a
scheme during the Depression to settle men from Durham
and other hard-hit areas on the land.

This particular farmer had, in a sense, come back to the
land, for his grandfather had been a farm worker and, ironi-
cally, his father had been driven *into* the town by the Depression. But farm management or ownership seems such a
closed shop unless you inherit a farm or have enough money
to buy one; could this, I wondered as I encountered many
more 'county council' farms, be the way into farming for
anyone who really loves it but has to start from scratch?

Well, not quite from scratch, as we shall see. The Wise
Report, which like a lot of those Stationery Office books in
their prim blue covers, combines a wealth of information
with a story of absorbing social interest, reviews the statutory (i.e. local authority) and LSA smallholdings and makes
recommendations for the future. It turns out that the LSA
which today has some 800 holdings, in various estates or
settlements (which have centralized produce sale arrangements) totalling some 11,000 acres, is small beer compared with the statutory scheme. In 1964 there were 15,212
local authority holdings, amounting to 426,478 acres. They
formed approximately one tenth of the more efficient agricultural units under 100 acres in England and Wales (for a
long time the basic smallholding figure has been thought of as
50; they are not so sure about this now). Some counties are
more involved than others; Cambridgeshire leads, followed
by northern East Anglia and the counties bordering the
Severn estuary.

There has been a statutory scheme since an Act of 1892, developed until now the Ministry can lend up to 75 per cent. But the origins are in the philosophy expressed by Sir John Sinclair at the Board of Agriculture in 1801 as 'three acres and a cow' as a means of helping the depressed day labourer after the enclosures and other agricultural changes of the eighteenth century. The smallholding scheme was conceived of as a 'farming ladder'; but in fact, over a recent six-year period only 330 smallholders did graduate to owning a farm. For many, concludes the Report, a smallholding was the highest rung of the ladder. The evidence submitted rings with claims and counter-claims. The pool of skilled agricultural labour must not fall dangerously low (from 527,734 in 1949 to 309,800 in 1964, a fall of 41·3 per cent. At the time of writing, early 1968, it is 220,000); yet the tide is moving against the small unit (80 acres is now regarded as better for a smallholding). But why should the State subsidize one kind of worker on the road to self-employment when he is in an industry where the proportion of workers to managers or bailiffs is already 1:1·12, a great deal higher than it is in most manufacturing industry? Why not provide a 'farming ladder' through a re-organized wage structure with proper payment for technical skills? In the waiting list (slightly falling) of some 4,000, 'preference' applicants are those with at least five years' experience of farm work *and* the ability to raise starting capital (some just don't like borrowing, don't understand the mechanism, or are afraid to borrow before applying, but many authorities think the ability to accumulate a little capital is *part* of the quality that makes a good smallholder). 88 per cent of successful applicants have come with not less than a quarter of the necessary capital; and average figures for such capital are given as £1,350 to £2,000 for an arable smallholding, £2,000 to £3,000 for a dairy smallholding. To get started you have, literally, to mean business, and the Report is fascinating about the qualities of the men who do make it, and on the network of mutual assistance of neighbours and relations that helps them to make it. At the same time, it points out, 2,500 fully qualified students leave agricultural institutes every year, and some of these are lost to farming, at a time when trained and efficient young men are needed, if the turnover in small-holdings remains too static. The Committee was dismayed to find one statutory smallholding had remained in the same family since the grandfather had it, and recommends that the waiting list be abolished and all vacancies adver-tised in the national farming press, since 'we consider that men who have had formal training would be more willing to move in order to secure a smallholding'.

*

It is always interesting, when one sees a group in a hotel who are obviously from some conference, to try and guess what the common bond is. Surely there is a Quaker face, for example; and a civil servant face. I'm inclined to think there's a soccer player's face too (there are certainly soccer player's knees). I don't think I've ever seen such an immedi-ately identifiable group as the Young Farmers Club that came into the comfortable pub in Sherborne; the only other thing they could have been was Young Conservatives, for there was a definitely well-heeled look about them (and why should there not be? The estimated profit in the farming industry for 1967–8 is between £350,000,000 and £400,000,000). Yet they were too healthy-looking to have been united by such an indoor thing as mere politics.

You don't have to be a farmer's child to be in the YFC. The other side of the management fence is represented. But a recent survey showed that if the figure of 55 per cent of members engaged in agriculture (urban-area clubs are growing and rural ones slightly declining) is itself broken down, 63 per cent of it comprises those working on family farms, 16 per cent owners or legal partners (and the average YFC member's age is 18½), and only 22 per cent hired farm workers. And the proportion of those with grammar or higher education is higher than the national average. Naturally there is a considerable amout of purely technical stuff in their meetings and excursions; the scrapbooks contain a lot of accounts of stock-judging competitions, visits to farms to see new equipment and the like. But there is also a very strong social and recreational side, and quite often the YFC is the liveliest youth organization for miles around, with quizzes and dances and public speaking competitions and exchange visits to foreign countries and all sorts of enterprising programmes:

February was a rather memorable month for the Young Farmers Club, because of the Juniors reaching the finals of the Junior Quiz and the Club being selected from the whole of Lancashire to stage a display of crafts at the Northern Area finals to be held at Durham.

(*Dunsop Bridge, Lancs.*)

And, not surprisingly in Wales,

The Young Farmers Club meet weekly during the winter months, and although there are only 14 members under the age of 25 in the Club they did extraordinarily well at the County Eisteddfod held at the King's Hall, Aberystwyth, by winning the W. G. Hughes Shield for the highest number of points, also the Geraint Howells Trophy for the winning choir conductor Mr G. Oliver at Llanavan. The Choir was also placed first at the Llanilar Eisteddfod Solo Under 21, Solo Penillion, Pop Song, Quartet, Unison, Hymn Singing, Action Song, Choir, Party Recitation

Under 25. The County Rally was held at Troederyraur. Llanilar was placed first in the Dairy Stock Judging Competition.

(*Llanilar, Cards.*)

*

The Ford tractor division produced a kind of 'our artist's impression' of the post-2000 farm in which, according to a *Times* report, there will be hovercraft, and 'wheeled or tracked giants doing long sequences of operations in one sweep – clearing one crop, processing the soil and putting in seed for the next.' It will be an affair of 'big open spaces' but 'the farmer has now no need to go outside. National and commercial services pour in accurate weather forecasts and market analyses, make printed copies for reference and swell the recorded data for the private computer which gives him all the answers to simple questions like the rationing of his stock and the best time to sell his produce . . .'

It doesn't sound such hard work as it is now. Not so much fun, either.

The Surviving Past

Memory implies change, and *vice versa*. If life were an undifferentiated, unchanging stream there wouldn't be any memory, or any anticipation either (how boring the conventional earthbound, timebound notion of Paradise is, a kind of endless fine Thursday afternoon!). Yet somehow we expect the countryside with its background of enduring natural life, cyclic but not changing – certainly not changing as much as the cities – to yield more in the way of memories.

But here we should distinguish between personal and communal memories. Let us take the latter first. There is certainly something rooted about country life that makes communal memories and customs resonate more than they do in towns, so intensely concerned with Now. In a town, revivals have a very self-conscious look; morris men may look pretty strange dancing outside a country pub, whether or not laid on for American photographers, but they look even stranger in the Wigmore Hall. Quite a lot of things in the country which people take to be age-old traditions turn out on closer inspection to be nineteenth or even twentieth century revivals – and none the worse for that, if they fit naturally into the 'long memory' of the countryside. What, for instance, could be more olde than the maypole? The first thing you see in *Aldborough*, a village now practically joined on to Boroughbridge on the A1, is the tall pole on the sloping, triangular village green surrounded by decent, comfortable Georgian houses; they have all been there a long time, on the edge of the fat plain of York:

The maypole is a ship's mast. There were only six maypoles standing in the area in the 1800's. This one dates from 1903. ... First we collected the children; girls willingly, boys reluctantly practised the whole of a cold windy March and wet April, with sodden ribbons and a portable maypole. The Fire Brigade put up our lovely new ribbons on top of the 45-foot pole with a gale blowing. They blew down and were put up much lower, so that the children could manipulate them. Plaiting was more difficult with the longer ribbons. Practice in the rain every night the last week in April. May Day the sun shone, the church bells rang, hundreds came to watch, and the children looked like angels and danced till they could dance no more.

This seems perfectly natural in a village as conscious of its history, which goes back to Roman times, as Aldborough:

Few people in Aldborough itself are entirely without feelings for these things, although perhaps many have neither the time nor the inclination to read about them much. There is a steady if small demand for books on local history at the Boroughbridge branch of the county library. Talks on the same subject are greatly appreciated and a good deal of interest is always aroused when excavations are going on in the village. ... Isurium Brigantum. The works of such well-known authorities on the subject as R. G. Collingwood and Richmond make fascinating reading to some of us who often find in our own gardens the relics of a civilization that flourished so many centuries ago. Most of us turn up pottery and sometimes coins and other small objects when hoeing our rose-beds or digging our vegetable patches.

The Hustings overlooking the green is a reminder of the days before the Reform Act of 1832. Here the 60 or 70 electors of Aldborough chose their Parliamentary representatives, a privi-

95

lege which a like number of electors in Boroughbridge, only a mile away, also enjoyed. Both boroughs were in the 18th century under the control of successive Dukes of Newcastle ...

Possibly living in a place with strong communal memories is also conducive to a more organized articulation of personal memories; possibly it is simply that there has been no urban equivalent of the scrapbook competition – after all, it is not necessary to live in a village to have personal memories; merely to be old. And of course most people do not make the formal distinction between communal and personal memory; one's own life, that of one's parents, and so that of one's ancestors, blur and merge in the context of a strong enough local tradition. It seems perfectly natural, again, when immediately after the Romans and the rotten boroughs the Aldborough book goes on

There is a pony in the village called 'Titus' and a dog called 'Roman' ... newcomers are not considered 'Roman' if they were not born in Aldborough. Nevertheless, as the new residents tend to increase and others move away a kindlier note prevails, and these may be considered 'Roman' after 25 years in Aldborough ...

Miss B. J. Mudd came to Aldborough in 1910 and ran the Aldborough Dairy for 45 years, up to 1960, during which time she entertained a number of celebrities. She showed butter and cheese very successfully at numerous shows throughout the country, and Miss Mudd's Cheese became known over a wide area and internationally, 'As Supplied to H.R.H. The Princess Royal.'

The Village Shop; 1913, Mrs Nicholson's father moved in. In those days things were very primitive. All the water for drinking and animals came from the village pumps. Besides the shop my father had a yeast round, going round all the villages in a 7-mile radius. We also had four fields in which were kept cows, horses, pigs and hens. He also took people to Boroughbridge station in the pony and trap, and the waggonette was used to take our village and local people to whist drives and dances. The same year, I was born and christened Minnie in our church. The shop opened at 7 a.m. till 9 p.m., and on Saturdays till 11 p.m.

Communal memories may be nothing more than local sayings, customs or superstitions:

It was the custom, which is now dying out, that when a person sells his stock and implements on declining farming they provide a meal for all persons attending the sale, whether they are buyers or not. They also provide stronger liquid refreshment for those who spend a good deal of money or are neighbours. It is also traditional for each neighbour to buy a piece of equipment at the sale, often the piece he borrowed most, and to pay over the odds, i.e. more than it is worth.

Burial customs: no member of the family bears the coffin; that is the duty of neighbours. No matter what the difficulties, the deceased must go out of his own front door feet first.

Local families give their sons family surnames as their Christian names, such as Wilson, Tyson, Dixon, Scott and Thompson.

Wedding custom: the bride and groom, on leaving the church, find the church gate firmly tied. The groom has to throw copper coins to the local youth before he is allowed to untie the gate and proceed to the reception.

When a farmer sells an animal not intended for slaughter he will give about one shilling in the pound back to the buyer in 'luck money', thus ensuring the animal's continued good health. Up until August this was deducted by the auction company from the selling price, since when several auction companies used by Drigg farmers have refused to deal in 'luck money', and it is now paid in cash to the buyer.

(*Drigg, Cumberland*)

Drigg may be on that romantic and still largely unspoiled coastline where the Fells come down to the sea, and a mile from Low Moor a signpost indicates a secondary road on the right, TO STATION AND SHORE. This road contains cottages, bungalows and houses . . . the houses peter out at the level crossing, and here is Drigg railway station which is threatened with closure. Next to the railway station stands the Victoria Hotel. The road . . . follows a circuitous route to the beach, over the lonely stretches of Drigg Common

but it is also a place where '36 per cent of the population are employed by the Atomic Energy Authority at Windscale and Calder works'.

. . . 4th of November 'Mischief Night', when children half believe lawlessness is permissible. Damage was done to road signs in the village.

(*Willoughby, Lincs.*)

On the other hand—

The old seasonal children's games have almost vanished in Willoughby. The primary schoolchildren had never seen the old wooden tops, nor knew how they were whipped. Those who still hoarded marbles did not know how to play with them. Inquiries about iron hoops brought one, blacksmith-made, out of its hiding place, and for a while it was trundled along the lane. But what good is one hoop without the fun of competition? Some sort of hopscotch survived, but it was admitted that games never really got going because of the arguments as to what the rules and methods of play should be. All skipping games were rare, outside organized games lessons at school.

Few old superstitions seem to remain, but a modern one very generally accepted dictates the proper procedure at the sight of an ambulance. The favourite is 'when you see an ambulance, hold your collar until you see a four-footed animal'. A less popular alternative is 'when you see an ambulance, lick your finger and put it on your heel'.

A living link with the 19th-century fairs was an old custom that was still observed in the lifetime of Dr Barry, who died in 1928. People coming to Grampound on those occasions used to come to the doctor's house and pay his bill, and if this came to over £1 they were offered a buffet lunch 'on the house'. In those days the doctor lived in Bon-y-Thon and those of us who remember the house as it was can picture the scene. There was a beautiful long mahogany table stretching the whole length of the staircase wall, and on this were cold joints of all kinds, bread, butter, pies etc., and on stands below the table casks of beer and cider. The late Mrs Barry used to tell us of the weeks of preparation, pickling beef, hams, tongues etc., and of the extra cooking when the great day arrived.

... one must not wash clothes on Innocents' Day, because you would wash your friends away. This is a bit difficult, because New Year's Day is also forbidden. One must never wash blankets in May. But apart from these you may go on happily on any day you wish.

(*Grampound, Cornwall*)

Grampound also has a Wassail Song which, for all the rustic vigour of its tune (below) induces a slight suspicion that this may have been one occasion on which the old days

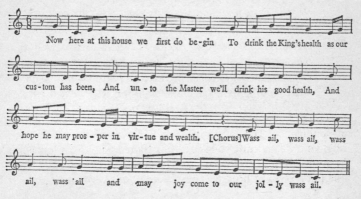

Now here at this house we first do be-gin To drink the King's health as our cus-tom has been, And un-to the Master we'll drink his good health, And hope he may pros-per in vir-tue and wealth. [Chorus] Wass ail, wass ail, wass ail, wass ail and may joy come to our jol-ly wass ail.

were perhaps a bit *too* spacious. If you looked out of the window and saw the singers approaching, perhaps swaying a little already, you would know you couldn't possibly get though all this in less than twenty minutes, if that:

> *Now here at this house we first do begin*
> *To drink the King's health, as the custom has been*
> *And unto the master, we'll drink his good health*
> *And hope he may prosper in virtue and wealth*
> *Wassail, wassail, wassail, wassail, and may joy come*
>   *to our jolly wassail.*

> *In a friendly manner this house we salute*
> *For it is an old custom, you need not dispute*
> *Ask not the reason from where it did spring*
> *For you very well know it's an old ancient thing*
> *Wassail, etc.*

> *Now here at your door we orderly stand*
> *With our jolly wassail and our hats in our hand*
> *We do wish you good health unto Master and Dame*
> *To children and servants we do wish the same*
> *Wassail, etc.*

> *It has been the custom, as I've been told*
> *By ancient housekeepers in days of old*
> *When young men and maidens together draw near*
> *They fill up our bowls with cider or beer*
> *Wassail, etc.*

> *Come fill up our wassail bowl full to the brim*
> *See harnessed and garnished so neat and so trim*
> *Sometimes with laurel and sometimes with bays*
> *According to custom to keep the old ways*
> *Wassail, etc.*

PAUSE FOR DRINK

> *Methinks I do smile to see the bowl full*
> *Which just now was empty and now filled do grow*

By the hands of good people, long may they remain
And love to continue the same to maintain
Wassail, etc.

Now neighbours and strangers we always do find
And hope we shall be courteous, obliging and kind
And hope your civility to us will be proved
As a piece of small silver in token of love
Wassail, etc.

PAUSE FOR COLLECTION

We wish you great plenty and long time to live
Because you were so willing and freely to give
To our jolly wassail most cheerful and bold
Long may you live happy, long may you live bold
Do we now say wassail, etc.

We hope your new apple trees prosper and bear
That we shall have cider again next year
For where you've a hogshead we hope you'll have ten
That you will have cider when we come again
With our wassail, etc.

We all hope your barley will prosper and grow
That you may have barley and beer to bestow
For where you've a bushel we hope you'll have ten
That you will have beer when we come again
With our wassail, etc.

Now for this good liquor to us you do bring
We'll lift up our voices and merrily sing
That all good householders may continue still
And provide some good liquor our bowl for to fill
To sing our wassail, etc.

Now for this good liquor, your cider or beer
Now for the great kindness that we have had here
We'll return our thanks, and shall still bear in mind
How you have been bountiful, loving and kind
Towards our wassail, etc.

Now for the great kindness that we have received
We return you our thanks and shall take our leave
From this present time we shall bid you adieu
Until the next year when the time do ensue
With our wassail, etc.

Now jolly old Christmas is passing away
According to custom this is the last day
That we shall enjoy along with you to abide
So farewell old Christmas, this merry old tide
With our wassail, etc.

Perhaps the deepest and at the same time taken-for-granted communal memories are some that have not been in the conscious mind at all, until some piece of specialist information relates a familiar scene with the past. One climbs a great hill out of Newcastle-under-Lyme in the scarred and grimy Potteries; at its summit, a sudden glory of sunset over Welsh mountains; one drops down again, under the M6 (it seems a natural frontier, like the instant change from Essex scenery to Suffolk scenery when crossing the River Stour on the A12, or the sudden view of all Oxfordshire from the edge of the stockbroker Chilterns – there are many such). And suddenly one is in Cheshire, where, as the book for *Bartomley* puts it,

although we are only two miles from the Pennine flanks, this S.W. prolongation of the Pennines re-curves from the Staffordshire to the Shropshire county boundary, and the sands of the low morainic hills which separate Shropshire from Cheshire, and the Weaver basin from the Severn basin, mingle here with the sands of a deltaic outwash ridge ... these bounding sands form rolling country of varied height, diversifying the level boulder clays and peat mosses.

It is all flat fields, cows, meadows, trees and heathland,

and snug half-timbered villages (where you may find a Rolls-Royce director or a railway executive from Crewe); and you notice a lot of high yew hedges:

In bow-and-arrow days almost all the cottage gardens boasted yew trees. Now we are within a bowshot of the M6 motorway.

Sometimes a mere menu or programme can give almost as much of the atmosphere of a tradition as a well-written account. One can *hear* this evening, just looking at the page:

Burns Club, 65 members (limited for space)

PROGRAMME

Toast: 'Sentiment and music.'	
Address to the Haggis	C. Scott and
	J. Armstrong

(No smoking)

Grace	Chairman
Toast: 'The Queen'	Chairman
God Save The Queen	The Company
Toast: 'The Immortal Memory'	S. Ridley
Song: 'There Was A Lad'	The Company
Appreciation of 'The Immortal Memory	G. Blackie

(Smoking allowed)

Toast: 'The Lassies'	R. Allen
Reply	Major Dance
Toast: 'The Visitors'	H. Wilson
Reply	A Visitor

(Five minutes interval)

Song: 'Green Grow The Rushes, O'	J. G. Dodd
Song: 'The Lea Rigg'	H. Jackson
Toast: 'Bellingham Burns Club'	J. Maughan
Reply	Mr Sumners

Recitation: 'Tam O'Shanter'	R. J. Steele
Toast: 'Chairman and Secretary'	W. Lawrence
Reply	W. Anderson
Toast: 'Singers and Speakers'	W. Charlton
Reply	W. Johnstone
Toast: 'Host and Hostess'	T. Armstrong
Reply	W. Foster
Auld Lang Syne: Pianist, T. Hedley.	
Piper: J. Tough.	

(*Bellingham, Northumberland*)

Of course for anyone over forty in Britain there is one area where personal and communal memories are inseparable:

The Second World War saw every man, woman and child fully involved as the Battle of Britain roared overhead, the skies streaked with white vapour-streamers from the planes. A girls' school was evacuated here from London. Refugees came in from the coast, soldiers were quartered in the larger houses. We were crowded out, and almost too busy to be frightened. Before D-day American airmen were encamped in the woods. And then, worst of all, the buzz-bombs, night and day, incessantly. A number of houses were destroyed and ten village people were killed, mostly women and children ... when a searchlight unit arrived during the war we could let them have baths, although there were barely a dozen baths available in Smarden ... we had our own official WI work, that of jam-making and fruit-canning. The first canning operation took place during the height of the Battle of Britain, in a farm outhouse, where the cans were boiled in a copper fed by billets of wood, while the planes roared and crackled over our heads ... the village swarmed with American airmen from the Thunderbolt aerodromes round about. They appreciated the dances we organized for them, but otherwise did not seem too willing to be befriended.

(*Smarden, Kent*)

The great hero of our time, through whom Britain and its countryside (and the whole Western world) were preserved, inviolate, for the dangerous future, was carried to a country churchyard during the year covered by these books, and there is scarcely one that fails to mention that steel-grey February morning when we *all* remembered.

... left by early morning train to the lying-in-state of Sir Winston. There was no impatience among the people at all. In Millbank Gardens the WVS were serving out welcome beakers of tea, which people bought and took along with them as they walked. At this point it could have been a queue for any event. The women outnumbered the men, and there were also lots of children, many obviously in a school party. Gradually one could pick out those who had probably served in the war, when Churchill was at his greatest. There were men who looked like veterans of D-day and Alamein, and in this age-group we somehow felt a bond. As we neared the great door of St Stephen's progress became slower, and people silent and subdued. We moved to the top of the steps inside the hall, and there the first striking fact to remember was the stark simplicity of it all. The raised coffin was covered by the Union Jack, and above it, on a cushion, was the Insignia of a Knight of the Most Noble Order of the Garter. There were six huge candles around the coffin, and at each corner of the catafalque stood an Air Force officer with head bowed and hands crossed over his sword, so immobile that they looked like wax-figures. It did not take long to pass through the hall. There didn't seem to be enough time for all our thoughts. Many were weeping over the loss of someone we all really knew, but as we emerged and brushed away the tears there was also a feeling of triumph and a great pride in being British and of having lived in his time.

(*Willoughby, Lincs.*)

A 90-year-old shepherd still cultivates his quite large garden and goes into Brigg, shopping for himself, on Thursdays. He and his wife, who died a few years ago, could tell many interesting stories of the hard life of farm workers 60 to 70 years back, and it was quite touching to hear her address him as 'shepherd'.

(*Wrawby, Lincs.*)

*

A red-faced, smiling man in a brown store-coat said, 'Ah knaw him well. He's mi father!' when I asked where I could find an old man mentioned in one of the Westmorland scrap-books. He took me across the street and opened the front door of a cottage. A splendid craggy old man with a white moustache was dozing over the fire. 'Here's a man from the BBC to speak to you,' said the son. 'No, I'm writing a book, about the country,' I said. 'Oh, aye, come in,' said the old man.

. . . and what about entertainment in those days?

Oh, I were a fiddler. Aye, I tried to play t'fiddle. Ah had a brother a good'n. Piccolo player . . .

. . . do you feel that people lived more as a community, or less, in the old days?

Well, they were more company for each other. There wasn't that bloomin' television.

You don't like television?

Augh, it's done away with all family life, because some people – 'put that off!' – 'no, but Ah want to hear this!' – well, there y'are, it's goin' and goin' and goin'. But then they used to sit down and – well, used to play games, cards, and different kinds of games of a night, you know. Or of course we used to get our fiddles out, and practise fiddlin' at home, you know, and dance around kitchen.

What did you dance in the kitchen?

Oh, polkas and schottisches . . .

*

There may be stronger communal memories in the country; but when it comes to personal memories what counts is the ability to express them. It so happens that the following piece has an urban background; yet it seems strangely redolent of the Lincolnshire village in which the writer lived. We are not told what the town was, but somehow one imagines a small town on the East Coast, where children grew up within reach both of fields and the sea . . .

My first childhood memory is the introduction of electric trams into the town where I was born . . . then that *ragbone!* We children received a windmill made up of a square of wallpaper, cut and pinned on to a stick, for a few rags. Another of my very early recollections is hearing my Mamma and Dadda with two other people practising quartets after I got to bed. I loved it. Whenever I hear *Two Roses* or *O, Dem Golden Slippers!* I get the same thrill I experienced then. We were a musical family, and how happily we all clustered round the organ on a Sunday evening after chapel! Mamma played, Dadda boomed out the bass, one sister sang tenor, another alto, and the two others the treble. We each had our own particular solo. Mine was that pathetic *Children's Garden*. As we got older, and one sister was out at work, our meal times got staggered, but we always had Saturday dinner together. After we had eaten we would sit where we were round the table and sing – songs, hymns, oratorios, forgetting time and place for at least an hour. Happy days!

What about that annual holiday in the country? I remember vividly waking at dawn and hearing the cockeril crowing, the clip-clop of the horses' hooves, and the jangle of the harness as they were led out to the fields – a heavenly sound to a town-bred youngster . . . a particularly vivid memory I have is of an unusual sound in my town. Perhaps in the middle of the night I would wake up hearing a hymn tune – like a trumpet of heaven, I thought – the sound coming nearer and nearer until it seemed to fill all the room, nay, all the world, with its music. It was a certain sea captain returning from a fishing trip, who had adapted his ship's buzzer so that he could play tunes, and on nearing port he let his wife at home know that he was on his way back. What a thrill it must have been to her! I know I was just entranced.

I wonder if anyone else remembers the boys making sparks by kicking the pavement with their protector-studded boots? I tried it out many times but never succeeded.

Just one more memory before I leave, though I could go on and on. Imagine a blazing hot day in town. It is too hot even to play. The dust rises every time a horse and cart passes, or a man with a hand-cart. All at once there is a shout goes up. 'Water-cart! Water-cart!' The boys scramble to take off their boots and stockings and roll up their trousers, and as the water-cart goes up and then down the street they jostle each other to get in the spray from the numerous jets along the back of the cart. How we girls wished we could shed our modesty and do likewise! What a wealth of enjoyment one gets from these memories, and what a wonderful Creator we have to give us this ability. We could be infirm, blind or deaf, but we can always 'remember'.

(*North Kelsey, Lincs*, a winning essay by Mrs Gibbons in an *I Remember* competition)

*

Having read the book of *Eglwys Fach* with several others, in the town of Denbigh, I drove over the mountains to the village itself; one of those roads where you can stop, and hear nothing but the wind moving through many kinds of rich, shining grasses on the wide verge, and the bleating of sheep. Down a 1-in-4 hill to Eglwys Fach, set snugly in the valley of a tributary of the Conway. I was directed to the little house of the 76-year-old Mr Idwal Jones, who had sounded as if he might be interesting. He was. I got not only a fascinating picture of life in rural Wales over half a century but a harp and song recital and tea and some particularly good Welsh cake. I slept in my caravan that night, in a field just outside the village. As I was backing out in the morning an elderly labourer got off his bicycle. 'Oh, now, you were right under a tree. If you're camping you never want to do that, you know. The lightning will take the tree if there's a storm, and come down into your van. Wait now, I'll guide you out . . .'

I cannot reproduce Mr Jones's delicious blooping harp music, which included not only *The Ash Grove* with its original words but *The Ash Grove* with Welsh nonsense words, consisting of the titles of a lot of Welsh songs strung together *but in a different metre*. But –

'. . . we all stood at a certain place in the village, and a pack of farmers stood in another place; and then the farmer called one, and they had an argument about wages. "Will you come to me for a week, or a fortnight?" "Yes." "How much d'you want?" "O, I want two pounds." "I'll give you a guinea." Half the morning would go in arguing, to try and get the price down, you see . . . and the first two to settle, they announced loudly over the village, "that's the wages for this week". And everybody would accept that. It was called "the cross", I don't know why.'

How long did this last?

'O, it was gone before the First World War. O, I remember going to a farm in the uplands [he pronounced it *iplands*] – we had our harvest early here, you see – and my father said, you can go out for a fortnight to earn pocket money. Well I went into a big farm in the highlands there, starting five o'clock in the morning, working two hours out in the field before having a bite, breakfast at seven, dinner at twelve, tea at three, and supper at seven; hard work, not sitting on a tractor.

We had an annual fair on the 11th of May. You couldn't go through the village; standings each side, shooting galleries, also coconuts and all sorts of things. And it was the waging period, you see. The farmers came down looking for lads for a place for the following year, you see. And the cattle dealers used to come here, and we used to take cattle down, and stand in a certain place, and the cattle dealers came round. I remember taking yearlings, and selling them for £6 per head. You get £28 to £30 for a calf today ...

... I went to Coventry to learn piano tuning. And while I was there I got a syllabus of the Eisteddfod in Liverpool, with *penillion* singing with the harp – O, I've sung in scores of Eisteddfodau, you see – then I made up my mind I would go there to sing under a certain adjudication – adjudicator – because he knew the chapel I come from. I started from Coventry, six o'clock in the morning, on a push-bike. I jumped off for dinner in Newcastle-under-Lyme, twelve o'clock. I jumped off the next time in Liverpool six o'clock that night, after riding a hundred and ten miles. I stayed with my cousin in Wallasey. In the Eisteddfod next day, there was eight competing. I cycled home after getting the first equal prize ...'

For many years himself an adjudicator in the unique Welsh art of *penillion* singing, he also wrote poems for the nurses when he was in hospital; and the following shows how capable he was of turning small events in a local community, such as would make did-you-hear-about-old-so-and-so tales in any village pub, into ditties in English:

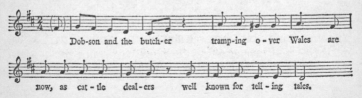

Dob-son and the butch-er tramp-ing o-ver Wales are now, as cat-tle deal-ers well known for tell-ing tales.

Dobson and the butcher
By tramping over Wales
Are now, as cattle dealers,
Well known for telling tales

They have a special chauffeur,
Very lucky chaps!
But like most other people
They also get mishaps

One day the noted party
Set out up Beulah's Hill
The motor turned a gypper
And stuck there, standing still

And Trevor bach was puzzled
He didn't know what to do
Until Bryn Howard's horses
Came forth and pulled him through

The famous cattle dealers
Were lucky, I can tell,
When the car just tumbled over
By Tyn-y-Groes Hotel

And Dobson, hanging over,
Was an interesting sight,
The butcher on the other side
Pushing with all his might

I'm told another story
That Trevor met a train
At Abergele Station
Which proved to be in vain

The train went through with Dobson
But left him in a mess
Hanging out of the window
Of the Holyhead Express.

*

Although even here the bungalows of the retired, English as well as Welsh, are spreading up from the sea and the Conway estuary, such a place as Eglwys Fach is to a certain extent protected by mountains. All the same, and allowing for the special tenacity of Welsh culture (the scrapbooks refer constantly to the problem of Welsh-speaking in schools, how this is fine in the middle school but makes things progressively difficult as sixth form level is approached), will there be such men, rooted in their local as well as their national culture, in another fifty years?

Memory and tradition, as these extracts have shown, is more than quaint thatched roofs. It is childhood, wars, luck money for auctioneers, yew hedges, schottisches in the kitchen; the whole texture of a way of life. In the nature of things older people are the ones who hand it on; but up to now it has been a continuous, living process. Is there now a tide before which even those protecting mountains will crumble, will the electronic village, in an irresistible process, worldwide, a mechanical and electronic culture, endlessly universal and homogeneous, obliterate the diversified life of villages as we have remembered them, all rural and all different? Let us see what is happening.

Changing, or Commuting

It may seem strange that a place like *Harden*, in Yorkshire, should have a branch of the countrywomen's organization at all. Although the secretary entertained me in a nice new house in a nice new estate at the base of a wooded hill (her husband told me how he had asked, in a rural pub on the North Yorkshire moors, where was the best place to see the salmon leap and was told 'by Whitby Gasworks'), the core of it contains several big old brick factories and mills:

Joseph Steel Ltd make springs of every kind; compression springs, tension springs, torsion springs, flat springs. Employs 120, mostly from the village.
Ellison Circlips Ltd make various wire clips.
V. and A. Spinning Ltd, spinners of hand, knitting and rug wools. This firm employs 26.
Intermark Ltd make Cloth Bunches for the textile trade and plastic covers for the printing industry.

It might seem at first sight the kind of place everyone was thinking about when the WIs were debating their 'nothing-over-4,000 rule' at their Albert Hall AGM. (It was repealed, but not without much heart-searching. Although there had long been anomalies such as a WI in *Wembley*, the new ruling does reflect today's blurring of the old village limits.)
None the less it is useful to start our survey of the new-comers to rural life, with their overwhelmingly non-rural occupations, with a place such as Harden, where one is re-

minded that before there were mill-towns there were mill-villages. From the Dukeries coalfields, up through a lot of country on both sides of the Pennines, right up to Newcastle, one is reminded that in the North, birthplace of the Industrial Revolution, the smokiest and gloomiest town is conscious of fresh moors and hills within a few miles. The modern urban penetration of rural scenes, the rows of house windows, on a distant shoulder of land, catching the evening sun as one enters some sweeping valley still composed largely of fields, seem less startling, more the continuation of an old process, than do new estates and light engineering works in southern villages. Harden is near Bingley, which is much too large *ever* to have had a Women's Institute; and in less than five minutes' drive out of Bingley one can be on a moor that feels like the roof of the world – stone walls, sheep, immense distant blue views. Something sparkles down in the misty middle distance; at first sight one thinks it must be a lake or reservoir, then one sees it is the glass roof of an enormous factory.

Just outside *Appley Bridge* in Lancashire one can stand on a slight ridge looking back over rolling pastoral views to Wigan, which from here does not look densely industrial; there is one truncated tip, one very high chimney, a couple of mysterious big green things, but the general impression is of a compact town sheltered under a high line of moor. Appley Bridge itself doubtless sends many of its youth to Wigan for technical and higher education, and itself contains industry:

The M6 cuts right through Calico Wood, through which runs Calico Brook. A rough private road goes to a large works, British Glues and Chemicals, known locally as 'The Bone Works' – always white (with bone dust?) ... products, tallow for soap, technical gelatine, animal feeding-stuff, glues, bone for china, cat-food, hair as used in mattresses for bedding, rubber glue used in 'Tuf' shoes, rubber backing for carpets, rubber glue used in atomic work . . .

Caravans are also made. Appley Bridge is built on a sandstone goldmine. To industrialists the white dust of the sandstone quarries shines like silver. The geologists claim it is the source of stone unique in South Lancashire for its high quality, invaluable in the making of pre-cast concrete. William Finch Ltd make 4,000 flags a day, 2,000 kerbstones per day. 70 men employed . . .

One of the residents, Mr Theodore Major, a painter, and friend of the painter Lowry, is quoted –

I came to live here because this is where the real beauty is; near the Bone Works. This is where real beauty is. When people try to make something beautiful they make a mess of it, and make it ugly. A factory is not meant to be beautiful, but it has a purpose, it's full of life. It's beautiful.

Yet Appley Bridge has a long tradition of community rural life, among people who have lived there all their lives; remembering the same teachers. Now the secondary modern is at Shevington, and

Altogether Shevington children have some very good tutors, and they appreciate them. There is no 'blackboard jungle' here; more like a well-ordered garden, with the children the flowers and the tutors very good gardeners. When Mrs Walsh retired, having taught for forty years, she was presented with a modern bookcase and a low fireside chair. . . .

. . . it seems a pity that our field paths are not used more frequently. There was a lovely country walk through Lucas Fold and the fields on to High Moor. Now the path, through disuse, is completely lost, with a heavy growth of bracken and willowherb, some of it growing much taller than oneself . . .

recently the Lancashire County Council have erected sign-boards indicating footpaths through the fields, and this is very suggestive and encouraging to us.

Some Lancashire dialect still persists among our over-60's, and the following is a copy of a poem sent at Christmas by one of our members in accompaniment of a present of a waistcoat she had knitted for a friend's husband:

TO JACK, AT CHRISTMAS

Does ta shiver? Well, tha maun't
So here's a ganzee, so tha caun't!
Dost feel t'caud? This'll keep it cawt
Neaw can't see whor I'm talkin' abeaut?

Bless thee, mon, tha'rt gettin' owd;
Tha maunt catch thi deoth o' cowd!
So pud id on, it'll keep thi warm
While wearin' this tha'll cop no 'arm.

And wen tha wears it, bear in mind
Tha'rt mighty lucky t'ged one o' its kind
So slop thi tay deawn if tha durst
And reckon wi' me tha surely must.

When tha swanks in't just tek care
Ah've no moor wool ner time ta spare
Neaw, by Gow, Ah've had ma say
So pud id on an' beggar away.

None the less, in spite of the familiarity of many northern villages with industry, here too the post-war mass influx of commuters (and, if it is a really rural village in an 'unspoilt' area, which could not of course be quite said of Appley Bridge, of retirers also) seems to be of a different order; a more wholesale and universal process:

1965 has seen the start of a new sewerage scheme, an event which in the long run will probably lead to bigger changes in the layout and character of the village than almost anything else that has happened in recent years. Our neighbours in Parbold have seen a dramatic increase in building take place following the completion of the sewerage scheme in their village, and we shall doubtless see the same thing happen in the next few years.

It is simply that when one looks at the occupations of residents in what might appear to be totally rural areas in the south, midlands and west one is somehow apt to be more surprised. The Somerset village of *Compton Martin* for instance, on the road from Bath to Weston-super-Mare, is on the lower north flanks of the Mendips; the water of two reservoirs in the long valley, full of characteristically melting west-country views, gives at times the feeling of being in a cosier, small-scale version of the Ardennes where they come down to the Meuse. The same succession of faintly holidayish villages with a lot of Edwardian wood, prospects of water, rich comfortable hills (here having splendid names like *The Wrangle* and *Browning's Tump*). You walk up a steep little path from the road to a fat, dark, solid Norman church (one of the pillars is fluted) in which there is a gorgeous wooden group of St Joseph taking the child Jesus for a walk; sturdy, foreshortened medieval figures. There is also the effigy-covered tomb of Sir Thomas de Moreton, Moreton being a hamlet now inundated by the Chew Valley reservoir. Local words include

barton: a yard round which buildings are grouped. *Dickered:* prolifically spotted. *Dimp:* stupid. *Dimpsey:* dark, twilit. *Drang:* a well-enclosed lane. *Flower-knot:* a cottage flower-bed.

And there are plenty of other evidences of antiquity, even if these are somewhat later than the fossils found here officially named *comptonensis:*

Ghost at Barrow Well, near the council houses. An old woman washing cabbages appears at midnight when there is a full moon. Ghost lady crosses the road from Highfield House to near Swan Croft. Ghost in heavy boots walks on Wrangle at midnight. . . .

But Compton Martin is only about fifteen miles from Bristol. In 1965 its population was 422; three adults to one child, a certain number of weekenders. Their occupations included the following:

Bristol Waterworks, Somerset highway authority. Architect, auctioneer, businessman, bank clerk, civil engineer, civil servant, corsetière, factory workers, catering industry worker, journalist, landscape gardener, lorry drivers, local government officer, nurses, postmen and women, policeman, poultry farmers, university professor, saw mill worker, shop assistants, sales representatives, teachers.

A press-cutting in the book tells a familiar story:

Country lanes in the commuter areas of north Somerset are providing new headaches for the divisional surveyors of the Somerset Highways Department. Near villages new homes are being built along many roads. Some of the houses are selling for high prices and they are equipped with most luxury gadgets of the modern world. But the entrances are often inches deep in mud. Water lies in great pools. Additional traffic is breaking up the road surfaces. New residents angrily claim that their homes have been highly rated and in return they should receive better amenities.

One of these storms has arisen at Undertown, a developing part of Compton Martin. Water and mud and cattle-trodden verges make Wellington boots a 'must'. Residents and visitors tread the mire up to the doors and it is not long before handsome new carpets lose that pristine look.

The new residents tackled the Parish Council. The Parish Council tried the Divisional, then the County Surveyor, but the lane is still as muddy as ever. People who come to live in the country expect things to be different from the towns. That, presumably, is why they come. But they draw the line at ankle-deep mud for weeks on end, and road surfaces that could break any axle at speeds of more than ten miles an hour.

Compton Martin's case is typical of many a divisional surveyor's problem, but they cannot do much because their allocations will not cover the additional expenditure. Many of the new homes are the most highly assessed domestic properties in their villages; often they suffer from the worst lack of simple amenities.

Within commuting distance of Bristol, says an advertisement. Surrounded by a large pleasant garden, double garage, kitchen with stainless steel double-bowl sink unit, plenty of cupboards and working surfaces including a breakfast bar. The kitchen also contains a Crane No 5 boiler which provides the central heating. The bathroom has a heated towel rail and a shower unit and stall, and the main bedroom is fitted with a wardrobe. Price £6,500 . . .'

The affair of the mud and the rating arguments are of course mere teething troubles in one particular example of a process which is widespread, complicated and above all *real*. It isn't only the mud that is real, but the carpets, the houses, the raw new gardens, the newly mobile people. They are the most important basic new fact about our rural life, and it is obviously useless for those who have already been in the country for a long time (or, very often, fifteen years, long enough to have become a much more fervent advocate of 'the country' than the most gnarled ploughman; I admit to this myself!) just to bury their heads in the thatch and hope they will all go away. They have just as much right, etc. etc. It has already been suggested that there *is* a basic classification of people, they are born naturally 'town' or 'country' as, it is said, thinkers are born naturally Platonist or Aristotelian; the new people come to the country by a positive act of choice. Perhaps the main tension, or one of the main tensions, is between their modernity and the idea, associated with the word 'village' in everyone's mind, of a small community where everyone knows each other.

A Grampound child went shopping in the village with a child who came from a large city. On the way down the street everyone they met had a cheery greeting, a smile or wave from them, and the shopping expedition developed, as usual, into a series of friendly visits. The city child, accustomed to the impersonal and frequently indifferent attitude of the people among whom she lived, became more and more interested, and at last she said to her hostess, 'do you really know all the people in Grampound?' This brought the immediate and astonished reply, 'why, of course I know all of them; they're my friends!'

By 'modernity' in this context is meant the fact that on the whole the newcomers tend to be in the younger age-groups and to come fully equipped with all the modern devices that make a home so self-sufficient, independent of local social structures: there is the car for excursion (and for taking the husband off to his work in the town anything up to twenty miles away), the television for entertainment. Obviously there is no clear-cut dividing line in this respect between them and the natives, who are themselves modernizing their houses in the biggest domestic revolution since Georgian architecture came in (and naturally doing it in a shorter period) – and as we shall later see, two of the scrap-books that gave the strongest impression of a classless and really living community were those of *Fairlands*, near Guildford, and *Cherry Willingham*, near Lincoln, neither of which look like villages at all in the conventional sense, but like what they mostly are – large housing estates. We are still a clubbable people.

In fact the newcomers are merely the spearhead of this domestic revolution, in which the most traditional interiors are, in the useful phrase of *Willoughby*'s book, being 'all contemporied up'.

The older houses, in the main, are constructed with the local red sandstone quarried in the district. Some have outer walls constructed of two thin walls about two and a half feet apart, the inner cavity being filled with rubble, mostly pebbles and huge boulders from the beach. The wall when completed is usually over three feet thick. Sandstone is porous, and these houses have no damp course, consequently all are somewhat damp inside. It is also suggested that the use of shore sand in making both mortar and plaster causes moisture to remain. The plaster in most of these houses is hygroscopic; it absorbs moisture from the atmosphere, showing damp before rainfall rather than after. Where central heating has been installed this manifestation has ceased.

The interior of most of the old houses is still decorated with wallpaper. It looks warmer, and people seem very conservative in taste. Two of the houses have wooden partitions instead of walls, and in one case these are left, but in the other, the old house on Cross Hill, the owner's wife thought it looked rough and covered with modern wallpaper some fine hand-chiselled boards. Very few houses built during the last two years have tiled bathrooms or kitchens. The clinical look has gone out of fashion ...

26% of the population are professional people. Only 5%, mainly dwellers in the older houses, are without a television set. Over 80% of all houses in the village have an electric washing machine

(*St Bees, Cumberland*)

Arrangements that would have been taken for granted in

the country quite a short time ago now, however objectively described, take on a curious air of the antique:

Most houses have bathrooms, but those that are still without have a washstand in the bedroom. This has a marble top, usually covered with an embroidered runner made of linen or cotton. On this stands a large shallow china basin with a matching jug. The full set consists of a soap-dish, toothbrush-holder and chamber pots. Sometimes there is an enamel bucket with a hole in the lid to take the waste water. This bucket is now more likely to be made of plastic.

(*Broad Chalke, Wilts.*)

Broad Chalke, incidentally, throws a wry sidelight on the absorption of farm produce into ever more centralized marketing systems:

Farm butter, like home-cured bacon, is just a memory, and the factory costs about 4/– a lb. New Zealand butter is cheaper. Fresh cream is a luxury unobtainable in the village unless ordered from the milk roundsman. Ice cream is much cheaper, and on sale at each of the village stores. Tinned and frozen foods and vegetables from all over the world are in plentiful supply and great demand. Although all houses have gardens of some sort it is easier and cheaper to buy vegetables ready for the pot, which means that garden produce is grown more for pleasure than necessity.

Milk, like beer, may not be sold without a licence, and it must be pasteurized and sealed into sterilized bottles. At present the prices are controlled at 9½d a pint. A delivery van comes every day from Salisbury. Expectant mothers and children are allowed one pint a day at half-price; every schoolchild is allowed one-third of a pint every day free, and this milk is delivered to the school. In this area none of the farms are licensed, but they are permitted to sell milk to their employees at a cheap rate, but to no one else, and it is one of the minor frustrations of country life that, surrounded by cows, one is unable to buy an extra pint once the milk van has passed by.

Pembury is a village which was once just outside Tunbridge Wells but is now, in terms of many of its new inhabitants, also just outside London:

The fast train services to Waterloo and the city and Tunbridge Wells (50 minutes, hourly) and from Tonbridge (40 minutes, half-hourly) have expanded the area in which it is possible to live and bring up a young family in the country and yet be able to follow a career which necessitates office hours spent in London.

In a village where there are still people who use expressions such as *emmet-cast* (ant-hill), *Jesus-flannel* (rose campion), *hop cat* (hairy caterpillar), *hop dog* (green caterpillar), *latchety* (loose or wobbly), *dreening* (wet through), *drackly minit* (very soon) and the self-explanatory *spatterarzing about*, they know all about the building breakthrough:

In many cases before the war the purchaser of an individual plot would have commissioned his own house, thus giving a pleasant and varied architecture to land such as Romford Road. Now in 1965 the pattern has completely changed. With the enormously inflated price of land due to the ever-increasing demand for houses, architects and builders are concerned to get the maximum number of houses to the area permitted by the local authority, and consequently estates now being built consist of a large number of houses of stereotyped design with ever smaller gardens but always a garage or carport. Usually some central heating. Only one fireplace, and, if space can be found, a downstairs cloakroom. Doors, windows and fittings are standardized for cheapness. The general effect of some estates is monotonous, e.g. the Pembury Garden estate, where a large number of terraced houses are being built, though these houses, selling at £4,650, are well planned inside.

Yet another estate has the stairs running up through the middle of the living-room. Surely in 1965 this impractical and comfortless idea could have been avoided. The largest and most expensive houses are four chalet-bungalows in Romford Road, which with four bedrooms and two bathrooms at £6,750 seem to provide good value for money.

Pembury is characteristic of many villages anywhere within a sixty to seventy mile radius of London, and could obviously be paralleled in correspondingly smaller areas round Birmingham, Manchester, or any other urban centre. Indeed a place has to be pretty remote nowadays for it to be out of range of employment for commuters. In the little village of *Trefnant*, between Denbigh and St Asaph

... employment other than farming. 6 men, Merseyside and North Wales Electricity Board, 7 men Denbigh and St Asaph Hospital, also 15 women in hospitals, 9 men Pilkington's Glass in St Asaph, 8 men Somers Steelworks, Queensferry, 6 men Courtaulds factory at Flint. Many women and young people work in light industries recently started in Denbigh – biscuit factory, clothing factory etc.

In all this ferment there are many cross-currents; clashes of public and private interests, idealism, greed, preservationism, philistinism, the loss of young people from village life, the need for providing them with attractive work:

Employment in the village is difficult to find, and young people leaving school find it hard to obtain the type of job they would like to do. Here in Bellingham this is certainly one of the main reasons why the younger people, young marrieds especially, tend to leave the area and seek employment in the surrounding large towns. The children, once they have joined into the village community during their schooldays, are loth to return to the isolation of farm life. For the child with talent there is little opportunity, and many go away to college and to hospitals, never to return.

(Bellingham, Northumberland)

This applies to the *really* young marrieds – the kids just starting out who are just never going to be in the market for a £6,750 chalet bungalow with a Crane No 5 boiler and the rest of it. The people who buy those aren't so young as all that. In fact, nowadays in all but the most remote or picture-postcard-preserved or retirement villages of any size there is usually one council estate – or there may be several. The three constituents of the average village are the Old Village, the Council Estate and the Development. And that might well be the order in which they depend on mobility for their livelihood. Mobility would defeat its own purpose if it led to a demand for a factory in every village (after all, practically everyone is mobile, if only with a scooter, the moment he is seventeen, if he really wants to be). Not every village has such a snugly truly rural factory as this:

Hammonds' Tannery dates back to 1600. It uses 4 to 5 thousand hides every year. It is one of the last three oak bark tanneries in Britain. Oak bark, which is made for the tanning of the hides, comes from Dartmoor and Exmoor, and is soaked for two months to extract tannin. In the tannery we see a survival of one of the old hand crafts of the country. Much of the work is done by hand, and many of the implements are the same as those used centuries ago. The leather from the tannery is used for various purposes, such as sole leather, harness, and for surgical use. One finds tapioca being used on the flesh side of bridle and stirrup leather after it has been stained. Valonia, which comes from the Turkish oak tree, is added to the oak bark; this is only used for sole leather.

(Colyton, Devon)

Quite often places in the council estate go not to young people anyway, but to people moved from old, possibly picturesque, but unhealthy and condemned property – often with an at first very unacceptable rise in rent. Those at St Erth (see p. 32) have already been mentioned:

The new council estate has twenty bungalows for old people. These are on a warden scheme, linked by a bell system to the warden's house. The old folks were moved from condemned houses, and they grumbled at the high rents of their new homes. Now that they have tasted the joys of all mod. con. they find it well worth the price.

(*St Erth, Cornwall*)

Demolition of old cottages built originally for old ironworks. They have only privies, and water for all purposes is obtained from outdoor stand pipes. Access to the one bedroom is in most cottages by way of an open step ladder, and to the roof of the bedroom, which is not underdrawn, the walls are only 4 ft 6 in. high. It was not until 1903 that small kitchens were added to the single all-purpose downstairs room. But despite the drawbacks not all the tenants are happy at being moved. Mr Edward Stephenson, who has lived in the middle of Percy Street for 47 years, said that the tenants were now paying only 2/9 to 5/- a week in rent. Naturally some of them were not going to be very happy at having to pay in the region of £2 a week for a council house. Mr Stephenson remembers being told that the cottages cost only £40 each to build ...

(*Bellingham, Northumberland*)

This whole process is called suburbanization by people for whom that is the worst possible term of abuse (those who, living in who knows what sophisticated penthouses, fondly told each other incessantly in print that the late Giles Cooper had really lifted the lid off suburbia with his play about housewives paying for the fitted carpets with immoral earnings during the afternoons. The raw truth about Streatham, they all thought it was). In fact it is a combination of modernization, mobility, and affluence, and although generalizations are dangerous it does seem, on the evidence of the scrapbooks, that basically the newcomers do like the *country*, still. But it is a real life-process, and like all life-processes it has its pain. Some preservationists are too angry, maybe merely selfish (and it is not unknown for landowners, farmers, builders or just people who own a couple of nice eligible fields to be on the committees of various official bodies, just so they can sniff what's in the wind). Some farmers want to sell. Some newcomers complain about mud and want orange street lighting put in too soon . . .

Refuse bins emptied once a fortnight. If the roads are bad those who live on the steep slopes are even worse off. The community's determination to retain its rural character was seen in the rejection by the Parish Council three years ago of a proposal for street lighting, but this may have to come in view of the housing development . . . until the first World War Station Road was a narrow road bordered by green fields leading from Bishop's Cleeve station (now closed) under the railway bridge to the little hamlet of Woodmancote. Despite much noisy criticism seven neat little bungalows were erected in the first field past the bridge. This proved to be the thin end of the wedge, and development in a variety of styles and materials was allowed. Every available space has been filled on the north side, though green fields will preserve an open space between Woodmancote and Cleeve on the south side. After 1945 an enclosed avenue of ten pre-fabs was erected, and a residential caravan site was established behind Oxbutts Farm in the early 1950s, where some of the 21 caravans still have the original occupants and well-tended gardens. On the village green the chestnut still stands, sheltering the seat on which the older inhabitants can daily be seen resting during their walk, but no longer does the old cottage in its half-acre of land lie beyond it. Instead, the cottage has been demolished to make way for four houses which have caused a tremendous amount of controversy in the village. The Parish Council fought their construction on the grounds that they were totally unsuitable for the village setting, but without success. Planning permission had already been given, the Planning Officer being convinced that they were a brilliant architectural achievement. These houses are far taller than any other dwellings in or near the green, and completely hide the view from neighbouring residents. The garages are built at road level, and the living areas of the houses are built over the garages ... inside the houses are most attractive, with clever use of space, the ground floor being on two levels ... the view from the bedroom windows really is superb.

(*Woodmancote, Glos.*)

Denbigh council revoked permission for building 100 houses on 50 acres. The man who wanted to sell the land, Mr Parkinson, said this would turn his high-class building land into a green belt, and sterilize it completely for development. Worse still, it would sterilize another 25 acres of land nearer to St Asaph, which might well be approved for building if 15 acres had gone through. The difference between the value of building land at £2,300 an acre and farmland at £300 an acre meant that on every acre he would lose about £2,000, he claimed. In addition, he would lose the profit from the sale of the houses through the building firm of Parkinson and Webster. Averaging £4,000 per house and a profit of 10% he would be making £400 per house, and houses would have been built at about seven or eight to the acre. All this, said Mr Parkinson, took no account of the losses through delays, for he had paid professional fees for the detailed layout and other expenses. The future of his company and the labour force of fifty men was now in jeopardy. 'What really makes me mad is that a democratic decision had been upset as a result of pressure by influential people outside the county. I have had a raw deal. I am going to ask the Secretary of State to look into this and find out what has been going on behind the scenes. I want the ratepayers to know what Wednesday's decision will cost them. The £120,000 I could claim would increase the rates by sixpence.'

(Press cutting from Trefnant, Denbighshire)

That is a classic example of the kind of row that has been going on in countless villages since the war. There is no denying that it is a complex, sometimes agonizing problem. The only thing that can be truly said in every case is that very few of those who argue so passionately and explicitly for or against 'development' can stand up to a simple *cui bono*? It is very easy to work up a fine moral indignation about the possible burden on the poor downtrodden ratepayers if you stand to 'lose' £2,000 an acre, not to mention another two or three thousand profit from the houses on each acre; many developers can say 'let the people have homes' with as much fervour as the most radical politician, and are equally ready to speak darkly of unnamed 'influential people' undemocratically opposed to the people's will. If you can't think of an argument in Britain, bring in class. Port wine drinkers, pheasant shooters, those influential people, every one. On the other hand, the preservationist movement *is* overwhelmingly middle-class, and not all of its members have enough moral sensibility to feel faintly foolish at having to say, in effect 'I appreciate this beautiful place, having been born in it, or having moved to it because I am sensitive to this kind of thing; I/we thought of it first, why do you people now all want to come pouring in here and muck it up?'

We don't want a film-set, thatched, stockbroker's Arcadia, and we don't want subtopia. Clearly at some point the preservationists have to stop being embarrassed by the not inconsiderable number among them who are prompted by nothing nobler than the desire to keep the dreaded People away from their evening rose-gardens and say 'thus far, and no farther'.

When, as happens fairly often, things *do* go farther, then clearly the whole community must change – it is almost as if the rule were 'hate them before they come, love them after'. Since this is the point at which argument, which is hypo-thetical, has to give way to living actuality, which is real, relations do move on to this level, and can bring very happy results, as the next chapter will show.

Many preservationists who do fundamentally care about the country are afraid to speak up because they are aware that nearly all public statements on the issue are loaded, and because they feel their mainly aesthetic arguments to be unconvincing against the economic ones put up by the de-velopers and the tradesmen on local councils, and because a lot of the old local population don't give a damn either way – and because 'it will happen anyway'.

It isn't often one finds an overwhelming local opposition to a scheme, except in such obvious examples of that special obstinate central-government bloodymindedness in some-thing really big and insane, like Stansted; usually there are far too many divergent interests, too many cross-currents. At first it did seem as though there had been absolute una-nimity in the Glamorganshire village of *Pentyrch*. You go northwards, about seven miles out of Cardiff, up a green wooded hill; on its far side, deeply eroded by quarrying, you drop down into another valley-conurbation, but here all is airy openness; snug 'old village' with trim lawns, spacious new estates. I sat on a public bench on the wide grass sur-rounding one such. Two old men, with metal toe-caps on their boots, sat there watching three small children tumble about. 'Ah the children here are like birds,' one of them said to me. There was an immense vista of sky, sea, distant blue

hills. I had been reading the Pentyrch book down in the
Library in Cardiff:

There have been many highlights in the chequered pattern of
village life, but 1965 will be remembered above all as the Year of
the Public Inquiry, into the proposed development of a new
town of 25,000 people ... 'it seems that town planning combined with the proximity of overpopulated Cardiff can succeed
where geology and geography failed, in destroying the age-old
rural and agricultural nature of Pentyrch. We Pentyrch natives,
who love every field and farm of our Parish, cannot help being
sad at the thought that the twentieth-century planners can
change these lovely fields into a featureless housing estate' –
Stuart Williams, Glamorgan historian ...
... inhabitants, 80 under 5, 100 5 to 11, 70 11 to 16, 95 16 to 21,
644 21 to 70.
... three farms vacated in 1965. Penllwyn, 'Head of the
Grove', with its origins at least 600 years old, standing gaunt and
defiant now, with the limestone quarries creeping ever nearer;
Caer yr Fa, 'Fortress of Arms', a Royalist stronghold in the Civil
War and a Bronze Age mound, no less, in the kitchen garden;
Caerwen, 'White Fortress' on the slopes of the Garth and overlooking the lovely valley ...
... near this farmhouse not so long ago there used to be an old
bench, on which the many poets of the village would congregate to compare their works and also to indulge in the spon-
taneous composition of the complex four-line stanza form of
Welsh poetry known as the *englyn*. This seat was aptly called
'The Bardic'; the comparatively isolated position of the village
has allowed it to preserve much of its essential character. Although no one pretends that it is the same place it was even
twenty or thirty years ago, the older people recall the time
when the saying *bit ryddoch chwi, wŷr Pentyrch* ('let it be
between you, men of Pentyrch') illustrated the opinion, not
always complimentary, held by the people of the surrounding
areas. This saying was prevalent at fairs, markets and the like

131

when trouble was started by adventurous young bloods from Pentyrch ...

... field names: *Cae Twm Tinker, Cae Moses Lewis, Llwyn-yr-eos* (Grove of the Nightingale), *Hendre scuthan* (Winter Abode of the Wood-pigeon), *Maes-yr-haul* (Meadow of the Sun). *Llwyn-y-brain* (Grove of the Crows) is explained by one of our older parishioners with his tongue firmly in cheek. One day many years ago a boy was engaged at frightening crows from the growing corn when a number of the birds perched on the big beech tree that grew in the middle of the field. The boy, having filled his blunderbuss with an assortment of tin-tacks, promptly fired at the intruders. The unfortunate crows were pinned to the branches of the tree and with a tremendous squawking and flapping of wings the tree was uprooted and taken with the flying birds up into the clouds. This strange ensemble landed in a field in Herefordshire, and so frightened a group of cows standing there that their faces turned to white. This was the origin of the white-faced Herefordshire cow ...

... for good or bad, there is an unashamed pride here ... speak to an elderly gentleman whose family has been in the parish for generations, and he will ask you into his cottage. He will show you the Welsh dresser made for his grandparents from an oak tree that had grown on the *derwen* field. Then you will see his pride. Ask someone who has quenched a thirst in summer at *Ffynnon Gruffydd* spring. Speak to someone who has seen the primrose carpet at *Penllwyn Isaf*. Find someone who has experienced the comforting warm air wafting out of the side of the Garth on a cold winter's walk along the mountain road. Ask a child who has seen fox cubs play in Tyncoed Wood, badgers at Llwynaddu, hares on the Forlan and squirrels in Parc-y-Justice, and you will see this pride. Best of all, rise early, climb to the top of the Garth, see the morning mist rise, see Llwyn-derw as the glistening gossamer hoar-frost lifts away to the sky; the sparkle from the birches will bewitch you, you will know then why our grandparents believed in fairies ...

Such a place, it may be imagined, did not take kindly to

having a New Town tacked on. In the Year of the Public
Enquiry:

What we are against is the indiscriminate herding together of
families at very high densities, so that the developers can make
very high profits. Of course people must have homes in which
to bring up their families, but it is our bounden duty to see to it
that planners always plan with the sanctity of family life upper-
most in their minds. As I understand it the proposed development is based on Leasehold, and we must regard this as
thoroughly bad. We must do all we can to protect future generations from the merciless grip of landlords in the awful leasehold system. The town would have twenty to twenty-five
thousand people crowded into about 800 acres ... a modern
shopping area would be where the Athletic Club is now ... the
cost would be about 35 million pounds.

'My opinion is that it would not be economic,' an architect,
Mr Raymond Gorbing, told the Ministry Inspector at County
Hall ... after interruptions during the hearing the Inspector, Mr
R. Harris, warned a number of objectors 'If I have any noise
from the back you can all go out.' When Mr Harris complained
later of outbreaks of laughter from some listeners Mr Michael
Gibbon, for the objectors, said 'those present here are ratepayers'. Mr Harris replied 'I can understand their feelings, but I
wish they would not express them publicly.'

Mr Gorbing said the Pentyrch proposal was intended to make
an immediate positive contribution towards providing homes
for people in overcrowded and unsatisfactory dwellings and to
accommodate new population in good environmental conditions. Dr Nathaniel Litchfield, a development, planning and
economic consultant, said it could be an independent settle-
ment, looking to Treforest Industrial Estate for employment
and to Cardiff for employment, cultural and other facilities.

(press cutting from *Pentyrch, Glam.*)

The Pentyrch book ends before the reader knows what

the result of the inquiry was. I didn't know when I drove up there. Perhaps I should find a Welsh Harlow already rising under the 1,000-feet Garth mountain, from which the view includes 'Glastonbury Tor, the Bristol Channel with the islands of Flat Holme and Steep Holme, Brecon Beacon and Radnor Forest.' Or would the people, including not only the '29 Davies, 23 Evans, 28 Jones, 6 Llewellyn, 25 Lewis, 32 Thomas' among their surnames but also 'Bertonani, Bosanko, De Swiet, Hopfenzetz, Pulvermacher, Zamastil and Szlumper' have won their case, stopped the development juggernaut and preserved what was left of rural Pentyrch? And if the opposition succeeded, would it have been mainly middle class?

I found that the great thirty-five million pound scheme by Messrs MEBC (Pentyrch) Ltd *had* been disallowed. In addition to the old quarrymen on the bench I spoke to a man in alpaca jacket and straw hat (it was a fine July day, high lazy clouds moving in from the Atlantic), who in fact beckoned and smiled as I drove past. When I stopped he said, 'I am so sorry. I thought you were my son. He has an exactly similar vehicle to yours. He is headmaster of a college in Burton-on-Trent, and he is coming down today.'

I asked him about the new town. He thought the opposition had come from new and recent residents. 'They called a meeting, you see. If they had left it to the Parish Council – I've been on it, I've lived here all my life – they'd have got it through. But Cardiff have allowed it; they came here and built these houses, they're the majority now, you see . . .'

On the other hand, one of the old quarrymen on the bench simply said, dismissively, 'Oh, that was just a money-making scheme.'

In other words, it is impossible to generalize, it is impossible to tell from a man's circumstances, class, birthplace, looks, or anything else, whether he is a total preservationist, absolutely against all new building, all council estates, all weekenders, all change from the *status quo*; or an unfeeling philistine tradesman, an unsociable subtopian whose brand-new house might just as well be in Brixton or Cricklewood for all his appreciation of the country.

These are, of course, a *reductio ad absurdum* of the two extreme positions. What can be safely said, now that we have had a look both at the old traditions and at the immense pressures of change, is that for most people in most villages as they now are the reality comes somewhere in between. In the scrapbooks one may perhaps see a certain ambivalence towards builders:

The Parish Council: seven members who were elected in a contested election in 1964 for a three-year term of office. The Chairman is a native of the village, a Parish Councillor for twenty years, the past eight as Chairman. A fair cross-section; local residents of long standing, a nominee of Compton Martin WI, a newcomer, others earning their living locally or working from the village. At present the farming community is not represented, although it was till the sixties. In contrast the Council now has three out of its seven members actively engaged in the building industry. This may be no more than a coincidence. On the other hand, considered in relation to statistics which may be produced by other villages, it may be indicative of the shift of emphasis in community life in villages like this within easy commuting distance of larger centres of population, and therefore subjected to great pressure for building development.

(*Compton Martin, Somerset*)

Here again, it depends what you mean by 'builder', a term which nowadays can mean anything from the London-based consortium which would have built the new town outside Pentyrch, to the traditional village family firm, very often having old headed notepaper with a curlicued, old-fashioned floral design telling you they are 'Builders and Undertakers'. In scrapbooks all over the country there are references, usually fearful, to the complete planned new town, which London will cause to spring fully armed from the bare earth; *that* kind of builder has all the terror of the unknown. Between them and our builder/undertaker there is a new phenomenon; many of the new estates of bungalows or small houses are built by recently-established firms which sub-contract most of the work – flooring by Messrs A, wiring by Messrs B, roofing by C Ltd, answerability in ten years' time by No One.

Some of this must cause ambivalent, not to say wry feelings in the older builders (who may or may not have tried to get planning permission for the same land). Here is a charming statement by a builder who is evidently a countryman too:

In 1930 Donald Olver took over the business of carpenter and wheelwright from Mr Arthur Coad, who had carried on for fifty years in what was once Mr Solomon's poultry-picking and egg-packing shed on the Truro side of the bridge. This building is now scheduled to be pulled down in the next five years as part of road improvements. The business was carried on under the name of *F. D. Olver, Wheelwright, Carpenter and Undertaker* until 1964, when a young man of the village, Anthony Mannell, was made a partner, and the business became *Olver & Mannell Ltd.*, with offices at Miranda. They carry on the business of builders and undertakers etc. with some casual labour but no permanent employees. They are the village 'factotums' and do everything from clearing drains to building bungalows, and whether you give their status a 'shove-up' by calling them Builders, or merely Country Codgers, they are typical of the few remaining village craftsmen, which are the salt of the earth.

Since the last war Cornwall has been invaded by many folk of retiring age who find the climate of this district much kinder than the cold North, and if the mass exodus of young people continues, by the turn of the century this last Celtic Outpost will have become an Eventide Home.

One has the impression that the only people who will benefit from this Cornish Twilight will be the Builders and Undertakers, so long live Olver & Mannell Ltd. – F. Olver.

(Grampound, Cornwall)

The Newcomers

In *Dalston*, four miles outside Carlisle, I was in a hall where old men were playing dominoes in a side-room, old ladies sewing and making tea in the main part; they spoke, in their lilting accents, of days when Dalston had a forge that made its own nails, and seven pubs that have since become houses (three of them were *jerries*, or alehouses); when they went in to Carlisle to dances that were 2d Ladies, 3d Gentlemen, with a Ball at the end of the season with tickets at 1/6; a violin and melodeon provided the music; when they carried lanterns with candles in them on dark nights.

What would you get for Christmas, as a child?

'Oh, apple, orange and some nuts.'

According to Mother Shipton when Dalston meets Carlisle it will be the end of the world. As it is Carlisle only just stops short enough for you to appreciate, when you come to the wide little square before the cross-roads, flanked by church and a few rather dignified shops, that here *is* a village, snug and solid, for centuries weathered by keen salty airs from the Solway Firth; for you will just have passed, on your left a Nestlé factory that takes milk from 900 producers within a fifteen mile radius (and where there is bingo every Thursday night, with a pies-and-peas supper at half-time for 1/3), and on your right a fairly expensive-looking estate (one of those which seem to be built on the maze principle when you are trying to find a particular house: it is extraordinary how one road doesn't lead to another – a further example, perhaps, of our talent for subdivision). In Dalston there is a

Home Beauty Service

At your invitation a trained and courteous Beauty Counsellor will bring her free beauty advisory service to your home, let you enjoy a practical demonstration with full trial of a comprehensive range of exclusive skin-care and make-up preparations, without obligation. Or introductory free facial. Try before you buy. Established for many years in the USA and Canada, the Beauty Counsellor Service is now available to you. Your Beauty Counsellor is ...

A large secondary modern serves a catchment area of a hundred square miles. Next to the estate is a very comfortable new block of apartments for old people (foyer gay with notices, northern wind humming comfortably outside, nobody seemed to be in; the lady I wanted was in that hall). There are no shops on the posh new estate. 'Ah, no they didn't want shops to spoil it,' one of the old men said.

But the Dalston scrapbook was organized by someone living on it.

*

I must admit that cheaper housing first led us to North Kelsey, and a detached cottage in its own ground offering privacy and plenty of scope for young, do-it-yourself minds was something of the materialization of dreams. Both my husband and I hankered after the open of country living, as we had originally come from village life, and the friendliness of such communities had left a deeper impression than we at first admitted. Our baby son was growing, and even with modernistic ideas, old-fashioned, we believed that the country was the place we wanted for our children, present and future, that they might grow with the freshness of mind and body we believed it endowed.

On our second trip to view the cottage I said to my husband 'it feels a happy village, I'm sure it would be lovely to live here'.

I was right ... I am glad to see the back of the large self-service supermarket ... I enjoy the 'small shopkeeper' service which is smiles and service born of a true desire to help and serve. So too for the school. Outside it appears small and out-of-date, but there is a headmaster who knows his children, works with them and for them, and for whom the commanded respect is won with hard work and patient understanding ... life in North Kelsey is basically happy, and the people of all ages are friendly and forthcoming. I soon felt 'at home', as if I belonged, and generally these people work, and work hard, that North Kelsey will be richer and more blessed by what they do; and here lies the secret, the true heart of this village. And if, as our children grow, blown by fresh breezes, free and happy, aware of beauty born of nature, surrounded by happy people who care, if we should feel smug who can blame us, for here in this little village of North Kelsey lies peace and fulfilment that if only all the world could share, we need never fear again.

(*North Kelsey, Lincs.*)

The year opened with the sound of little children singing at my front door at 8.15 a.m. The old custom of *calenig* is dying out but I will always remember these young children wishing me a happy New Year ... this book is written in English, to conform with the rules of the competition sent out in November 1964. It is a great credit to some of our senior members who have written in English although their first language is Welsh ...

... my home is in Nottingham and I moved to Llanilar after I got married. Before my marriage I was a teacher in a secondary modern school in Leominster. I completely failed to find a teaching post in the Aberystwyth area and so took a job as a technician in the University college ... husband is manager of a 230-acre farm. Llanilar I found to be very friendly. It is the first village we have lived in and we were quite delighted that on the day after we arrived it was awarded first prize in the Best-kept Village Competition. Although we could hardly claim any credit for this we attended the ceremony, and the concert and the tea afterwards ... two children, David, 15, and Lynneth, 10, have settled in quite happily at their new schools. David, coming from the boys' grammar school, had to get used to having hundreds of girls about the place at Ardwyn; this seems to be no great hardship. Lynneth had to adjust herself from attending a school of 300 to one of 35 or thereabouts ...

In my younger days I would sit for hours looking out to sea from the window of a holiday cottage where one could relax mentally and physically and watch the ever-changing scene of the same stretch of sea.

On coming to Wales a few years ago I was so thrilled with the scenery that we chose a site on which to build our house on the south bank of the river Ystwyth. The house is not in the conventional style and lies at an angle of 75° to the road. The lounge with its 22-foot long window lies at the back, facing south, whilst the windows of the less-used rooms face north. Now I can sit by the window overlooking the panoramic view of the glorious Ystwyth valley. The view is never the same on two consecutive days and as I sit here I think of the words of the famous hymn, 'When I survey the wondrous cross', but instead I survey the wondrous valley. Above the house, to the south-east, stands the ancient Saxon encampment, a curious protruding hill, on the lower two-thirds of which are used to pasture a herd of the famous Welsh black cattle; they graze lazily, reminding one of the toughness of their breed, for they are out in all weathers in this exposed valley. The upper third is barren. Gorse bushes grow here and there amongst the shingle. A symmetrical saucer-shaped edge forms the top, and with very little imagination one can picture the Anglo-Saxon soldiers defending Cardigan Bay. I recall Coronation Day, 1953, when the young and energetic members of the village carried tons of wood, tyres and oil into the encampment and at sunset lit a beacon the flames of which were seen from Portmadoc.

The cheerful voices of the children direct my attention, and I look down the hill to the playground alongside the 100-year-old school with its modern windows painted blue. In the adjacent asbestos building, looking rather out of place, there is a school canteen where hot dinners are served daily. The music of the children's voices ceased on the clanging of the bell rung by the schoolmaster warning them it was time for lessons. The long, new green bus came slowly down the narrow high-hedged road, stopping to put down a little fair-headed girl in a bright red coat.

A hundred yards from the school stands the parish church, which was built in the tenth century. The weathercock, indicating the prevailing wind from the west, stands above the square Norman tower, which houses the clock, the chimes of which can be heard throughout the village. The path from the wicket gate to the oak door beneath the arch winds through the old parish cemetery where tombstones dating back to the fifteenth century can be seen appearing above the uncut grass. At the side of the church the tidy rows of modern graves can be seen, and the colourful flowers on the first corner indicate a recent funeral.

As I look from the church across the deserted village square I can see the village shop with its untidy advertising signs, wooden five-barred gates, bundles of wire and various pieces of farm equipment standing alongside. Opposite this is the 'local', where the red-and-white sign of the 'Falcon' can be seen swinging above the blue door, which is contrasted with the freshly painted white walls. A small red post van is making its way along the narrow winding road, leading up the hill to the cluster of trees surrounding the whitewashed cottage which often has 'golden windows' at sundown, reminding me of the old fable. Beyond this the roadman is leisurely cutting the grass verge; the wind is blowing his two red flags, near one of which stands his bicycle, raincoat, and tin box of food.

The ascending hills are covered by forest plantations. The bright sun accentuates the glorious autumn colours of the beech and Japanese larch trees standing by the belt of dark green Norwegian pine trees. The leaves of the Canadian oak have now turned bright red and can be picked out at regular intervals.

Beyond the forest stretches rolling land, cut up into fields of various sizes and shapes, some green, some yellow, some brown. In one field the sheep-dogs can be seen obeying their master and rounding up the sheep. Lower down the valley black-and-white Friesian cattle are being turned out from the square farmyard surrounded by its buildings, scattering a flock of white geese which are making their way to the Afon Fach, which bubbles over the rocks with its creamy foam before joining the river Ystwyth. The farmer's boy is driving his blue tractor pulling the trailer containing milk churns which he is taking to the concrete stand on the main road, where an impatient driver in a peaked cap is waiting to load his famous green milk lorry.

Returning along the main road to the village I notice a row of severe grey stone houses with roofs of slate. These houses have all three windows upstairs, two windows down, and the front door in the middle. They were built many years ago and have withstood the strong winds and heavy rain so prevalent in this area. They contrast with the estate of white modern council houses with their colourful curtains and small neat front gardens, built to an oval shape designed around a new village green which is planted with ornamental trees. Looking away from the village I follow the river Ystwyth leaving its steep rocky head and broadening as it meanders its way in an S-shaped pattern slowly towards the sea.

The railway embankment lies between the village and the river, and I can see a diesel train winding its way like a caterpillar between the trees. Nostalgically I think back to the days when the Great Western cream-and-chocolate train with its puffing-billy steam engine chuffed its way along. At the station along this track I can see the roofs of the low, irregular station buildings, but above these stand two large signs clearly displaying the words LLANILAR and GENTLEMEN. This will soon be a thing of the past as the line is doomed. One would like to live in Utopia, where all things would be peaceful and beautiful, but alas, as we take our place in this modern world we must give way to progress; the uses of the station yard are being changed. Ugly erections are being put up in the midst of heaps of untidy loads of timber to house the sawmills which provide local employment. As I stand by my window in this peaceful haven my thoughts wander back to the busy town, to the hurry and bustle, dirt and smoke, and to the brick walls seen from most windows; and I am thankful that nothing can spoil God's beauty.

(*Llanilar, Cards.*)

*

Coming down the long thin valley from the Peak District to matter-of-fact Derby, headquarters of Rolls-Royce, must be, even for the thickening stream of car-borne commuters, a slight daily throwback to the childhood feeling of return from a holiday. For the casual driver on a summer morning there is a curious poignancy when the bricks and mortar give way to wooded hills glimpsed across a meadow, a sparkling river, then close in again. An influence from the free moors and the wild rocks is felt, but now wandering and discovery cease, this is a place of settlements. What do they all *do*? GLOW-WORM, says a sign, vouchsafing nothing else, over a factory all by itself against a hillside; it has two red metal chimneys with bulging-out bits. There is a sense that they know each other all along this road, as along that valley from Lampeter to Carmarthen. Rock closes right down to the road, then opens out again. A shiny old-red-brick factory, ENGLISH SEWING THREAD LTD. A good way down the road, ENGLISH SEWING THREAD COMPANY SPORTS GROUND.

Duffield has the last (or, of course, first) golf course on the Pennines. A man said when I parked my car 'Have you locked it? They open the windows an' they get in there. We caught two on 'em, ten an' thirteen. The trouble is, ye canna dust them.' A colour photograph of Duffield taken from the Chevin, an overlooking hill, shows almost entirely green, rolling country. When the church was restored carvings known to exist on the cross-beams were examined; above one of a sombre-looking face – two round eyes, long blob nose, the whole thing very primitive, a kind of white West African – was the name.

BOB JAC^KSON

thought to be the master carpenter in 1621.

There is still a nucleus of the original population, who live and work in the village. Many of them belong to local families whose names persist in the district, e.g. Cooper, Lomas, Yates, Bowmer. But there is also an entirely new population who have come from all parts of the country, mainly younger people with young families who are rapidly being absorbed into the community. Most of them say they find Duffield a friendly place. This is largely due to the activities of the WI, the WEA, evening institutes and other cultural organizations, to say nothing of the innumerable coffee parties, wine-and-cheese parties and other social occasions. Class distinctions which existed before are fast disappearing, and it seems that Duffield is becoming an example of the classless society fostered by the Welfare State . . .

. . . My first impressions of Duffield were very pleasing. I loved the surrounding country and the river. There seemed to be footpaths everywhere just asking to be walked on. I found the people so friendly and helpful, and the many social activities really surprised me. There was something for all ages, from Brownies to the Over 60 Club. Duffield seems to be very go-ahead; many new houses are spreading across the fields and two new schools have been built. I didn't expect a Fire Brigade, but it is a very satisfying thought to have one so handy. Whilst being in the country we are very convenient to the town for shopping, and the bus service is quite good; I can't say the same for the trains. There are excellent facilities for sports, and the golf course is in a lovely spot, on the last hill of the Pennines. I think I can be very happy here . . .

The Newcomer

O village in your fair twin valleys
Between the Derwent and the Ecclesbourne
With mellow cottages and alleys
Would I were 'Duffield bred and born'!
No longer do I seek in dreams
With reckless spirit, restless feet
New faces, places, reckless schemes
My soul fulfilled, my life complete –
For who would not be happy here
Or come more pleasantly to rest
Where there is wholesome worth and cheer
(For in this village all are blessed
In haunts of peace, or so it seems)? –
Accept me, haven of my dreams.

The beach estate and subsequent housing development is looked on with alarm by many St Bees people, who fear that the place may lose its village character and become merely a dormitory suburb of Whitehaven or Egremont or even, eventually, of Carlisle. On the other hand the people who are coming into the village are often young, intelligent people who have had their fill of urban life and suburbia, and are prepared to forgo some of the advantages of town or city life – mainly cultural activities – so that their children may grow up in a healthy atmosphere. They appreciate the community life of a village and will oppose the introduction of industry and the development of the area into the very thing they have escaped from. Let us welcome these off-comers, who have much to contribute to village life. Those who have nothing to give or who do not settle happily here will soon depart, as have several families already. The future lies largely in the hands of our young people, and we can only hope that we have imbued them with the right spirit to keep our village beautiful, not as a stagnant pond may be beautiful but as a fresh lake with a constant renewal of vigour and life.

(*St Bees, Cumberland*)

The Oil in the Beard

Ultimately there is no point in living in the country unless, for all the unsociable conveniences of modern self-sufficient domestic life, the institutions of traditional village community life can continue, in however modified a form. Otherwise one might just as well live in any anonymous megalopolis or suburbia. Given an unlimited increase of mobility and industrial devolution there is no purely *practical* reason why there should not simply be a huge Los Angeles covering the whole country; a house every hundred yards from Land's End to John O'Groats. We have already seen that the old distinctions have been considerably blurred: nevertheless our old instinct for subdivision, for separateness, for modelling landscape, for creating inner space, is still strong. The expression 'in-filling' (building inside villages – indeed, between houses – already there, instead of just anywhere) which occurs in most planning documents is no doubt often prostituted, like all words; but it is a healthy sign that the village is still the real unit, the nucleus of possible community. Hence the title of this chapter, which is from Psalm 132, 'How pleasant it is for the brethren to dwell together, like the oil in the beard of Aaron.'

As we shall see, village community life is a dynamic and changing thing; some institutions decline, others take their place. But there is no doubt that this idea of community is closely linked with memory and tradition, and not with change. Where there is change and the rapid growth of new population a community can, in favourable circumstances, start a really thriving life almost from scratch; the second and third examples in this chapter will be of this kind. But all village community is influenced, if only subconsciously, by the idea we all have of the older, more closed and familiar, childhood-to-death form, the form of nursery and folk tales or indeed of literature (even if there isn't going to be any more such literature; the declension Hardy – John Cowper Powys – *Cold Comfort Farm* seems a final one). And perhaps it is not without significance that the obvious choice for the first example, a chronicle of village life of this older kind, should come from one of the scrapbooks which is about as far from London as you can get.

1. *The Familiar Village*
   Llanedwen, Anglesey. Diary kept by Miss Pheena
   Thomas, Sub-postmistress, in her own hand, 1965.

Jan. 2. The church room teaspoons are lost!

Jan 6. Church room spoons found. The Vicar had borrowed them for a tea party held at Llanddaniel Fab. Mr Williams the joiner has been busy. He has made three coffins this year. Mr Williams, Tan Bryn Farm, had a few words with the local newsagent for leaving his paper on the roadside instead of taking it to the door. It ended in Mr Williams stopping the papers and receiving them by post.

Thursday Jan. 14. Funeral of Mr T. Williams, from Llanddaniel, was at Llanedwen churchyard. Mr R. Blakeley not very well this morning; he has got a very bad cold.

Friday Jan. 15. Dave Williams of Chicago arrived at Rose and Thistle to stay with his uncle Mr R. Williams the joiner. Mrs M. Roberts bought a new electric stove. Manwel came a day earlier than they said to instal it in and collect the old one. They took away the Sunday joint as well. Mrs Roberts had to phone for it back.

Jan. 22nd. Mr R. Williams the joiner has made three coffins this week. Mr H. Hughes of Ysgabor Fawr Farm has applied for permission to have a caravan site on his farm. The Town and Country Planning Committee were round this week. Mrs —'s lodger left today. She had three, but they left because all the food they had tasted of onions, and no fire to dry their clothes when they got home wet in the evenings, they found lodgings nearer to Wylfa nuclear station where they work. Mrs M. Williams of Gwyl Mor, Porthamel, had a new door and window put in today. Mr R. Williams, Rose and Thistle, was the joiner. Mrs Bauler came home from Llandudno Hospital today. She has been in since a week. I did not know that she had gone in. She is feeling better. One of our postmen, a van driver, took the evening mail down to Plas Newydd. He had a small parcel which was badly damaged. He tried to explain to the Spanish girl who answered the door that he hadn't done it. She just stared at him for a moment and then burst out telling him something and waving her hands up in the air, postman just turned heel and ran back for all he was worth.

Feb. 15. Mrs L. Williams of Bryn Fellten and myself received our sailing tickets to go to Ireland for our August Bank Holiday weekend.

Feb. 19. Two coffins were made at the joiner's this week. A very small coffin was made at the joiner's this morning for a baby (one of twins). Llanedwen kiosk was painted today. Mrs Davies of Plas Llwynonn went in to phone. She came out quicker than she went in, her hand and coat covered with red paint. She was very angry, she had not noticed the wet paint sign.

March 4. Snowstorm. Today is a day not to be forgotten. Snowdrifts everywhere. I, Pheena Thomas the local postwoman, got to work by 7.15 a.m. Mailvan did not arrive till 8.15 a.m. with only a few local letters, he could not get any further than the Finger cross-roads because of road blockage Anyway the council workers cleared the road so traffic started to pass through round about 10.30 a.m. I walked the round, cycling was out of the question. I tried to reach Plas Llwynonn flats but had to turn back, the snow was too deep. Anyway, everybody was very kind, some took letters that they could deliver on their way to work, and others offered me cups of tea and biscuits, everybody seemed more helpful and cheerful in the snow except for one old growser.

April 3rd. Grand rummage sale at Llanedwen church room in aid of WI funds raised quite a lot of money. A lovely day.

May 17. A gentleman came to our door today asking for a loan of a spade to dig bait to go fishing, he offered me his watch as security, as he had been three times last year, we did not need any security so lent him the spade. Mrs Williams, Bryn Fellten and myself went with Cefn Bach Chapel Sunday School trip to Rhyl and we enjoyed ourselves very much . . .

Mrs Williams and I arrived in Ireland this morning. It was a bit rough crossing but we managed to have a good night's sleep, as we got on the boat early (11.30 p.m.). We arrived in Ireland round about 7 a.m., we had breakfast and then took a bus to Dublin, we did not like it very much, too much traffic and too many people. We went from Dublin to Bray, stayed there for a bit. Nice place, Bray, and then took a bus back to Dun Laoghaire and went to the theatre and had a lovely time. We went to the pictures in the afternoon and on a bus tour in the evening and we enjoyed every minute of it. We had very nice lodgings, a nice talkative lady who had a lovely mother of 88 living with her, also staying with us was a German family of three, a Mr and Mrs Morris, a Miss Mullen from London and Mr Byrne, a retired schoolmaster. We paid 16/- bed and breakfast, very good breakfast too. We have eaten a lot of cream cakes since we have been here, they are delicious.

. . . just as I was going home from work I took 28 pounds of chick food on the carrier of my bicycle, as I was going down the hill I heard a shee-sheeing noise from behind me, and the bicycle getting lighter, I jumped off to investigate and saw the chick food coming in a straight line down the hill, anyway Miss H. Owen of Bryn Amel was coming home from the bus, and she helped me to salvage some of it, we got quite a bit too, I took that home and came back with a broom and a pail and managed to get another pail full, so I did not do too bad after all, but I really felt like a thief, going up with my broom and pail, I was lucky nobody passed me . . .

November 18. A nice Ayrshire cow died at Fodol Farm, but the little calf is all right. I received a letter and Christmas card from Mrs Humphrey this morning, in the letter she said she had some visitors from Anglesey during the summer, Mr and Mrs Coulson, Mr and Mrs Harborne, Mrs Drakeford, also Mr Allen from the flat at Plas Llwynonn, that was news to me and I am supposed to know everything that is going on around me to put in this diary.

December 31st. We have come to the end of our Jubilee year and diary, but Mrs Hughes, 2 Bryn Amel, Mrs Jones, Bryn Hyfryd, and Mrs Thomas, Mael-y-Don, have all asked me on their behalf to thank all WI members for their kindness in giving them coal for Christmas, which was very much appreciated by them, and wishing them all a very happy New Year. Earlier in my diary I mentioned a gentleman coming to the door to borrow a spade. I am sorry to say that I have not seen him or the spade since, so ladies, beware of nice young men coming to your door to borrow things.

I am sure that WI members could have found somebody better than me to write their diary, as my English, spelling, and wording of sentences are very poor. I wonder who will be writing one in another fifty years? My hobbies are gardening and gathering firewood when I have time.

Mrs Lilian Parry left Plas Llwynonn flat, no, not on the last day of the year but on the first day of 1966.

THE END

(*Llanedwen, Anglesey*)

2. *The place off the Guildford-Aldershot road*

Here you are only just out of the area where the only spaces not occupied by bricks and mortar are parks or reservoirs or cemeteries or London Airport. For the first time you begin to see horizons, quite suddenly you can be on heathery commons, golf courses, the army exercise country where

the horizons of youth were once over seas crossed by confi-
dent troopships. Turn left off the too-narrow, crowded main
road, and almost immediately go round a huge traffic island,
as big as two tennis courts, into the self-contained *Fairlands*
Estate; central block of shops, well-kept gardens. At six in
the evening a constant stream of cars coming in, people getting off at the bus stop; the men returning, the evening meal,
almost as if it were a walled town.

Clearly this is a new community as Llanedwen is old:

Fairlands is named after Fairlands Farm. Brock's Drive takes
the name of the family which farmed at Fairlands Farm; Gumbrell's Close is named after the shepherd, Mr James Gumbrell, at
the farm. Another road derives from the maiden name of Mr
A. B. Johnstone's mother. Mr Johnstone was the man who com-
menced development at Fairlands in the 1930s.

Gumbrell's Close is a small road of some 34 families. Various
dwellings; houses, bungalows, detached and semi-detached of
both sorts. There is a wide section of society represented. The
jobs of the menfolk vary greatly. We have two architects, one
doctor, one official from the Dutch Embassy (a Dutchman, of
course), civil servants, various office workers, one bank official,
one carpenter, one decorator (these two self-employed), a chef,
a fireman, a butcher, one or two employed by Vokes, and one or
two working for BAC at Wisley. Of these, nine work in London,
only one driving all the way back while the rest travel by
train.

There are 27 children, most of them four years and under.
Several couples are childless but in these cases the wives work.
No mothers work, but one or two are considering doing so
when the children are of school age. All possess a washing-ma-
chine, spin drier, fridge, TV and modern gas or electric cookers.
Several wives collect trading stamps, welcome free gifts. Ready-
prepared baby foods are widely used, also frozen foods. Most
wives buy cakes and preserves, a few still do their own baking
and jam-making.

Methods of home heating (may not be entirely accurate); seven homes have central-heating, one oil, three gas, the others electric (two off-peak). Of the others, many have changed their open living-room fire for a gas or electric heater. It looks as if open coal fires are on the way out in England at last. All owners seem to be intensely house-proud and are constantly decorating and gardening. Everything new for the home is chosen with taste and care, resulting in a more attractive interior than a generation ago. Our parents gave much less thought to this kind of thing. Everyone says they are hard-up, but compared to the last generation we are affluent. Only three households do not have a car, and these probably do not want one; one newly-weds, one an elderly spinster and one a retired elderly couple. Several wives can drive and find it handy for shopping, visiting friends and transporting children to and from school. Most families have annual holidays; those with children to the sea, others abroad. One older couple will visit their daughter in South Africa soon, another couple are going on a Scandinavian cruise. Two young couples with small children will camp, two others hire caravans. Only four families are native Guildford; the rest come from a variety of places, mostly London suburbs. Some wives find this area too quiet. The road has been built five years, and already there have been 17 changes of ownership. We are more restless than our parents, all searching for the perfect house, the better neighbourhood.

This is a typical road in an area that appears to consist almost entirely of such roads; a place, one might think, where most of the energy was directed inwards, to the home and domestic life:

Family of two adults, one child and cat. Semi-detached bungalow, 3 bedrooms and 1 living-room, not centrally heated. Husband engineer with BP Research at Sunbury-on-Thames, 18 miles daily by car. 7.30 a.m., rise and dress, feed cat, cook breakfast, 8 a.m. husband leaves for work, wash up, put washing to soak, make beds; 8.30 a.m. child's breakfast, finish washing, housework. Prepare lunch, shopping. 11 a.m. child sleeps, time for interests – dressmaking, knitting, embroidery etc. 1 p.m. lunch, wash up, amuse child. 2.30 pm. take child for walk or visit friends. 5 p.m. child's tea and bath. 6 p.m. husband arrives home and puts child to bed. 6.30 p.m. high tea with husband. Most of vegetables are home-grown. Husband buys potatoes and washing-up liquid in bulk and pays for fuel for car when used for shopping. Almost all mother's and child's clothes are made at home. Cakes are mostly home-made . . .

2 adults, 2 children (3½ and 1½). Detached, 3 bedrooms. Husband accountant in City bank, leaves at 7.15 a.m. to catch train to Waterloo; he either cycles or takes the car to Guildford station. Morning spent in hectic housework, minding children – own and sometimes others'. Lunch at 12.30 p.m. in kitchen, as children still at messy stage. Afternoon shopping. Twice a week have friends to tea or visit families – all have families so there is always a large gathering of children playing together. Bread is delivered to the house daily. Visit Guildford to buy items unobtainable locally, e.g. clothes, shoes, dress materials, wool, presents. Tea with the children, 4.30 to 5. Children bathed and in bed by 6 p.m. Husband arrives home, time varies between 5.45 and 7.45, and has meal similar to midday lunch. House-keeping allowance £7. Evening spent sewing, wife makes most of own and children's clothes; knitting, reading, watching TV and listening to records. Husband is secretary of the FLG Bar Committee, wife secretary of WI.

The last sentence is the important one. FLG stands for 'Fairlands, Liddington Hall and Gravetts Lane' Community Association. Perhaps *because* of the newness of the whole estate, this is an extraordinarily flourishing affair, the centre of a very real social life. On Bonfire Night there was a vast children's torchlight procession from the shops to the field adjoining the Community Centre, and in the scrapbook there is a very good colour photograph of a Boxing Day pram race, lots of people in an open landscape, all smiling in the sun. There is no pub on the estate. I asked why not.

'For the simple reason that we think it would be detrimental to the residents,' said the Association's secretary. 'If we had a pub it would attract strangers on to the estate, it would attract a lot of undesirable people, whereas we as an Association can furnish for our own needs, with a licensed club to do as we like.' There is an ecumenical service every Sunday morning, taken by ministers of different religions each week. Mondays, youth club, Tuesdays modern dancing class, and handicrafts, Wednesdays WI monthly, Young Wives monthly, or a lecture, Thursday old-time dancing –

The Old-Time Dance Club has 60 members. We have now a very delightful and efficient professional couple, George and Arlene Bagley, giving instruction, and they seem to enjoy it as much as the members. So far we have attempted about twelve dances, which we do reasonably adequately, the enjoyment being as much in the learning of the dance as its actual performance. Everyone makes mistakes in the sequences, and this is all taken in great good humour, especially on one occasion when a certain foursome managed to interpret the instructor's promptings to the extent that two gentlemen were seen at one time to be dancing together.

– Friday bingo in one half of the hall, licensed club in the other half, Saturdays licensed club. Everybody wants baby-sitters on the same night when there is something big on, such as a play.

The Fairlands, Liddington Hall and Gravetts Lane Community Association opened a £12,886 Community Centre at Fairlands. It started in 1935, and ten years later had bought an old army hut for £7/10/–. The purchase of the new Centre was helped by several grants; over £6,000 from the Department of Education and Science, £1,183 from Worplesdon Parish Council . . .

155

Fairlands may *look* just like a suburb; but it has the compactness and the clearly defined boundaries of an old-time village (although its Community Centre does in fact serve two other adjoining areas), and in such a place, more than in many traditional communities, people who are lonely here (if there are any) have no real excuse.

3. *The Village that sounds thatched but isn't*

In any short-list of euphonious village names suggesting the classic, calendar-picture old English village (my own absolutely top favourite, which I have never visited lest the reality should spoil the illusion, is *Lydiard Millicent*) a place could surely be found for *Cherry Willingham*. Yet, if one tries to visualize them as girls, it is Cherry Willingham who also sounds like a girl one might meet in the High Street ('I ran into Cherry Willingham in the library'); Lydiard Millicent is too delicately preserved, fictional, seen for a moment on the edge of a scene in the Pump Room in *Northanger Abbey*. In fact Cherry Willingham is merely the almost-vanished village that gave its name to the large Lincolnshire version of Fairlands which swallowed it:

This is not an attractive village, in spite of its pleasing name. As long ago as 1842 it was mentioned as 'an indifferently built village', so it is not surprising that the older cottages have no particular architectural charms. One fine view, though, is that of farm cottages at the top of Church Lane, with the austere Georgian church in the background. This contrasts greatly with the post-World War II housing estate which has been grafted on to the former tiny village. Cherry Willingham is now a densely inhabited island amongst acres of arable land. Between it and Lincoln stretch field upon field with only a tiny scatter of farm cottages at Greetwell. From there as one crosses the high railway bridge one can see an almost solid block of houses in the distance. This density of houses is the result of partial in-filling of a triangle of ribbon development along Church Lane, Waterford Lane and Fiskerton Road. On the far side of the level crossing a similar development is taking place, covering the flat, windswept field between Croft Lane and Hawthorn Road, with detached houses, chalets and bungalows which will take several years to lose their raw appearance . . .

. . . retired people in the village, many attracted from far beyond Lincolnshire by the low cost of housing . . .

. . . I first saw Cherry Willingham during a rainstorm in 1961. On the train northwards I had noticed its name in a newspaper article about the appointment of the Vicar of Cherry Willingham to be Custodian of the Treasures of Lincoln Cathedral. At most I thought that his parish had an attractive name, never dreaming that I should be one of his parishioners. My first pleasure here was that we, who had only managed to afford a two-bedroomed bungalow in the south, could here live in a three-bedroomed house with a garage. We were lucky enough to live on the edge of the estate, so we are very aware that though a great mass of houses lay behind us all around stretched the acres of farm factory which was how we came to regard Lincolnshire . . .

. . . a constant sprinkling of FOR SALE notices shows how mobile is the population. The headmistress has found that there is a 25% mobility among the children who attend her school.

This mobility is in part accounted for by nearby RAF airfields. As in many new centres, capacious new school buildings (a primary and a secondary modern were both built in 1955) provide a focus for a great deal of social life; a drama society, for instance, was started in the same year. There are plenty of people, of course, who don't want to join anything at all, and seem, in their chalets or bungalows, to resent any suggestion that they live in a community, however potential:

Of 650 questionnaires distributed [for the scrapbook] only 156 were returned ... much discussion and gossip had taken place about the 'audacity' of the questions. Determination to refuse to complete the questionnaires spread amongst the housewives, and some husbands objected too. Much of this lack of support was due to the fact that many husbands work in Lincoln and have little interest in the affairs of the village.

They were pretty innocuous questions. *How many adults in the household? What is their occupation? How many children? Which schools do they attend? What is your religion? Were you or your wife born in Lincolnshire?* (29% said *yes* to this last). Nevertheless, even if there is nothing quite on the scale of the Community Association at Fairlands, Cherry Willingham is quite well organized enough socially for any newcomer who makes an effort to fit in to enjoy life; or perhaps the following extract was prompted by purely personal social contacts, for not everything can be achieved by institutions:

Most newcomers find plenty of social life in Cherry Willingham. Indeed it is very easy to become involved in so many evening activities that either husband or wife are out for several evenings each week. During the day one normally meets the mothers of nearby children, good relations with them being essential in case of childish tiffs. To me, this will always be the village where I have made many friends, some of whom have already moved away again. It has been the place, above all, where I as a complete stranger have been able to enjoy a wider social life than ever before.

In the great majority of villages life comes somewhere in between the foregoing extremes – the old and settled community where for a fellow-villager to have been in hospital for a week without one's knowing is a noteworthy surprise, and the two practically brand-new estates. Most places that

one still thinks of as villages *do* have less than 4,000 people;
and most of them have some non-farming new inhabitants.
The mere fact of those new inhabitants having moved there,
the decisiveness of this act, implies some recognition, however rudimentary, of the village as a community; but it is
possible that to these new residents, slightly more than to the
older, native, unthinking heirs of shared customs that have
grown out of the local soil, the whole idea of 'community' is
something of a paradox. One drives over magnificent bare
sweeps of Dorset, over land obviously, immemorially destined to *be* bare land; in spite of the pylons, the forest of
mysterious aerials outside Shaftesbury, in spite of the diffuse
sense of human history – Druids, peasants, Saxons, fairs,
monks, redcoats, journeys to India, tears, births, historic tea-
rooms – the wind over those bare ridges tells us we can know
nothing; and where the single farmhouse, the marvellous
human homestead, appears in the only possible place, the
uniquely right site in the cleft of land, it seems a private
domestic statement, one man and his secret, enclosed family
giving meaning to nature. It is a primary and clear impression. The villages, when they appear, no doubt have the
same original inevitability and rightness; but there is a blurring, a randomness, intersections, confusions of period. One
drives through, up the hill, past the lights; one village after
another; old cars, children on windy evenings outside council estates, maiden ladies in cottages full of polished things,
gardens neat or scruffy, gravelled pub car parks, halls of
corrugated iron, grand withdrawn Georgian houses ivied
behind white posts with chains, littered garages where a
fortyish man with a humorous face, woollen cap over blue
overalls, tinkers with a tractor. On sunny afternoons, driving
westwards one is aware of the Atlantic weather, solid dark
clouds against the sun in a bright sky, shadows moving over
combes, copses and towns. In the Fells, a man washing a Mini

with water from a clear gushing spring in a pure stone village like a film set – perhaps they do, all, know each other here. Bulldozers and earthmovers, the effortless motorway disregarding the old lie of the land, swishing past the huddled roofs; can the one reality know the other? The communities are secondary, derived, evolving, they cannot be fully known, described, generalized upon. They are one and one, each different, each changing; and each more, or less, real and living. People, surrounded by misty evening fields, coming together.

Entering Oxfordshire from Northamptonshire, the road surface abruptly changes (and here, on unfenced land with an ex-airfield look about it, is yet another mysterious array of aerials, interspersed with little huts, stretching away over the horizon); the landscape becomes dominated by horizontals; marching lines of light separated clouds with unvarying base lines that echo the hedge trees on ridge after ridge. There are broad grass strips between the road and the hedge, or sometimes it is unfenced. The village of *Beckley* looks from a secret wooded ridge over Otmoor, described in the nineteenth century as 'a dreary waste and coarse aquatic sward'; it commands the view which suggested to Lewis Carroll his chessboard in *Alice Through the Looking-glass*.

It is a haunted landscape, like many in this country; Dorset is haunted by something old, the Fell country by something older still, there are curious shut-in low valleys in Suffolk haunted by forgotten but nevertheless later miseries – the Black Death, perhaps, something closed-in and mad. Otmoor is certainly haunted, like all places where the Romans have been (a Roman road which once ran from Dorchester to Bicester crosses it, partly as a muddy track). One R. Hussey first noticed a stony ford in a little brook near Merton, and elsewhere there is a field called Struttle Mead, the 'street hill' of the Roman Road. Field names such as

Rushy Meadow, the Flits or Fleets, Moorleys, Pill's Ground, tell their descriptive tale; a *flit* is a marshy hollow, and a *pill* is an accumulation of quaking bog. Otmoor has 'seven towns' – Beckley, Noke, Oddington, Charlton-on-Otmoor, Fencott and Murcott and Horton-cum-Studley. It is haunted too, by the Otmoor riots which stemmed from the Duke of Marlborough's petition in 1801 to enclose four thousand acres. A Parliamentary committee authorized the fixing of notices to the church doors, but because of hostile crowds at Beckley, Oddington and Charlton this was only done at Noke; a possible origin of the rhyme

> *I went to Noke*
> *But nobody spoke,*
> *I went to Beckley,*
> *They answered directly.*

And Oddington bells, according to Robert Graves, are supposed to ring 'Hang Sam Gomme, Save Will Young', the former being a spy for Lord Churchill's troops of yeomanry which in September 1830 were used to round up Otmoor men who were destroying the new fences, the latter being a ringleader.

In the saloon bar of the pub people from miles round were eating scampi by candlelight. In the public bar I found only one local man, born in Beckley in 1888; he remembered the hiring fairs at Thame, where shepherds had a bit of wool in their buttonholes, and carters a bit of whipcord; Beckley had then a shoemaker (Mr Amos Wing), a blacksmith (Mr Auger) and a baker (Mr Gatz) who 'used to cook our Sunday dinners for us at $1\frac{1}{2}$d a time. We would take the joint and the batter along on our way to church – we all went to church then – and pick them up after service. Every cottager would have a pig and they would never be short of bacon or lard. You would see the flitches of bacon hanging from the beams in the kitchen.' He met his wife at the fortnightly dances in the school. 'We had all the old dances, lancers, quadrilles and waltzes. Amos Wing, he became the postmaster, used to play the piano for us, and before he learned to play we had Mr Obadiah Cripps of the Windmill, Wheatley. Mr Chaundy played the cello and Mr Haynes the piano. All the young men wore white gloves and buttonholes.' He was with Allenby in Palestine. He worked as a carrier and later as a woodman. 'They were hard times for us all after that war – not like this one . . . it is not to be wondered at that so many of the old village customs came to an end when the young men were called up and never revived again after the war.'

Yet there the village still is, overwhelmingly as it has looked for two or three centuries, in spite of the bungalows. Do they live there now, like the oil in the beard of Aaron, where

21 own or manage farms or smallholdings, 13 are agricultural, forestry or estate workers, 1 is a publican, 3 are builders, 1 is a baker, 1 is a glazier, 2 are school helpers, 7 are small traders, 17 are at Pressed Steel, 9 at Morris, 15 at small Oxford firms, 6 work for the University, 7 for other educational bodies, 5 for Oxford hospitals, 4 are builders, 4 own small businesses, 4 are sales representatives, 2 are servicemen, 2 are civil servants, 1 works for the GPO and 1 is a solicitor?

A picture in the scrapbook shows fair-haired school-children smiling at the camera from rows of chairs between two honey-coloured buildings; framed in the gap behind them are those blue rolling horizons of parallel hedge-trees:

The school swimming pool is the outcome of a really successful community effort and we are proud of it. In 1961 a meeting of parents resolved to raise the money needed and in eighteen months over £300 was collected to purchase and instal a Purley plastic-lined pool. Since then it has given great pleasure and many children have learned to swim. In the past two years every child leaving for secondary education has been able to swim ten yards ...

Most of its children are a focal point in any community (and the voluntary efforts to provide a swimming pool are, incidentally, the story that recurs with most frequency in the scrapbooks I have seen); but this is to anticipate. Let us look at the other and most consciously organized adult end of the community; even though

realization that the future depends so largely on forces outside our own control is conducive to apathy

in Beckley, as anywhere else, the first and most obvious aspect of a community is the external one of formal government.

The civil parish forms part of the Bullingdon Rural District. The present chairman of the parish council is Mr Lankester, Surveyor to the University, and the other four elected members are Mr Bowring (retired), Mr Tilbury (builder), Mr Tompkins (farmer), and Mr Young (Instructor at the College of Technology), giving a reasonably balanced representation of the village community. No woman has yet been elected to the parish council; but since women are much concerned with the kind of business which comes before it, this is something which the WI is thinking about. In addition to its routine duties the council has recently taken charge of the maintenance of the playing field and pavilion and it has interested itself in the definition of rights of way. Although the council has no powers in the thorny matter of planning permissions, it is now invited by the planning authorities to comment on the applications they receive; but so far there has been little evidence that any account is taken of the council's views.

In a way it must take more sense of duty to be a parish councillor, forever discussing bus shelters, graveyards, tree-lopping, lighting and other minor matters, than to aim higher at the RDC or the county council itself. Yet very often there *is* a sense of continuity with the higher echelons:

The parish council is the lighting authority, also for wayside seats and shelters. It has powers to provide recreation grounds and open spaces, allotments and village halls, and can spend the equivalent of a penny rate on things not authorized by laws or regulations provided those things are for the benefit of all, and not for one particular section of the ratepayers. Housing is the prerogative of the rural council, but the parish council of Duffield has always enjoyed happy relations with the rural council, who always ask the council for recommendations when they are selecting tenants for housing or bungalows. The final say does of course rest with the rural council, but it is interesting to record that in the past a very good proportion of the parish council recommendations have been accepted.

(Duffield, Derbs.)

For this very reason, however, lower echelons of council service are invaluable, because they are concerned with small, personal details of everyday life of a community; the parish councillor is the opposite of a bureaucrat.

The parish council is continually busy. In the autumn it began walking the footpaths of the parish to see that they remained accessible rights of way, and that stiles and bridges were in repair. Parishioners bring their complaints of dangerous trees, road defects and failing bus services to the council. The rural district councillor is consulted informally at all hours, over beer in the pub or while he does his garden.

(*Radwinter, Essex*)

Radwinter either will be, or would have been one of the places doomed by Stansted; when the Concord gets going they won't be able to hear themselves speaking like this:

Well, how are you together?
Half tidy, like. How's yarsel'?
Middling, mate.
Bill tell them he hev to go right up them filds to wock, so I had to take my vittals with me. After I got hom I had me tea and a pipe of bacca, and I went in the garden and howed my taters, and stuck my peas. They owd budds hev picked em all to pieces, the varmints. Well, mate, are you goin to hev another one afore you go?
No thanks, I better be agoin'.
You ent goin' hom yitt?
. . . mornin' mate. Ain't it cowd! It wuz a stinger last night. It friz my water tap, an' then it snew pourin'. I had to clear a path to my hinnas. I think we shall git some more afore long. We shall hev some Thaxted snow. I shan't goo much fudder today once I git aginst that fire. There, look at they owd boys snowballin'. They'll hut theselves, then they'll be blaring . . .

Also overhead at a WI meeting concerned with supper recipes:

My husband wouldn't it that owd codge.

No one would claim that regional cultures must be preserved in aspic. Radwinter, like a good many other charming places in north Essex, is of course a special example; when, to the ordinary pressure of urbanization that exists in varying degrees all over the country is added the unique,

Whitehall-created problem of a vast international airport (in an area whose special quiet, untouched and remote charm is precisely due to skimpy communications!), it takes a bold imagination to conceive of any kind of community at all surviving, let alone a traditional one. Nevertheless Radwinter makes a brave, resigned and hopeful attempt:

Older people living in poor conditions have been re-housed by the council, but for younger people, unless they are fortunate, there is nothing at all. The tendency, then, is for Radwinter and other villages to become communities of older people. No industry has appeared to replace agriculture as an employer of labour. In Radwinter the turkey farm and the mushroom farm [started by a Pole] provide some employment, and there are also places for a few people locally in road maintenance, the postal service and odd-job work of various sorts, but generally there is no employment in the village, just as there are no houses for younger people, and inevitably they go elsewhere. The shops find difficulty too. The near-by towns bristle with cut-price shops where the cost of travelling out of Radwinter is amply compensated. The mobile grocery shops sent out by the town cooperative societies are a boon to people living out of the village centre, but they are an additional competition for the village shops to which the same people once walked. The village inns, on the other hand, have been made busier by the growth of motor traffic; Radwinter Red Lion is visited by people from a very wide area.

An idea of what is happening is given by the fact that the school population is steadily declining, and seems likely to go on doing so. In the entire parish there is only a handful of under-fives to enter the school in the next few years. It is true that many of the better-to-do people send their children away to school. Nevertheless the child population is diminishing. Schools in some villages have been closed for lack of pupils. The recent modernization of Radwinter school makes it improbable that this will happen here. Probably instead its intake will come from an increasingly larger area.

Our picture, then, is of a tranquil village in which people are happy, but aware of many uncertainties for the future. In particular, the population is an ageing one. Younger people leave, largely through the necessities of housing and employment. The tendency, though not as pronounced as it has become in some villages, is towards a residential grouping rather than the preservation of a working community with its roots in the countryside. The establishment of the airport at Stansted would undoubtedly damage tranquillity. Radwinter is outside the area in which there would be intense noise, but it would hear a good deal, and become aware of increasing activity on the roads as well. The prospect is far from agreeable. Yet the same development would provide jobs in the area and lead the way to better amenities. The higher income from rates at Stansted would lighten immensely the problem of providing improvements all over the Rural District. And improvements are needed. There is nothing picturesque about cesspools, or elderly people fetching water in buckets from standpipes.

Prophecies have been made of the disappearance of the countryside under the pressures of traffic and population. Ideally a community should be able to select what is good from the new while preserving the best of the old. Such choices are seldom possible. Local authorities can try to control development but can rarely dictate it. What a community can do, however, is to interpret trends and try to prepare for what is coming. Here the Parish Council has a valuable part to play. Its purchase of the recreation ground, for example, has ensured that whatever changes come there will always be open space in the centre of the village.

What we would wish for Radwinter, then, is its preservation as a living community. If it has to be touched by modern times we hope for the touch not to be heavy-handed. Certainly, amenities and conveniences must come, and we should want housing and work as a means of keeping young people in the village

167

and so preserving our heritage of tradition. But whatever changes come, we want also to have fields and trees around us; to hear the birds singing; to take pride in our farming; and to feel that our village is, for each one of us, unique.

Membership of a parish council can be undertaken for many reasons, ranging from what is left of traditional upper-class 'sense of responsibility', or even merely wanting to have an ear to the ground and an eye to the main chance, to genuine desire to serve the community and make it more real and articulated. Democracy, after all, began as a city-state idea, not an affair of vast nations, and obviously, in theory at least, a *village*-state, where everyone actually knew everyone else, would provide an even better example of the beard of Aaron:

The Parish Council, that down-to-earth, rock-bottom example of democratic government, jealously guarded from extinction or even amalgamation, once a year holds an open meeting for parishioners, at which they hear reports of last year's proceedings and proposals for the coming year, and themselves then make suggestions, criticisms and decisions; and for years and years this meeting has been held at the school, a building very closely associated with everything that has happened in the village.

What memories hang round this gaunt old room, with its tall windows, its faint green walls and iron girders from which, high up in the roof, glare down the unshaded electric bulbs! Memories not only of schoolchildren with their daytime hullabaloo, but of every kind of gathering – dances, whist drives, WI meetings, plays, concerts, and Saturday afternoon rummage sales, wedding receptions or flower shows. So all our lives through, from schooldays among the desks and blackboards to the time when, as pensioners, we come here for the Old Friends annual party, the school has been the centre of our social existence.

Before official business the Chairman reports that a gentleman (unnamed at this stage, but we all know it is Ron Cornes) has sold his meadow behind the school to the Parish Council for so small a sum that it can be considered a gift. This means they can finish playing football on the cricket pitch ... discussions about the village hall ... the meeting ends, and so home earlier than usual. We have had an amusing evening in the name of duty performed, and, as ever, some of the matters we have been burning to discuss are kept till we get outside. At the schoolyard gate little groups of twos and threes are hard at it, their figures dim under the trees among the bike lamps, their voices drowned by the revving up of car engines.

(*Smarden, Kent*)

In fact it is probably true that the parish council is the last expression of a rural community. Whether it is, like Belloc's don, 'remote and ineffectual', or whether it enjoys a lively and personalized relationship with the village, is something that depends on many other factors – and not entirely on the preponderance of unassimilated newcomers, either; as we saw in the case of Fairlands, it is perfectly possible to start a very real community spirit from scratch. And, *per contra*, there are doubtless many villages as old and tra- ditional as Smarden which could not provide as pleasant an account as that just quoted. The community makes the council, not the other way round.

These 'other factors' are those details of everyday life – transport, shopping, medical service, in fact *all* services – which in spite of all changes, are still quite different from those of the city. The relationship between the people and their postman, district nurse, grocer is part of a social con- text quite different from that of the city, because such func- tionaries are all very much more likely to be known outside their function. To be known as people, in a community.

The Sociable Services

The Scrapbook Secretary, in her sweetshop, often spends anything up to ten minutes helping tiny children to decide what to buy. Sometimes after all this time they will say 'I'll go and see what Dick has.'

(Askrigg, Yorks.)

This is everyone's picture of the village shop, and may easily be visualized in a place still so coherently a village, fine solid Georgian houses set against the sweeping Dales (for most of it was built either around 1760 or in the first half of the nineteenth century), where everyone has a nickname:

Mrs M. Weatherauld	*Mary Michael*
Mr H. Kirkbride	*Lile Harry*
Mrs Robert Bankes	*Our Tan*
Mr John Percival	*Bogey*
Mr W. Sharples	*Nobby*
Mr Jack Metcalfe	*Molly*
Mr John Metcalfe Jr	*Young Molly*
Mr Norman Dinsdale	*Normy Joy*
Mr G. Halton	*Pills*
Mrs Joe Chapman	*Maggie Joe*
Mrs C. Dinsdale	*Mary Colin*
Mr J. Thwaite	*Swol*
Mr K. Weatherauld	*Pop*

Mr J. Metcalfe	Postman Jack
Mr G. Calvert	Dick
Mr W. Sharples	Buff
Mr F. E. Chevins	Shev
Mr J. Fawcett	Fawcey Fowce
Mr John Metcalfe	Slip'oy
Mr Jim Dinsdale	Flute
Mr W. Metcalfe	Willy Lug
Mr Jack Percival	John Jacket
Mrs A. Hodgson	Hoddie
Mr V. Wilkinson	Uncle
Mrs. J. Foster	Jinny Bob
Mr Welsh	Jock
Mr J. Halton	Jim Dick
Mr R. Halton	Shimmy
Mr J. Kirkbride	Jack Slack
Mr J. Abraham	Our John
Mr J. Abraham	Our Jim
Mr W. Chapman	Coney
Mrs S. Bell	Gilgate Mary
Mr T. E. Metcalfe	Tucker
Mr Carl Metcalfe	Splash

... as people we accept newcomers at first not enthusi-astically, but later after a few years and after taking stock of their worth we welcome them. At the same time we are ex-tremely loyal to our own. It is a very outstanding incomer who is accepted with the same loyalty. We are proud of our heritage. We are, or have been, members of a working-class community. There are no ladies or gentlemen on the moor. There are no ladies or gentlemen of the manor in the village, no class dis-tinctions. There are groupings based on different ages, incomes and interests, but no snobbery.

Shopping, as several extracts have already shown, is one of the first areas in which newcomers to the country are struck by the sense of something much more personal and relaxed than its urban equivalent; and curiously enough at least one of the modern replacements of the sell-everything village shop, far from being 'impersonal', is if anything less so – for what could be more personal than a shop on four wheels calling at your door?

Practically everything is delivered to the door, including the car when serviced at the garage. Food is delivered from shops in Holmbrook, Seascale, Ravenglass, Egremont and Whitehaven. Travelling shops bring round bread, groceries, vegetables, fish and meat on different days of the week ... furniture and hardware is delivered from Gosforth, Egremont, Whitehaven and Carlisle. A lot of households buy through mail-order catalogues.

(*Drigg, Cumberland*)

In the majority of villages, especially the smaller and more traditional, the village shop stands in no danger from such modern practices, since its natural function as social meeting-place and notice-board both visual and oral is reinforced by the fact that it is also the post office. *Willoughby's* book, revealing that '6 people in the village run mail order clubs' also gives an impressive list of village post office business:

Postage, savings and insurance stamps. Postal orders, money orders, premium bonds, development bonds, savings certificates, savings bank, parcel post, inland and foreign. Licences; television and radio, gun, dog, game (£3 for whole season, £2 for whole season less first month), gamekeeper's dog exemption for working dog (4 issued); pensions – old age, national assistance, family allowance, Army, Navy and Air Force allowances, Army disablement, sickness and unemployment. Registered and recorded delivery, C.O.D. 1964 was the first full year when letters were no longer date-stamped by hand at Willoughby.

The same book provides some very good and characteristic examples of the personal element in rural trade and shopping.

During the early part of the year a weekly shoe-repair service also operated from Scunthorpe, but this was discontinued when the firm's van was smashed. No one who had seen this van being driven round the school corner was surprised at its fate. . . . The unusual Sunday greengrocery round of Brown's of Alford is due to their being Sunday newsagents also . . . in 1965 Alford Market made a comeback, with a lot of Cheshire farm produce as well as locally produced fare; many people came home on the 11 a.m. bus, but for those who stayed until 2 or 2.30 p.m. the auctions starting at noon offered both bargains and entertainment. Bakers, butchers and grocers all deliver. Milk consumption varies widely from one household to another, so that if an average were worked out it would demonstrate little. No household had more than a regular six pints daily, but with one lone householder consuming two pints daily and another household of three sharing one pint between them milk consumption appears a very individual matter. Pasteurized milk had the biggest sales but there was also a large demand for sterilized. This long-keeping milk was popular with (1) people living alone who did not use a whole pint a day and wanted it to keep fresh, (2) in summer time and close weather families with no refrigerators preferred its long-keeping qualities, (3) the very few (five) households to which milk was delivered only once a week and had no choice but to buy it, and (4) the surprising number of people who preferred its unusual flavour in tea, or who found it more economical as it 'went farther'. . . . Free gifts are not as good for sales promotion as they were, especially gifts of cheap polythene items . . .

A photograph shows the milkman, Bob Riddington, with a little cart pulled by his bicycle –

Whistled hymn tunes with the rattle of milk bottles; a life-long passion for railway engines of the steam era; and ability to play, in the right key, with accompaniment, any tune he has heard a few times – that's Bob. Musical scores mean nothing to him. 'Notes,' he says, 'are just so many black dots,' and his early music teacher soon gave up trying to get him to understand them. But the Methodists, the Mothers' Union, the WI, the old people at Virginia House and many more are delighted with his skill as a pianist and his willingness to play for them. Nothing seems dull or ordinary to Bob, and his enjoyment and obser-vation of his daily rounds are always new, from the barn owl on the post blinking in the sunshine to the dew-hung autumn spider's hammock.

All this seems somehow *extra* snug and human set against the background of Lincolnshire, the second largest county in England; even in high summer, there is something raw-boned, fresh, open, earthy about it, something particularly domestic about tree-sheltered Tennysonian rectories set in folds of the cold wolds. At Alford, I arrived at the big-roomed, at first slightly gaunt-seeming pub (on a dignified little square with a huge flagpole on which a Union Jack thrummed in the wind) at the late evening hour which people are always telling you in England will cause scowls if you ask for a meal. In fact, the lone diner in a big old room full of stiff white tablecloths, a great sideboard, tremendous talk from a parrot heard every time the service door swung open, I was very courteously served with excellent chops. And it was a very snug bar. And the first thing I noticed in Willoughby the next morning was a neat little brick box of a house, its lawn fringed with lobelias, called *Emoh Ruo*. Wil-loughby, incidentally, is the birthplace of John Smith, founder of Virginia; hence the name of the old people's home.

To some extent villages are obviously less self-sufficient than they were in the past:

A talk given at a WI meeting on the village in 1846 with the aid of a directory of that time proved that the village of a hundred years ago was much more self-sufficient. Today the village is served by one general store and post office, and the baker's, butcher's and tailor's have all disappeared one by one. Most of the village people work in Lutterworth, the nearest market town, where the main industries are hosiery and engineering. The village school is still open, but only just over 20 children attend, mainly due to the fact that many young married couples move out of the village as the houses are very hard to get. Not much building has taken place in recent years, and many houses have become derelict and some have been demolished. Although there is only one shop there are several *mobile* shops.

(*Kimcote & Walton, Leics.*)

At *Hovingham, Yorks,* a village dominated by the Palladian Hovingham Hall, home of the Worsley family, to which the Duchess of Kent belongs, the scrapbook tells of cricket played here for more than a hundred years and shows pictures of Sir William Worsley with Freddie Trueman, or King Haakon of Norway ceremonially planting a tree; and here

one in three housewives belong to clubs like Littlewoods, Brian Mills or Trafford for buying clothes. They enjoy the glossy magazines and catalogues . . .

Even so, the shopping pattern of villages is less diffuse than that of the town dweller. There are fewer imponderables, less impulse buying, making it possible for the scrapbooks to provide some very informative budgets.

Hovingham offers a very practical, Yorkshire, do-it-yourself piece of economic research:

January 1st. ½ lb. Danish bacon, ½ lb. New Zealand butter, 1 large white loaf, ½ lb. lard, 1 packet frozen peas, ½ lb. Cheshire cheese, 1 lb. sugar, 1 packet cream crackers, ½ lb. currants, ½ lb. beef sausages, ½ lb. shin beef, 1 pint milk, ½ dozen eggs, 1 box matches, 1 lb. washing soap, 3 Oxo cubes, postage on two letters, 1 *Yorkshire Post*, 1 Kemp's chocolate wafer biscuit, came to £1. On December 31st exactly the same things came to £1/2/7½.

Fylingdales gives the budget of a pensioner of over 70 and his wife, income £460 p.a., including £370 pension.

Weekly expenditure groceries £2/13/–, meat £1/10/–, fish 5/–, milk 7/–, eggs 5/–, fruit and vegetables 7/–, TV hire and relay 7/6; postage, chemist etc. 10/–. Personal allowance (hairdressing, tobacco) for the year, £52.

It adds up to £459/10/10 and is followed by the note

To play with: 9/2.

And here is a classic example of the kind of budget which Mr Micawber knew would bring 'result, happiness':

We are grateful to the wife of a gamekeeper for allowing us to reproduce her weekly budget. There are five in the family, including three children of school age. They keep hens and grow their own vegetables, cook by electricity but use mainly wood for heating, so that their fuel bill is small. They are not in the habit of going away for holidays but enjoy excursions in Mr X's car. The children earn extra pocket money in the winter months by acting as beaters. Mrs X makes many of her own and the children's clothes, and runs a clothing club. She is also the family hairdresser. Income: housekeeping money from husband £9, Family allowance 18/–, own earnings £3, total income £12/18/–. Average weekly payment for food £7/12/4, clothing club £1, savings £1/2/6, fuel and electricity 10/–, coal 5/3, sundries £2/7/1; total payments £12/17/2. The bigger items of food expenditure are meat (to include sausages and bacon) 35/–, bread (8 loaves) 10/6, milk (22 pints) 15/11, school dinners 15/–, 10 lb. sugar 8/9, 3 lb. butter and 1½ lb. cheese 6/–, cooking fats 4/8. All cakes and jams are home-made. Sundries include papers and comics 5/3, children's pocket money 11/–, dog food 11/–, as well as chemist's necessities, shoe repairs etc. The large amount of regular savings will be noted. The family does not believe in buying on the never-never, but rather in saving for what they want. Their television set is their own, and each week 7/6 is paid into a Christmas club, 5/– into a grocery club, whilst 10/– goes direct to the bank. Total savings, 22/6.

(Clapham & Patching, Sussex)

Grampound, that mine of information, even gives the relative prices of basic foods in five different countries, France, Germany, Sweden, England and Cornwall:

	France	Germany	Sweden	England	Cornwall
Steak per lb.	£1/1/–	9/6	£1/0/7½	10/–	8/6
Cauliflower	1/3	1/7	2/2	1/8	we grow them
Butter per lb.	7/6	4/5	4/7½	3/3	3/8
Tea per lb.	£1/6/–	18/–	14/4½	6/8	from 6/–

Perhaps it really *is* cheaper in Cornwall, for in *St Erth* (where, incidentally, the village shop is run by a Pole, called Ivanowsky; while I was in it buying bacon a little girl came in and bought a bicycle lamp, a pack of playing cards and a toothbrush) we read –

There is a butcher's shop which is only open in the morning. Mr Stone is not expensive, as his customers are not very wealthy. His fillet steak was 7/– a pound when it was 17/– in London.

Very often if you want to get a message to someone who cannot be reached physically or by telephone but is known to be somewhere in the village, the place to make contact is the village shop; and of all village personalities there is none so likely to be that someone as the district nurse. In many ways she is coming to occupy the place in people's minds that belonged to the country GP in the old days, simply because modern medicine often means that when a patient reaches a stage that in the old days would have meant frequent visits and close attention by the doctor, he is now whisked off into hospital in the nearest town. The district nurse's life is one long round of visits – looking after the old, giving regular injections, and, above all, acting as the central and indispensable figure when – a line in the local paper for others, but for one household a day of tension ending, literally, in a bloody miracle, a baby is born. Sometimes, after everything has been tidied up, when that immense, universal force has swept through the house, *this* house, like a mighty wind, a strength leaving this weakness, a cry, a tiny baby's sneeze, a mysteriously identified and unique little face still wrinkled from millions of years in the oceans of time, she accepts a cup of strong tea and goes to the telephone to report to the doctor. 'It's a BBA. Everything OK. A boy.' It stands for Born Before Arrival.

The actual availability of medical services varies widely. *Broad Chalke* (*Wilts*), with a population of a mere 560, has a doctor and surgery in the village, whereas many places with over twice that number are sometimes lucky even to have a weekly surgery held by a visiting doctor. Most good-sized villages have regular pre-and post-natal clinics. In *Compton Martin*

the doctor sent in his resignation from the clinic, owing to over-work in his practice. The Council asked them to carry on the clinic without a doctor for the time being.

Some ancillary medical services shade off imperceptibly into voluntary enterprise, such as the hospital car service with its roster of volunteers, or perhaps the provision of premises:

Through the auspices of the Morpeth RDC's Old People's Welfare Department twelve old people had their feet attended to by a chiropodist who visited Longhurst on January 7th. Mrs Nancy Thomas kindly allowed the use of her home on this occasion ... *Chiropody sessions every six weeks. Please attend for your treatment at No. 8 Longhurst Villlage, Thursday April 1st 2 p.m. Fee 2/6 (if you are a diabetic you must inform the chiropodist).*

(*Ulgham, Northumberland*)

We are really quite adequately served as far as our doctors are concerned, but the greatest lack in the area is a dispensing chemist. There has not been a qualified chemist in the village for about sixty years. Now that the number of inhabitants has increased so much we are really in need of one. It is very hard for those without their own transport to obtain medicines prescribed for them, but for very urgent cases most of the doctors carry a small supply of drugs to be used as an interim measure. A lady in the village until recently allowed prescriptions to be left at her home before lunch on Tuesday and Friday. These were collected by a chemist from Egremont and the medicine returned by early afternoon. This service had been given for some years, since a doctor ceased to hold a surgery at the house, and had proved very helpful. The explanation given us for the cessation of the service was that the Pharmaceutical Society had said that the chemist concerned was getting more prescriptions than he was allowed to make up. No one seems to have heard that there was any limit to the number of prescriptions a chemist may make up. It is possible that other chemists in surrounding districts have complained at one of their number seizing a monopoly.

(St Bees, Cumberland)

In all these widely varying conditions the district nurse is the unvarying constant; and the account of her activities in *Llanilar*, where

Dr Thomas does his own dispensing, entailing a lot of extra work but giving a better service to his patients

may be taken as typical, both of the work and of the cheerful and observant women who do it:

A great deal of our work, unseen and unheralded by the general public, is concerned with filling in forms and statistics about our patients, the dreary weekly, monthly and annual returns that are always waiting to be completed. Have you ever wondered where the local paper gets the printed facts regarding 'the number of old people over 70, the diabetic survey, the prevalence of certain diseases in different areas' etc? I think quite a lot of credit for the statistics must go to the district nurses. A DN's greatest pal is her car, or in my case a Mini-Minor van, and her next-best friend is the friendly garage which gives her good service, for without this her work would be impossible. The County Council pay running expenses and depreciation allowance, but only for a small car. It is no use the glamorous or ambitious would-be District Nurse seeing herself with the latest sports Jag, as finances would soon come unstuck. Police and the public generally are always helpful to the DN on the road. They never swear at you, at least not to your face. I must admit the uniform has saved me a few fines from parking offences.

It helps if the DN has a husband to answer the ever-ringing telephone when she is out. However, as the said husband is not paid for the service he does not feel obliged to write down or remember the messages very clearly. It is embarrassing when one follows the messages up to find that the new baby you call on, complete with maternity bag and equipment, turns out to be an old man of 82.

Most of my work is concerned with the elderly and the very young. The week-ends can be quite hectic with accidents from people following leisure pursuits – cut fingers, sprained ankles, foreign bodies in eyes, noses and ears are commonplace. In a country area the biggest problem is that of age. We are an ageing population, and the young people are leaving the area to find work elsewhere. The elderly patient is never really well. They are confused, they eat the wrong foods, they are always inclined to be constipated or, worse, suffer from diarrhoea and other digestive ailments. In winter they are always cold, and in our climate suffer from various chest complaints. Many of them are also very poor and live in old, insanitary, damp houses. Most of all, they are lonely. The WI in all country areas I cover are always kind and helpful to the elderly. It helps to have a Meals On Wheels service, but in remote areas this is not always possible.

On first calling on the elderly patient living alone one is confronted with a bedside table containing twenty or more bottles of tablets of medicines of all colours and varieties and diverse instructions, such as *Take every four hours*, *Take three times a day*, *After meals*, etc. Sometimes they have the patient's name on the bottle, sometimes they have been passed on after first being prescribed for some well-meaning friend. It never fails to amaze me how well these old dears stand up to all this medication. I don't want to give the impression that I resent the good GP's work; on the contrary, I have worked with about twelve different GPs and they are all wonderful and never resent my calling them out at any hour of the day or night, their only fault being that they tend to kill the old people with kindness, if you will excuse the pun. One dear old lady I recall had a nasty rash on her abdomen and the doctor prescribed a pressurized antibiotic spray. Imagine my consternation when I found the patient spraying her tummy, with great glee, with a delightfully perfumed silicone furniture polish! All medicines and cleaning materials were being kept in the same cupboard. The rash cleared up in no time at all. I wonder what impression the antibiotic spray made on the furniture.

Perhaps the nicest part of our work is the midwifery side. There is a boom in the birth-rate at present. People are getting married at a much younger age. Mothers are younger than they used to be. Some parents today are still at school or university. The older generation may frown at this state of affairs; I can only observe that the younger mothers have the healthiest babies. They have them more easily, and they have more patience to bring them up. . . . I have the privilege of teaching the young mothers mothercraft in a weekly class, where they are also taught relaxation and prepared for labour by psycho-prophylaxis, a method devised in Russia and taken up by Dr Lamase in France. It is pioneered here by Erna Wright, a mid-wife sponsored by the National Childbirth Trust.

This profile would not be complete unless I paid a tribute to my greatest helpmeet in these busy times. No! I do not mean the GPs, bless them, but the Industrial Chemists and Inventors of all the new disposable equipment, syringes, plastic drawsheets and disposable enemas, catheters etc. which lighten our load and help to make the unpleasant tasks of nursing bearable. So a big cheer for the new Plastic Age, and the age of labour-saving devices, as long as we don't go too far and find the computer robots have taken over our jobs.

Transport

In no field has the modern revolution been more intimately bound up with the revolution in country life than that of transport. It is among the first things suggested by the word 'services' but it would be idle to pretend that country life, relying as it now does on ever-increasing use of private transport, dwindling bus services and threatened rail services (where these are not actually defunct) could now count it among the *sociable* services described in the previous chapter.

It is impossible to drive very far in any direction today without seeing some weed-grown line curving away into woods, a derelict station flanked by desolate sidings, a lonely and useless embankment forming a stark skyline which meets the road at a non-bridge. It is not necessary to go all the way with G. K. Chesterton –

> *Wild weddings of strangers*
> *That meet and not mix;*
> *The town and the cornland;*
> *The bride and the groom;*
> *In the breaking of bridges*
> *Is treason and doom*

– to feel a loss of something which has nothing to do with economic categories; something curiously social. The railways could be considered, certainly, as working outwards from a place, as the primary instrument whereby modern national self-consciousness was, for good or ill, intensified;

there was something pastoral, invertebrate – one might almost say, after the iron, steel, metallic wars of this century, innocent and peaceful – about countries before they were stiffened by these iron bones. And it became exciting for one region to explore and recognize another. But they can also be considered as the means by which one returned home, *with others*. There was something very social about the village station. As the *Fylingdales* book puts it:

Brow Side, or Stoup Brow was in the thirteenth century the largest vaccary in Whitby Strand. It is now no more than a scattered community of farms and holiday cottages. It has no direct road communication with the other centres of population in the parish, and with the closure of the Whitby-Scarborough Railway in March this year it became even more isolated. The railway was the only direct route to the villages of Fylingthorpe and Robin Hood's Bay. Now the nearest public transport is a two-mile walk away by lane and road, but residents get a Walking Permit to use the railway track, which saves a mile or so . . .

The passing through Robin Hood's Bay station of the last train sounding its bell like a death knell and with people standing round to pay their last respects, made me think of a funeral service in church where many friends had gathered to pay a last tribute to an old friend. It certainly marked the death of a railway line as a sad day for the people of Robin Hood's Bay who were dependent on the railway station as their 'gateway to the world'.

They realized that life would never be quite the same again. Many of the residents are retired people who used the railway as an easy means of transport to visit friends or relations in their home towns. Many too are young people receiving education at the renowned Fyling Hall School. At term end they travel to many parts of the British Isles, and return at the end of the holiday plus luggage to school again.

Residents in all walks of life will be greatly affected, including the sailors. One of the joys in life was arriving at the station after a long absence from home and finding loved ones on the station platform to welcome them. A few years ago I was meeting a friend from the train and said to a girl who was in the Waiting Room, 'Is your sailor brother coming on this train?' To which she replied, 'He may be, but he asked me to meet every train so that there would be sure to be someone to meet him.'

The waiting room was quite a social centre. As people gathered to await the arrival of the train, they would meet friends and inquire about the anticipated journey. Perhaps it would be a relative or friend the other person knew and they would take the opportunity to send greetings. The newsagent could be there, also the local fishmonger and the other tradesmen waiting to collect their wares from the train.

In the event of a breakdown or bad weather, arrangements would be made by the Stationmaster for a good fire to be burning and the late Mrs Ascough, wife of the Stationmaster, would bring hot tea for the delayed passengers.

Many distinguished visitors have arrived at the station to take a restful holiday. Artists keen on capturing the unique scenes and beauty of the district. Students from Leeds University attending courses in Geology found the railway an easy means of travel. The skill and devotion of the staff gained the Station garden many first and second prizes for the best kept station on the line.

Great efforts were made by the local Council, backed by many residents, to keep open this beautiful line and when the closure was announced there were strong feelings expressed.

Fylingdales, incidentally, gives what must surely be a unique example of the sad farewell, for most railways had had a much longer period than the Whitby-Scarborough line in which to become part of the local life:

Young Fred Meynell stood on a stile at Robin Hood's Bay and jumped for joy as he watched the first trains on the Whitby-

Scarborough line go by. The local headmaster had given Fred
and his fellow-pupils at Thorpe Church of England school one
hour off school to mark the occasion. That was eighty years ago.
On Saturday Fred, now 91, stood on the platform at Robin
Hood's Bay station and watched the last train go by.

Perhaps it is significant that although real regret is expressed over and over again about the disappearance of
branch lines the note is atmospheric rather than coldly practical, so that a note on railways perceived as an unquestioned economic tool (albeit carrying ore rather than
people) comes as quite a surprise:

The Trent, Ancholme and Grimsby Railway, which goes from
Doncaster to Grimsby, is a heavy freight line, and may therefore
survive. Its main cargoes are (1) English iron ore transported
from the iron ore mines of Colsterworth and Kings Cliffe, i.e.
South Lincolnshire and Northamptonshire iron ore fields, to
Scunthorpe blast furnaces, (2) foreign iron ore via Immingham,
mainly from Sweden, to Scunthorpe, (3) coke for the blast furnaces, from the Yorkshire coalfields, to Scunthorpe via Barnetby, (4) manufactured steel going to Immingham for shipment
to many lands, much of it to Canada, (5) coal for shipment at
Immingham Docks, (6) iron ore empties returning to Colsterworth and Kings Cliffe, (7) oil from Killingholme and Immingham to refineries in N.E. England, although a good deal of the
oil imported at Immingham is now carried in tankers by road.
Also, gas made from the waste products of the oil industry is
now piped from Immingham to Leicester, and just skirts our
northern boundary, passing through the land of Mr Watson.

(*Wrawby, Lincs.*)

This area, Lindsey, the bit of Lincolnshire just south of the
Humber, is flat, Fennish (but quite well-treed) country, humming with the summer pastoral airs of Delius (who knew

the tenor Gervase Elwes, of the local great family; hence *Brigg Fair*). It sees nothing but distant wolds, but hears and feels rumours of industry all the time. What other pipelines and lorries will it know after the North Sea gas, and the proposed new city by the Humber, when already

Heavy commercial vehicles on the way to the ports of Immingham and Grimsby, private cars and public transport, the traffic swollen in the summer by endless streams of coaches from the industrial Midlands travelling to Cleethorpes – with all this Wrawby, alas, has little chance to dream.

It wonders about the future of its local Elsham station, but its picture of the reality of the railway is the earlier, primary freight picture. This is, after all, how the railway began, as a coal-carrying system. No one was quite prepared for people's enthusiasm for travelling; it was not till 1862, in fact, that passenger revenues caught up with freight. Now, in spite of a few crack businessmen's trains and car-carriers to Oban or Penzance, it seems as though the liner-trains are at the core of the railway's survival policy. Wrawby's list of all those clanking wagons with their heavy and useful loads coming through the meadows, through junctions which exist because of the awkward but true estuary shapes of England, to distant prospects of cooling towers and tank farms on misty low horizons, has a powerful sense of continuing reality.

There are, of course, many villages where nostalgia for the sociable village railways is combined with a genuinely practical sense of the loss of a real service, which the all-conquering motor car cannot easily provide; the commonest complaint concerns school journeys:

Bellingham is a very pleasant place to live in, surrounded by moorland, the beautiful North Tyne river wending its way from the Scottish border to the mouth of the Tyne near Newcastle; but there are certain drawbacks to these rural surroundings. We miss the little train that used to chug up the valley three times a day. Our bus services have been much curtailed. Children who have the opportunity for a grammar or technical school education have to travel 34 miles each day into Hexham or Haydon Bridge.

(*Bellingham, Northumberland*)

The question whether the railway makes industry or industry makes the railway is very much a chicken-and-egg one; and when not only economic but political considerations are involved it becomes impossible even to look at a simple relief map in a simple way. Have we been wrong all these years in assuming that, except for the south, most of the valleys in Wales are east-west ones? For Drs D. J. and Noelle Davies, in *Can Wales Afford Self-Government?*, a Plaid Cymru pamphlet, say uncompromisingly 'All the Welsh transport arteries seem to converge on England, as though the object of their designers were to make it easy for English goods and governors to come into Wales and for the Welsh people and profits to be driven out of it' (here, I say, wait a minute, what about them bringing Lloyd George and Nye Bevan and Welsh coal to England and English tourists to Wales, one wants to say; fair's fair!); but if a railway is mainly a passenger and not an industrial one, even such a blamelessly north-south Welsh line as the Aberystwyth–Carmarthen seems beyond saving; the effort to do so involves pushing against a huge inertia, like running through treacle. It is all very well for a Plaid Cymru candidate to say

it has taken only one short year for the Labour Government to break its pre-election promises to the county. The Aberystwyth-

Carmarthen line has been closed and is being torn up. Our roads are shockingly inadequate, and mid-Wales has not yet been designated a development area ...

(press cutting from Llanilar)

– or for a Tory candidate to say it, or for a Labour candidate to say it about a Tory government, as they all have and doubtless will. But

Aberystwyth Borough Council's Town Clerk told members on Tuesday that he had advertised in local papers the need for anyone suffering hardship by the closure of the Aberystwyth-Carmarthen railway line to come forward, but there had been no response of any kind.

(Llanilar)

There seems an inevitability about the whole thing. The railways will never, to borrow a phrase from Catholic opponents of the flat-prose English and four-square hymns which have now replaced the rising-and-falling Gregorian chant and sonorous Latin of the Mass liturgy, be desacralized completely. In centuries to come there will hang about those cuttings and embankments something haunting and domestic (as something haunting and military hangs about the old Roman roads), something incidentally caught in that marvellous little D. H. Lawrence poem *End of Another Home Holiday*:

> *The moon-mist is over the village, out of the mist speaks*
>   *the bell,*
> *And all the little roofs of the village bow low, pitiful,*
>   *beseeching, resigned.*
> *—Speak, you my home! What is it I don't do well?*
> *Ah home, suddenly I love you*
> *As I hear the sharp clean trot of a pony down the road.*

Succeeding sharp little sounds dropping into silence
Clear upon the long-drawn hoarseness of a train across the
valley.

The light has gone out, from under my mother's door.
That she should love me so! —
She, so lonely, greying now!
And I leaving her,
Bent on my pursuits!
Love is the great Asker.
The sun and the rain do not ask the secret
Of the time when the grain struggles down in the dark.
The moon walks her lonely way without anguish,
Because no-one grieves over her departure . . .

Though the village station be turned into two smart flats and the public geraniums become private, the area whether Welsh or English will be as numinous as a graveyard, haunted by ghostly arrivals and departures. It is something not to be exorcized by thin, clerkly, Byzantine end-of-an-era cyclostyled letters such as this:

Pont Llanio to Aberystwyth Branch Line

Dear Sir

As you know, the above line is now closed, and I have now been instructed to undertake the disposal of redundant property. I see from plans which have been sent to me that you occupy property severed by or adjoining the line. As it is a general rule of the Board, except in certain cases, to give the owner of the adjoining freehold the first opportunity to purchase the part of a closed branch which is contiguous with his boundaries, I should be glad to know whether you are interested in the railway land which borders or severs your property. If so, perhaps you will kindly let me have a sketch or plan showing such property, confirming you hold the freehold to this area, when I shall be pleased to say, after completion of certain preliminary inquiries, whether I will be able to treat with you. I may say that I am approaching all the adjoining owners.

Yours faithfully

*

The railway is most ambivalent of all at a terminus. These lines go to enormous cities, full of lighted halls and hotels and shops, but here, by this wooden platform on a low shoreline, where sea grasses move in the wind and birds wheel over evening mudflats, the whole thing ends at a pair of buffers. Where will the travellers go now?

You never see freight at the station at New Holland, ferry station on the south bank of the Humber; passengers from occasional diesel trains go down the ramp with motorists to the blunt paddle ferryboat, all duckboards and slatted seats; there are satisfactory reciprocating steam engines with enormous polished connecting-rods, *clunk-cha, clunk-cha CLUNK* and a saloon where you can have a Guinness during the absurd little voyage, past occasional merchant ships moored or moving abstractedly at half a knot, almost always with water being emptied down the side (but this is the sea, that goes to Bombay, Coromandel, Fiji, and of course New York). On the other side, the Yorkshire Customs, green woodwork and windows, tea urns and tickets. A notice says

TICKETS MAY BE PURCHASED AT THIS STATION
FOR LINCOLNSHIRE AND STATIONS BEYOND

and under this someone has written

THE MOON

*

Perhaps a solution for retaining the elusive social character of the branch lines would be to cultivate them all into long, thin botanical gardens:

The stationmaster, Mr Cramb, has won thirteen awards for the best-kept station competitions of British Rail. Even though the competitions no longer exist he still endeavours to put up a good show. At his own expense he raises most of the bedding plants in his greenhouse, and porters Jim Newton and Jock Smith bed out about two and half thousand plants, mainly in their own time.

(*Riding Mill, Northumberland*)

On the embankment are some attractive additions to the local flora. They come from seed carried in cinders etc. tipped out here from the line near Knockholt; Evening Primrose, Basil Thyme, Toadflax, White Mullein, Angelica.

(*Smarden*)

*

It would be idle to pretend that as the Evening Primrose spreads over the rural lines in the twilight of practical and economic life, their power is confidently seized by the Young Turks of transport, bus services using the flexibility of their medium to bring timetables wonderfully, individually tailored to the details of local life.

Transport for the elderly, those on small incomes and the young is deplorable. The railway has been closed to passenger traffic between Barnetby and Market Rasen. As from the 1st of November the nearest stations are Brigg and Barnetby, each approximately six miles. The bus services are too few and wrongly timed. The Parish Council, Caistor Rural District Council and the local MP have all protested, but without any useful result.

Approximately fifty per cent of the adult population own some kind of motor transport.

(*North Kelsey*)

It is, of course, that last sentence which gives the clue as to why efforts to obtain a reliable, all-hours-of-the-day local bus service also have the feeling of running in treacle. No doubt the figures for private transport vary from place to place. In *Colyton*, first village in Devon when you come in from Lyme Regis (another natural frontier; suddenly, after all those bare sweeps, there are high hedges bordering the road again), a comfortable, neat townlet where the streets are still unofficial-looking, arbitrary spaces between little houses where, perhaps, many maiden ladies, daughters of old farming families, live under their magnificent church with its octagonal lantern, only 'out of the 2,000 population 12% own cars'. In *Little Houghton* (*Northants.*), on the other hand, '59% of the villagers have cars. Some are 2-car, some are 3-car, and one is a 4-car family.'

*

Because bus and train services are inadequate most families own some kind of vehicle. In some cases each member of a family has a means of transport, e.g. one house has two cars and two motor-cycles, each vehicle belonging to a son. Their mother uses a bicycle.

(*Drigg, Cumberland*)

*

Whatever the proportion of the population having their own transport at the time the scrapbooks were written, it is a pretty safe bet that it will have risen since then. Some villages (not surprisingly, especially those on main roads or near towns) report satisfaction with their bus services, even though fewer of them are like this remembered one

We used to enjoy the pleasures which come from personal contact. The newspaper, for instance, might be delivered by the bus-driver-conductor at gates en route. Parcels, even including fish, could be put on the bus at Ambleside and delivered to Hawkshead, or perhaps if a certain schoolchild was missing from a usual bus stop the driver would wait until reassured by some passenger that the child would not be coming because of illness or some other reason. Alas, although some parcels can still be carried, inevitably we have now been standardized in the way necessary in large towns, and the luxuries of such homely country habits have been lost.

(*Outgate, Westmorland*)

Also not surprisingly, Outgate, almost as far from London as you can get and still be in the area covered by this book, provides some good examples of the ability of the bus to undercut the railway on really long distances:

Travelling is comparatively expensive. The return train fare from Windermere to London was £6/12/−, but there was a cheap mid-week return for £3/15/−. The motor coach return fare from Ambleside to London was £2/13/3.

The bus companies do not, as the railways did, enjoy revenues from goods as well as passengers, and are therefore even less able than the railways to finance regular schedules which suit minority groups as well as the rush-hour majority. They are required by law to be commercially viable, and they therefore do make profits, usually in the 2 to 5 per cent region. They can only do this by thinning out the uneconomic services. Sunday services, for instance, have been dwindling for years, and support for weekday evening services has also been falling off. Paradoxically, although peak hour traffic has increased in many areas it is not always possible to take advantage of this; as one company told me, in the old days you could use a bus to take workers to a factory and then use the same bus to take the children to school, but nowadays they are quite likely to start at the same time; or end at the same time, especially on Fridays.

One or two of the scrapbooks tell of bus strikes. Strikes in this industry are always news because of their socially widespread effects:

One bus instead of three arrived at 8.30 in the morning, which was full up by the time it reached Little Houghton. Many people were given lifts, some hiked and some went home to wait for later buses. The school afternoon buses were cut down, so many pupils were let out earlier. Workpeople catching the 7.20 had to catch the 8.10. Different buses were cut out each day, and only by going to the bus station did one know which buses would be running. The strike affected only the Bedford crews, and things were back to normal within a fortnight.

(*Little Houghton, Northants.*)

There is not really much room for manoeuvring about wages in an industry where the profit expectations, in general, are of the kind which 'well, would make other industries laugh,' as one spokesman put it to me, and a lot seems to depend simply on personalities (it always seems to be assumed that all strikes are concerned with money and possibly politics, instead of boredom and inconvenience and many other aspects of day-to-day work). The bus industry is holding its own, but only by applying the iron rules of profitability to its services; many think the day is coming when towns, at any rate, are so choked with private traffic that buses only are allowed; *then* they will be profitable all right. But in rural areas there is no doubt where the reality lies; in the motor-car.

This, of course, is a field where there is no distinction between the city and the country dweller; we are all motorists now, although the pleasure/frustration ratio is surely higher for those living in the country. There the thing stands, outside your house, your 'ride' begins the moment you start, not after you have fought your way through ten miles of suburbs. All the same 'the traffic' is something of which you are not a part when it is thundering past your own house:

The cottages in the past have been owned mainly by two big landowners. As they fall vacant they are usually put up for sale and fetch a very good price, often between £1,000 and £2,000. The buyer frequently spends as much again, or more, in modernizing. This is done usually without altering the outside appearance, so that through the years, with a few glaring exceptions, Corfe Castle village has not altered in appearance, and remains the charming grey village so popular with the sightseers and beloved by its inhabitants. In the summer three times traffic came to a complete standstill. The tempers of the occupants of the cars were frayed, and the constant grinding of gears wasn't the sweetest sound to be heard on a fine summer's evening. It was four long hours on some occasions before the weary travellers at last managed to start their engines to a possible thirty miles an hour and head for home. All the lovely Purbeck stone which is mined in the nearby villages has to be conveyed through Corfe Castle, and stone lorries are not the quietest of vehicles. This added to the coal which now has to be moved by road instead of rail makes the main street, East Street, very noisy, and shakes the poor little cottages. We all look forward to the day when a by-pass is built and more police control deals with the parking problem and we can return to a semblance of the good old peaceful days.

(*Corfe Castle, Dorset*)

Certainly there must have been dramatic changes in villages where for years it has hardly been possible to cross the road; suddenly, on a day which may or may not begin with some gold-chained or other vaguely recognizable figure cutting a ribbon across the two virgin lanes of the new by-pass, all that frightful noise with which they have lived for years becomes merely a soothing distant swish and hum. The communities on either side of the road which had become more and more sealed off now begin to mingle again, conversations are actually possible in the High Street, property values declining for years suddenly shoot up; a place which has been pitied by neighbours with only the standard amount of noise now becomes the most desirable place of all, a village with no through traffic. But the road to *that* kind of return to the 'good old peaceful days' is a long, painful and uncertain one.

In fact it is not exactly as it was in the good old peaceful days, for the motor car has of course come into the life of the village – and the lorry. Village carriers and hauliers range far afield nowadays:

The haulage contractor employs thirteen local men. Lorries leave Askrigg at 4.30 a.m. and go everywhere, like Cornwall and East Anglia. The loads carried are extremely varied, and this year one driver has carried tinned fruit, babies' plimsolls, toilet rolls, cowhides, ½-lb. packets of lard, tins of stomach powder, potatoes for crisps, soap powder, drums of cable, steel, plastic, lime, timber, empty sacks, chemicals, fresh fruit, cattle food, sugar beet, hay and straw. These loads are usually of ten tons' weight.

(*Askrigg, Yorks.*)

... centre of a big haulage network which ensures that milk from the remotest Mendip farms finds its way to doorsteps in London, Bristol and other large centres of population every day. Although his fleet of lorries travel thousands of miles in all weathers throughout the year collecting thousands of gallons of milk from farms all over North Somerset, Mr Ted Dury, who runs this complex business with the administrative assistance of his wife and a son, is very firmly rooted in his native parish. All his lifetime his home has never been more than 200 yards away from his birthplace, the Blue Bowl Inn. His family share his attachment to the locality. His sons and daughter and their children have made their own home a stone's throw away from Mr and Mrs Dury's own modern bungalow adjoining their extensive business premises. Consequently, regardless of what other official title it may still have on the map in 1965, this particular part of the parish is now commonly known as Dury's Corner. He started it forty years ago with one lorry collecting milk for private farms.

(Compton Martin, Somerset)

If the life of villages be likened to the pattern seen in a kaleidoscope (although of course it has never had that symmetry; no life is symmetrical), the old pattern was like the kind where all the little bits are huddled close together, and the result is like a tiny, dense, rich, dark rose window. The coming of the motor car is equivalent to the larger, lighter and more radial design you get after giving the thing a good shake. But there is a shape, and the shape still has a definite centre. In spite of the motor car and the building explosion and all the other changes there is still a centre to village life. In spite of nationwide television networks and the creeping spread of cultural (if that is the word) uniformity there they are still, seemingly as well differentiated as ever – those local characters, local dialects, local jokes, local words. Perhaps they have almost as much power to absorb as to be absorbed (indeed, some of the most popular television programmes rely for their vitality and therefore drawing-power on what used to be called 'provincial' cultures). Now that we have examined the elements that go to make a village today, therefore, and before we look more closely at the texture of its social life, let us see what kinds of personality – and speech, the expression of personality – have flourished in it, and are still flourishing.

People and Words

Swallows dart under the old brick bridge over the Thames at Clifton Hampden, just before you get to *Long Wittenham* (*Berks.*) – those knolls with clumps of trees which dominate that landscape for miles are the Wittenham Clumps. At the Barley Mow Jerome K. Jerome stayed while writing *Three Men In A Boat*. Until the county council bought the bridge in 1946 a board at the side gave the toll charges for, among other things,

> ... every Horse or other beast drawing any Coach, Stage-coach, Omnibus, Van, Caravan, Sociable, Berlin, Landau, Chariot, Vis-à-vis, Barouche, Phaeton, Waggonette, Chaise, Marina, Calèche, Curricle, Chair, Gig, Dog-cart, Irish Car, Whiskey, Hearse, Litter, Chaise or any like Carriage, Six Pence.

The lock-keeper at Little Wittenham who retired in 1965 had a Hungarian wife, whom he met after the First World War while on the Danube Patrol; after thirty years in the Navy desire for an outdoor job had led him to these willow-fringed, gravel-soil meadows. Of Long Wittenham's 194 people, in a one-fifth random sample.

26·3% born in Long Wittenham, 35% in adjacent counties, 38·7% in more distant places. 2 from Australia, 2 from Canada, 2 from Germany, 1 from Italy, 1 from Jamaica, 1 from Jugoslavia and 8 from Poland. Enough from Scotland to make a hilarious New Year party. Several families from Wales settled during the depression. From Ireland, too, come people who have liked us and stayed.

And in Long Wittenham I met Mr Roy England; a scholarly, quiet-spoken man with steel-rimmed glasses. He runs a totally convincing and compelling little museum, in a couple of rickety-roofed sheds down a riverside *cul-de-sac*; it is partly a model village and partly a collection of railway antiquities. In one room is a model railway set in an extraordinarily elaborate landscape. Everything is perfectly set in the late Victorian period. The line runs from Madderport, past meticulously-made warehouses and pubs, a garden with a handmade rubbish dump including 200 tins carefully made from bits of plastic tubing. There are tiny sausages in a butcher's shop, old De Dions and Daimlers wait, at level crossings,

Leaving Much Madder by river and proceeding past the mill and round the bend just beyond the village we come to Cuckoo Island. This has quite a history, for it once formed part of the ancestral estate of the Gammon-Hogg family. It happened that one of those Gammon-Hoggs – Sir Hugo probably – set out on the Grand Tour to Italy and Greece. This young man returned to prosaic England with his head buzzing with visions of classical antiquity. So moved was he by the wonders that he had seen during his travels that he engaged an architect to build a folly in the form of a Doric temple. That sort of thing was a fashionable amusement in those days, and nearly everybody did it who could afford it. There he kept his fishing tackle, and on summer afternoons he would repair to the temple to meditate on the wisdom of antiquity, with an edition of Plutarch or Livy.

And there it all is, the little temple, the train trundling below, a tiny sign pointing through the trees TO THE SUMMIT.

This model was the life work of Mr John Ahern, who was also a skilled photographer, an FRPS, and Mr England now maintains it. Passing the small but evocative display of real railway antiquities – a copper-banded engine chimney, a stationmaster's hatbrush with the letters GWR worked in bristles of a different colour, a bottle once provided for first-class ladies, its label saying *Great Western Railway, VOLATILE* – you come to Mr England's own creation. Here too there is a scenic model railway which runs over a replica of one of Brunel's famous viaducts, but the main exhibit is a village typical of those between Wantage and Swindon, along the White Horse hills, as it would have been around 1930, before television aerials and Snowcem.

'There's a lovely old chain of thatched villages along those hills and in the Vale that's getting ruined now,' he said. 'Nobody bothers, they never repair anything. Cottages get dilapidated and are pulled down. They cut down the trees and sell the timber, and so it goes on. It's not any actual village, this model, it's composite. Look at this one. That comes from Wanborough, a village at the other end of the Vale. It's nothing new. It's just a cottage, they took off the thatch and put on a pink asbestos roof. The eaves are now quite straight, a hard straight line, and the ends are cut off square like a matchbox. There's a roughcast front and the whole thing is topped by a television aerial; unbelievably ugly. This is a farmhouse near Uffington (also spoilt now, but still very nice inside). I took 250 colour photographs. We measure everything very carefully, of course, and survey the ground to get the slope right. I use cardboard for the walls, water-colour for the paint, and human hair for the thatch.'

It is actually Chinese human hair. 2 lb. of it cost £11, whereas the same amount of English hair would cost five times as much. It is, of course, straight, which makes it good

for thatching, but black, which does not; so it had been dyed
the right colour at Leeds University (free). One cottage has
4,300 tiny tiles on its roof. There are beautiful sunflowers,
gladioli and hollyhocks in the cottage gardens, made from
blackbirds' feathers, among other things. Sawdust is good
for making elm foliage, some trees are better from foam
rubber cut up very small. A couple of rabbits turn out to be
made of brass, with phosphor-bronze ears. Mr England, who
is helped by one or two young enthusiasts, reckons the village will take thirty years to complete.

In the Long Wittenham scrapbook he has this poem:

The Presence

These meadows, soft hills, and the friendly places –
The rock-raucous woods and the hare-frolicked glades –
Orchards untrodden, the crops' sweeping spaces
Of jade turning amber, the unexplored shades
Of elm-gathered farmyards, the huddled dull village;
   All have their spirit
An intimate presence, unworldly, that graces
The life of the land more deeply than tillage.
Moors and the uplands, the harsh and the lone –
Skies in vast reaches, their dawns unattended
Save only by buzzards; snow and mists blown
Over waste mountain passes and crags unbefriended;
Towns brimming dark as a demon's lost chalice –
   All have their spirit
Ineffable presence with power to atone
For the sigh in the wind and the thunderbolt's malice.
Streets of close medley, jostle of trade –
Signs, traffic, noise: gaily cruel city
Making or marring. Dense cavalcade
Of brick-bounded hordes not asking for pity –
Some ill, and some feloned despairing unknown –
   Even slums have their presence –

An indwelling spirit: unsensed, yet unstayed
By our folly from making earth's sadness his own.

There follows a poem about the church bells by an 88 year-old bellringer, then this:

The Notice on my Back Door

If I'm not here I beg your pardon
Maybe I'm just up the garden
So if you are a maiden fair
Please don't go, you'll find me there.
If you're a man, please go away
And call again another day.

R. ('Curly') Didcot.

HYT SEMETH A GRET WONDUR HOUGH ENGLYSH THAT YS THE BURTH-TONGE OF ENGLYSCHEMEN AND HERE OUNE LANGUAGE AND TONGE YS SO DIVERS SOUN IN THIS YLAND. – Higden's *Polychronicon*, 1387.

Too-thri: a few days
Edge o' dark: dusk
Baggin: mid-morning snack, elevenses
Thrutch: push
Scrike: shriek

(Dunsop Bridge, Lancs.)

Mrs Joseph of Penally Institute decided she was going to present the Queen with some Pembrokeshire early potatoes. We told her she could not get them into the Palace. Anyway we came to the Palace door and she handed them to the footman. He said he would do his best to see that the Queen received them. During the afternoon Mrs Joseph was standing near Prince Philip and he said, 'Pembrokeshire?' Mrs Joseph said, 'I have taken some new potatoes from Pembrokeshire and left them at the door.' He said with a broad smile, 'Thank you very much, I'll see that I get them. It's about time I gave Pembroke-shire a visit.'

(Uzmaston, Pembs.)

Thomas Brecons, although he isn't aged, is the only man in Bellingham who plays the Northumbrian pipes. Northumbrian pipe-playing was revived in Bellingham in the 1920s ...

... Mr Andrew Murray, aged 77, an outstanding character. Educated at the small St Oswald's school, he has educated himself further by reading. He is most knowledgeable on almost any subject and will talk for hours. The watches he had to repair usually took about a year to do because he spent so much time in talking to every customer who came to his shop. He is interested in music, photography, history, especially Scottish history, and ancient buildings and churches. He is a member of the Photographic Society, which has brought him in contact with people of many countries. He is visited by people whenever they are visiting England. He is often asked by tourists to accompany them when touring Scotland, to point out the historic places; they learn from him the stories of their history, which he can relate for hours on end.

(Bellingham, Northumberland)

*

Goodnerstone (pronounced *Gunston*) is hidden in a sudden wooded fold of land in the mysterious bit of Kent that can always surprise anyone turning off the main road anywhere below Canterbury; chalky lanes through un-fenced fields, a road bordered on one side by woods that look as if even the Romans never bothered about them – such solitude, tiny hamlets, gentlemen's parks, drinks outside white weatherboard pubs in a golden evening radiance, an hour or so by train from London! It is dominated by the

stately mansion known as Goodnerstone Park, the home of Lord and Lady Fitzwalter and their five sons; it has been in the family since 1703, when the village was almost entirely feudal, as all the inhabitants either worked on the estate or produced the food or materials for its upkeep. Though the system has persisted for many years the system has gradually changed, mainly since the war, for although the present Baron owns nearly all the houses and the land many of the people work elsewhere ... the village is named after Earl Godwin, father of King Harold; it consists of one road, The Street. 173 inhabitants, 6 council houses. Most of the buildings were erected in the eighteenth century and indicate by their name the industry carried on. e.g. The Weavers, The Saddlers, The Old Forge, The Brick Kiln etc.

Huge plumes of smoke were rising from the churchyard straight into the calm summer evening. Two young men were scything the long grass and burning it. They asked me if I would like to go up the tower. Below us we could see the village; the one who did the talking pointed out to me the ex-coachman's house, the ex-forge. On the other side from the village, the long-walled garden, formally well-kept, then the great house, the whole folded in by woods. In the distance the slag-heaps of Betteshanger colliery. Then we went into the clock loft; my informant, who was an engineering draughtsman who worked in Chatham, said, 'Look at these eight-sided nuts. A man from Bristol came and took photographs of this clock one night. It's by Thomas Tompion, I think. I've got to wind it up.' There was a complicated arrangement of cogs and cams and pulleys. He arranged a cam and said, 'Now, it will go like this at five to nine (mind your head against this bit).' There was a throaty whirring, a lot of things changed position, then pulling the clapper against the bell, which was in a chamber above, he made it strike nine. 'Now it will do that again at five to ten; but we won't let it do it though.' But before he re-set it it struck two, clanging across the little valley.

There are no people in the village with very pronounced dialects, though several have slight accents, e.g. those from the north emphasize the syllable *con*, as in *con*dition, more than we do in the south, and there are a few cockneys. The real Kentish people in the village use some quaint old Kentish words: *shave*, a small narrow wood; *shucky*, cold; *libbet*, a short stout stick; *brishing a baging-crook*, using a sickle; *spuddling the gratten*, breaking up the stubble; *shock*, a stook of corn; *foracre*, headland. They also speak of a *chatteration* of starlings.

During road-mending operations a few years ago the remains of a woolly mammoth were found by a workman called Darky Hogben. A lady told me the local doctor was extremely interested in this, and they were *pithering about* for a week, but the council was impatient for the digging to be finished.

*

Wherever you ask about local humour, someone will usually tell you 'Ah, there's something very special about Devon/Yorkshire/Suffolk/Northamptonshire/Westmorland (or whatever it is) humour. Very sly, they are, like to score in their quiet way ...' e.g., party of walkers in Fells call farmer down from 2,000 feet contour, one says, 'Can you tell us the way to Mardale, John?'
'How did you know my name was John?'
'We guessed it.'
'Well, you can guess way to Mardale.'

*

A Cornishman's gift: I don't want it, you can have it.
A bleating cow soon forgets her calf.
Her face is like a gaol door.
Good fences makes good neighbours.
... Mr Charlie Chapman, of Creed, was the last professional

dowser in Grampound, and it was fascinating to watch him at work walking along holding the hazel twig in both hands and repeating the Lord's Prayer in French. He was a most picturesque figure with his white hair and white beard, wearing moleskins and a navy-blue jacket. This had faded to a wonderful plum colour with years in the sun. I wonder if the use of French indicated Channel Island or Huguenot ancestry?

(*Grampound, Cornwall*)

A little girl who had just started school said when she came home,
'What does *silence* mean?'
Mother: It means *stop talking*. Why?
Child: Mrs Meadows kept saying *silence, children*; I didn't know what it meant.
Mother: What did you do then?
Child: I just siled.

When Churchill was ill one of our family turned on the TV and the words *Churchill bulletin* were given out. Small son of the family: *Mummy, who shot him?*

(*Askrigg, Yorks.*)

How to tell the difference between winter and summer in Wales: in summer the rain is warmer.

(*Laugharne, Carms.*)

Irby is a gentle climb up from the south shore of the Wirral, the estuary-bounded bit of Cheshire underneath Birkenhead and Liverpool; before the high concrete-posted street lights come on, that arrived with the new bungalows that surround the old village, one may look westwards over gently falling fields to the sunset over the Irish Sea, or southwards to the estuary of the Dee. There is speculation in their scrapbook about the vanished port of Dawpool which once had a flourishing trade with Ireland, and about a proposal to build a barrage across the fast-silting estuary and put a new town of 80,000 people on it. There is a jolly picture of some WI ladies at a Christmas concert dressed as the Beatles, whose somewhat older home town is a few miles to the north; and there is this, by the Lollipop Lady:

The first month was something of a nightmare. There were a few bad moments, such as when a dear old lady thought I was holding up my sign to show her that the road was all hers and, chugging gaily through, scattered 60 ten-year-olds in all directions. A brightly-polished little boy brought me a rather tatty bunch of daffodils. Smiling politely I thanked him and asked if they were from his garden. 'Yes,' he said, 'I got them off daddy's compost heap.' Entertaining motorists, too; the one who slowed down to avoid a couple of courting sparrows. The man in a hurry, shaving as he drove along, no doubt pleased with himself for the extra five minutes in bed.

*

A fair number of the thousands of Poles who found that after the war their country did not exactly enjoy the kind of freedom they had been fighting for can be found happily integrated with our village life. They are usually in some enterprising field like mushroom-growing or running a shop; in *Willoughby* (*Lincs.*) – that county of haunted wartime airfields, broken runways and rusty Nissen huts among the cornfields – I found the village pub had a Polish landlord, ex-RAF; a big, expansive man, full of *concern* for the way drinks were made up ('Let me recommend *this* gin. What you think of it, ha? You ever taste gin like that before?'). The shade of the lamp on the bar was covered with silhouettes of his regular customers. On the walls were a collection of old farming implements and tools; a penny in the blind box if you couldn't guess what they were for. This thing like a glass teapot was an early barometer; that thing was for castrating horses. This little wheel affair with a red mark on it for measuring the circumference of cartwheels, for fitting iron bands. It was a gift to the landlord – Polish ('The Germans exterminated my three brothers'), familiar with cosmopolitan life in Paris and Cairo, in this English village – from his friend Frank Wright the blacksmith:

The blacksmith looks after about 30 horses. Forty years ago there were about 250 horses to be shod regularly, in spite of the fact that there were other forges (now closed) in nearby villages. Not all the shoeing could be done by daylight in winter, and Mr Wright still treasures this heavy iron candlestick, which could be used after dark and stood on the floor wherever it was needed, the height of the candle adjusted by a spring clip. The pressure of welding and implement-mending gives him little time for the wrought iron which he loves to do. He made his own front gate and there are many people who would like to persuade him to make more. He also makes weathercocks. He has a pattern waiting of a stallion, to be made in sheet metal, to be the vane of a weathercock for a Sloothby man who once 'walked' this horse round the district. He has just finished two iron footrests awaiting delivery to the local pub. Mr White is a tidy-minded man, and his shop is a model of neatness and method. This is somewhat disappointing to eager 'bygone' hunters, who hope to find some interesting and forgotten 'junk' there. His magnificent bellows are over fifty years old and are maintained in perfect working order. They are irreplaceable, and their failure would mean he would have to buy electric ones. His hammers and anvil shine with good use, and his swages, for bending and shaping wrought iron into all manner of curves and angles, stand clean and uncrusted. In one corner stand various shapes and sizes of tool handles, for he is an expert at 'putting a handle to it', and many are the broken hedge-slashers and garden tools that come to him for repair, and many is the time one sees a broken child's toy, pram or scooter waiting its turn. Nor, one suspects, will there be anything to pay when a small owner comes to collect. Frank White works as older craftsmen love to work, the hours it suits him. I well remember one summer Sunday evening when he stopped for a word on his way home from work. 'Ah well,' he concluded, 'now I'll go wash and change my shirt, and call it Sunday.'

Laal, little; *thrang*, very busy; *gang yam*, go home; *hair in cotters*, hair in a tangle; *galluses*, braces; *kytle*, denim working jacket; *sneck*, fastener or latch; *fratch*, quarrel; *yow-yowlings*, edible root of the pig-nut, *conopodium majus*; *booing*, ragwort.

(*Drigg, Cumberland*)

*

How extraordinary it is to listen to (say) the Dutch radio and to hear gales of laughter at a comedian's jokes! In a Welsh book there is a joke in Welsh with the pay off line kindly translated (and I hope I've copied it out right):

Aelod o'r WI a'i gŵr yn mynd am y tro cyntaf ar daith trwy dre fawr, yr oedd dwsinau o foduron o'u blaen. Ceisiodd y gŵr dorri allan o'r ciw i basio rhai o'l flaen. Ataliwyd ef gan blismon a dywedodd 'You can't do that sir.' 'Of course I can,' meddai'r gŵr, 'because I am not in this funeral.'

It helps to know that *blismon* means 'policeman'. The story, it will now be perfectly clear, concerns a WI member and her husband driving through busy city traffic, overtaking a double queue.

The book also tells of a well-attended winter course of lectures about the village and its history. They were given by an Englishman, Mr Tunstall, who is headmaster of a special school run by the Liverpool Education authority at Colomendy, a few miles away. I drove over the mountains to see him, and it. A drive led past the lodge, past pens full of sheep, tractors, cows, parties of young people with rucksacks. It was a hot July day, promising indeed to be steamy down in this wooded valley, but it would be cooler on the great blue hills that rose on all sides. In the parking area in front of the house and the cluster of huts there were double-decker buses, and signposts: WORKSHOPS, ADMINISTRATION, STAFF ROOM. And brightly-clad teenage children all over the place, all talking exactly like the Beatles. The school worked at various levels. A group of 15-year-old schoolgirls were doing work in preparation for their CSE biology. They were staying a week. 'They're visiting the Forestry Commission this afternoon; yesterday they were studying food chains in the woodland. There's another group from a secondary modern school, doing a very much more varied course; a little bit of biology, a little bit of geography, a little bit of geology and so on – more or less environmental studies, for a fortnight. The other group we've got in just now are an educationally sub-normal – actually they've gone off to Chester Zoo today. But they, at their own level, too, get an enormous benefit from this new environment, this completely different experience. The idea of this place is to put children out of a city into a completely new and exciting environment, and to use the stimulation of these new experiences to teach them . . .

Is it too early yet to ask if there is any evidence at all of people's choice of life or career being affected by a visit here?

Oh yes, I think this does happen. Last year I was doing my Sunday afternoon policeman act (you wouldn't believe how many motorists want to come in here and picnic) a woman I had never seen before came up to me and said in her best Liverpool, 'Do you live here?' so I said yes, and 'Do y'ave anything to do with the International Camp?' so I said yes.

'Did you take them to the quarry in 1958?' So I said, well, probably I did. If anyone did, I did. 'O,' she said, 'well, thank you very much. My daughter is now in her second year of geology at Nottingham University. It was the first time she took any interest at all in geology and rocks.'

*

Mr Sargent, driving his red lorry, can be seen in and round Bransgore almost any day. He holds a B licence, which permits him to operate within a thirty-mile radius, as the crow flies, from Christchurch Station. His chief loads are of sand, gravel, manure and logs. Whenever anything has to be moved we turn to him for help, whether it be an old piano, left-overs from a jumble sale or apparatus for a gymkhana. How often we hear the remark 'Ask Mr Sargent, he will know', or 'Mr Sargent will do it' – *it* usually being some awkward moving job.

(*Bransgore, Hants.*)

... if you see someone running in the village, it is usually Nan, running to give someone a helping hand.

(*Uzmaston, Pembs.*)

... the Pageant, *Methodism Comes to Wensleydale* at Bolton Castle. The castle courtyard will have seating for five hundred for next week's performances. The JP who wrote the script in Dales dialect, Mr Robert Sidney Hunter, of Castle Bolton, said that when one of the preachers sent by John Wesley to Wensleydale was preaching in a public house the floor collapsed during the singing of *Vain delusive world, adieu!*, and the congregation fell among the beer barrels in the cellar. Investigations showed that the main beam had been sawn almost through.

... *fog*, second growth of grass after mowing; *glishy*, bright sunshine in early morning, too bright; *swinway*, climbing zig-zag up a hill; *twitchbell*, earwig; *whumell*, a gimlet; *wengs*, shoelaces.

(*Askrigg, Yorks.*)

213

To each his county. Very well, then, there *is* something very special about Suffolk humour. It is wonderfully direct, and is helped by a marvellously earthy language. East Anglia is a great deal bigger than people think it is. I live over sixty miles from London and am barely half-way to Norwich (and there's a lot more of it after that); a composer friend who was having a piece performed at the Norwich Festival and was staying with me was astonished when I got the car out at six; 'they don't begin till eight,' he said. We just about made it, through a grand thunderstorm and sunshine, tumbled rainclouds and apocalyptic sun-shafts and marvellous dramas of light over that never-quite-flat, simultaneously infinite and homely landscape. East Anglia has never been on the way to anywhere except itself; at the next village to mine, Stratford St Mary, all the letters of the alphabet are let into the flint flushwork at the base of the buttresses, and there is a Latin quatrain for the benefit of priests going up to Norwich on horseback to the effect that although they might not be able to say their office while travelling it was all there in the 26 letters of the alphabet.

Stonham Aspal gives some of the basic Suffolk terms:

Frawn, frozen; *that fare as if*, it seems that; *that hully* (wholly) *fake me*, I have a pain; *lithe*, of a wet consistency, as in a cake mixture; *pingle*, to toy with food; *push*, a boil; *that howd cowd*, it's cold; *rafty*, cold (said to date from watches in the marshes against Napoleonic invaders); *hucker*, to stammer; *nannicking*, fooling about; *spink*, chaffinch; *hodmedod*, snail; *on the sosh*, askew; *dwile*, a house-flannel (the revivers of the Suffolk sport of *dwile-flonking* achieved world fame recently); *doddy*, small; *duzzy fule*, (obviously) fathead; *troshel*, threshold.

Another friend took a party of Suffolk schoolboys on a trip to Belgium. In Antwerp, while the party were looking at something, one boy detached himself and, overcome by rich continental food, was sick into the gutter, at which a kindly old lady in black sprinkled some eau-de-cologne on his handkerchief and wiped his fevered brow. He rushed to the teacher and said 'Sir! Sir! Her in the black's put suthin' on my handkercher an' that hully stink!'

A. O. D. Claxton's *The Suffolk Dialect of the Twentieth Century* gives an exhaustive list, and some good stories. A doctor had the misfortune to knock one of his patients off his bike. He hastily got out of the car and asked him if he was all right. 'Yes, thank 'ee, doctor, 'cept for a bit of a cowd.'

Old labourer, to chapel congregation when the pastor had not turned up: 'He fare t' be hully late, shall us hev a hack at a hymn?'

A girl swimmer was in difficulties at Aldeburgh; having called a boatman to no avail, she finally managed to struggle back. When asked why he hadn't come he said 'The last gal I helped only gave me half-a-crown. We git five bob for a body.'

My own favourite comes from another source, the *East Anglian Magazine*. An old farmer's wife lay dying, attended by the parson. She said 'When I'm gone, don't yow git married agin. Yow promise me yow'll niver git married agin, cause dew yow dew, I'll scrat me way out of the grave an' come an' *harnt* yow. Yow promise me now.' The husband duly promised not to remarry. Nevertheless, some three years later, he decided to marry again. The parson said to him, 'Are you ever worried by Hannah's threat that if you married again she would scratch her way out of the grave and come and haunt you?' 'Oh, no,' said the farmer. 'Oi buried that face down'ads, so the 'arder that scrat, the fudder down that goo.'

*

East Anglia, until well on into this century perhaps the most silent and unconsidered part of England, a perfect setting for the slow and inward growth of a regional culture, has some claim to be the most countrified county. Now of course it is subject to the universal pressures of change and the breakdown of isolation. Indeed in some ways the pressure is greater, since it is the last area in the south-east where there is room for growth. London 'overspill' towns are planned at places like Thetford, Haverhill, Cornard and elsewhere. There was a grandiose plan to extend Ipswich practically to Colchester. Dual-carriageway roads by-passing the pink and white villages are changing it as the trade routes changed Africa; but a stanza from some verses in the *Stonham Aspal* book expresses what anyone who loves life in a village knows will always be true; that all people are knowable characters, but there is a limit to the number you can know comfortably:

> . . . *Planned for countrywomen only*
> *Today it's townfolk who are lonely*
> *Living in our country places*
> *We must welcome all new faces.*

Nobody quite knows where the process is going to stop; and in any case the scrapbooks, although they contain a section called 'Hopes and Fears', are primarily concerned with the actuality, as it is now. It is not possible to formulate, to classify exactly, to produce some theoretical schema which would lay down what should be the differentiation between rural life and urban life in the twentieth century; everyone would have a different formulation, and in any case life does not follow formulations. It is clear from what we have seen already that the old distinctions of type are blurred; the farmer, with his machinery (and his television and his car) has become very much the same kind of person as the new country resident whose car has now made it possible for him to choose the green fields.

For the most part it has been a free movement of people; and although particular and local problems have been met with particular solutions – green belts, national parks, reports and committees, recommendations by the Fine Arts Commission (which may or may not be heeded), town and country planning regulations – it is quite possible for these to become isolated rocks, or even mere sandcastles that crumble at the first touch of that tide of free movement, not only of people but of money, the money to be made out of leisure in the country, as well as life in it. Eventually, some godlike, universally accepted formulation and division will have to be made.

The scrapbooks, and this distillation of them, make no such godlike claim. They merely mirror what is. Britain, convoluted and differentiated internally by history and geography, is diverse. Coming over the Cornish rocks, a traveller passes from single trees all bending one way, to clumps with a top line that appears planed off, finally to relaxed rich inland woods. From the wild Welsh mountains, or the gaunt downs behind the carpeted southern hotels or from little weatherboard towns low on the North Sea horizon, the road is into regions still diverse and particular enough for subtopia not to have swamped them. In thousands of villages they are not formulating at all, or if they do they stop quite often; to get on with living.

Life

In many ways the attitude of the average Englishman to the church (and especially perhaps to the *village* church, standing as it does for so many historical, aesthetic, merely romantic or other not specifically religious associations) is similar to that of the old Dublin woman to England during the blitz. 'Ah, 'tis a good thing to see the English gettin' a taste of their own medicine,' she said. Her companion suggested that if England were invaded it might be Ireland's turn next. 'Faith, an' what'll the British Navy be doin' then?' she exclaimed indignantly. People like the church to be *there*, even though it has an accusing giant wooden thermometer outside showing progress towards the £14,000 urgently needed to combat the ravages of the death watch beetle in the tower.

These are the days of the television interview, when everyone is expected to have instant, clear-cut opinions; no room for ambivalence, guilt, search, doubt, mistrust of language, sense of imponderables, humility. People who drift into church, either knowing or just hoping it's all right, learn not to say anything about it to certain kinds of people at parties, who pin them in a corner and say 'All right then, prove the existence of God. . . .'

You can't treat it as though it were algebra, and to that part of the modern consciousness that thinks you ought to be able to there is something irregular or irrational (and therefore, by an easy declination, hypocritical) about the social importance which the church still maintains in village life. In fact purely on the physical level, in thousands of villages the church is the biggest and most beautiful building; it is a symbol of continuity with the past –

Thanksgiving for restored tower: a special service. At last everyone has gone, and one might almost say that the tower alone remains standing now, silent and majestic, its ancient stones shining golden-brown and cream in the light of the flood-lanterns. But everyone has not gone, for here, in the dense shadows of the houses opposite the church there stands an equally silent figure, the figure of one of the old and respected villagers of this place. 'Yes,' he says gruffly, 'yes, she looks well,' and he shuffles off into the blackness of the night. Words, perhaps – but words which echo the feelings of us all; feelings of deep gratitude that we in our time have been privileged to restore again this ancient tower, so that it can continue to stand for years to come as it has done through the centuries on the hill at Houghton.

(*Little Houghton, Northants.*)

The reasons for which it is attended, or at any rate the terms in which those reasons would be expressed, would be as personal, diverse, and incapable of reduction into Gallup Poll statistics in a village as in a city; nevertheless it is obvious that an old church in a settled village – and very often its associated hall, as the only room large enough for social functions – exercises a kind of natural force of gravity which churches in towns have largely lost. This is not to impugn the motives of rural churchgoers; a great deal of rubbish is talked about the alleged pharisaical motives of some of them. You really don't have to go to impress the Squire these days (he probably won't be there anyway).

The Church was rebuilt. In 1350. By Sir Guy de Briand, Lord High Admiral of Edward III. There used to be a board on which the Ten Commandments were painted; it is recorded that this was taken down and given to St Clears, 'as no further use for them in Laugharne'. The present number of communicants is 238. The choir is 60 strong. Mothering Sunday service this year was conducted entirely by the children. They brought posies of Spring flowers to give their mothers and read the appropriate addresses and prayers. A really thoughtful and lovely service. The children again conducted the service on Palm Sunday, April 11th, with Heather Pearce, only 10 years old, as organist. The Congregational Church in Laugharne is now the only Nonconformist chapel now opened, being served by a full-time lay preacher, 50 members and a Sunday School of thirty scholars.

(*Laugharne, Carms.*)

The average attendance at church for morning and evening services together is 36. The number of communicants on Sundays other than Easter is 18. About 25% of the usual congregation is men.

The Methodist Chapel has a congregation of 15 to 20, of whom 12 are over 50, 4 are 25 to 50, 5 are 15 to 25 and 1 is school age.

(*Willoughby, Lincs.*)

The population of Laugharne is given as 1,000, that of Willoughby as 541, so that in the showing of these two (admittedly very random) samples the churchgoing proportion varies between nearly 30 per cent and just over 10 per cent.

The day religious statistics are really organized and computerized will be a sad one for the Church of England, indeed for any church. Those marvellous old buildings, smelling, at Betjeman puts it, of 'hassock and cassock, paraffin and pew', their graveyards where you hear the cold winter wind in the yews, or summer birdsong in the surrounding elms, and often the deliberate tick of an enormous pendulum in the tower, speak in their mere stones of a time-scale different from our tiny little lives, our absurd and glorious localization in time (Sunday) and place (this actual building) of God, and they are wiser than the centuries of *odium theologicum*, they have not been surprised to hear Catholic and Nonconformist ministers speak ecumenically from their pulpits. They do not ask questions till one is ready. Theirs is not the world of the survey and the instant answer – but it isn't the world of 'don't know' either.

St Augustine once said that so long as no one asked him what Time was, he was quite certain of the answer, but that when he was asked he was unable to offer a satisfactory definition. Something of the kind might also be said of the Anglican communion. It is not an entity in itself; it has no formal constitution – no distinctive faith, no central administration, no ultimate authority to which appeal might be made. Rather it is a loosely knit brotherhood of eighteen self-governing churches, which have in common their communion each with the other, and all of them with the Mother Church of England, and in particular with the Province of Canterbury. – from an article in the *Guthlaxton II Deanery and District Church News*, in the scrapbook for *Kimcote and Walton (Leics.)*.

This may sound supiciously like 'don't know'. The Anglo-Catholic wing, for one, would not care for the phrase 'no distinctive faith', and there is a happy and relaxed air about the statement which one suspects, also, would not please those who have read their Woolwich and are trying to come to terms with the Ground of Being, or Mr Brian Wicker who writes those splendid anguished articles in the *Guardian* – 'yet such outrage is also an expression of the sense we have that an otherwise intelligible order has been shattered ... Aberfan ... there will still be a gap that cannot be filled except with legitimate outrage, if not against other people then against life itself . . . not a hope based on the evasion of suffering . . . it is only through real death that resurrection can come.'

The people who go to village churches have presumably had the same quota of outraged feeling at uncomprehended human suffering as anyone else, and no doubt polishing a splendid brass eagle or a Jacobean pulpit isn't the essence of 'religion'. But what is? Is putting daffodils on graves? Is singing?

In addition the chapels have held *gymanfa ganu, eisteddfodau* and *gyngherddau* . . . the first a special getting-together for hymns; perhaps six chapels will come together and sing hymns which they have specially rehearsed, in full harmony; the second is a competitive musical and poetical event, the third more a straight concert.

(Eglwys Fach, Caerns.)

The Rechabites of the Pentyr-garn Tent have had a successful year under the leadership of Mrs K. Taylor, who has worked hard for many years with Miss Greenwood. In 1965, as in previous years, the young members took part in competitions for the Cardiff Area held at the Cory Hall, Cardiff, Saturday, February 13th. These competitions included painting, embroidery, knitting, cookery, handicrafts and writing as well as elocution and singing contests. In the evening a concert was given to an enthusiastic audience which filled the hall. Pentyrch won many prizes, and for the sixth year in succession won the special prize which is given for the Tent with the most points.

(Pentyrch, Glam.)

There are many ways of saying the unsayable. A Swiss poet-artist with the beautiful name Diter Rot has said, I read in an article about typographic poems, that 'what is tautology for Wittgenstein is *repose* for me'. All those village churches are tautological to the insulated motorist; another tower, another spire piercing the trees. Yet how diverse and particular they are – how one can describe the place itself, this unique font, that faithful bellringer, that children's Easter garden with a little empty tomb and a Plasticine angel, that watery light through a clerestory? And how the unity behind that diversity (a unity most of which lies in uncertain fields of hope and futurity) is as impossible to describe as Time was for St Augustine! Meanwhile,

The traditions in our village are mostly church traditions. One that has still carried on over many years is the Bellringers' Supper. The money to pay for the supper was left by an old bellringer of the name of Fred Stock. After the supper of bread and meat and mince pies and beer the ringers pass the time away singing carols and ringing the handbells until it is time to go up the tower and ring, on the eight bells, the old year out and the new year in. They are a joy to hear, ringing out over the countryside.

Every year our church has a Spring clean. The men sweep the walls and beat the carpets. Next day the women scrub and polish. Refreshment is provided for the men at the Red Lion and the women have tea in the Parish Hall.

(Radwinter, Essex)

John Betjeman, in the indispensable *Collins Guide to English Churches*, after describing various places where one should look for the key of a locked church, writes '... if there is no sign of the key and all vestry doors are locked, call at a house. If the path leading through the Churchyard to a door in the vicarage wall is overgrown and looks unused, you may be sure the vicarage has been sold to wealthy unbelievers and there is no chance of getting the key from there.' Several of the scrapbooks tell of three or more parishes sharing one clergyman. There are mysterious little churches standing all by themselves, far from any sign of habitation – sometimes left stranded by the Plague, when the entire village was rebuilt somewhere else, sometimes the private chapel of a mansion now owned by some electricity board or other, sometimes without any real explanation for their position. They may have a service once a month, or even once a year. There are closed churches. Chapels, too, have been closed or amalgamated. In *Wrawby* (*Lincs.*), the Primitive Methodist chapel had been closed, and the other Wesleyan Chapel was being repaired to serve both congregations. But down the road at *Horncastle*

A new Methodist church was built in one year. It has an average congregation throughout the year, both for morning and evening services, of 90 . . . the vicar of St Mary's, which is a C. of E. church, loaned Holy Trinity Church to the Franciscans after the Methodists had vacated it. This action was hailed by the national press as a fine example of ecumenism.

*

In the Yorkshire village of Crayke, on a slight escarpment giving wonderful views over the plain of York, I got into a conversation, with the landlord of the *Durham Ox* and two draymen in company-styled green overalls, about all those street games of one's own childhood. I discovered that the game which we knew in Coventry as *tip-cat*, where you have a little stick sharpened at both ends, one of which you give a clout with a long stick, so that it shoots in the air, where you give it another clout, this time directional (you hope), was called in Yorkshire *knur and spel*, in Cumberland *piggy-stick*. The landlord went out and came back with a brand-new, unused, forty-year old acetylene bicycle lamp, complete with little red light on the right and green on the left; and one of the old mineral water bottles with a glass stopper. 'When I were a lad,' he said, 'there would be fifteen or so of us in the cobbler's of an evening – we haven't got one now – and we'd play put-and-take with matches. Nothing else to do in those days. But I'll tell you, the kids are bored now when they're fourteen. Now how can you be bored at fourteen?'

'Ah, they've been *modernized*,' said the younger drayman. 'It's not like in your day.'

From the Crayke scrapbook:

The village of Crayke was given to St Cuthbert by King Egg-frith, so that he had somewhere to stay on his many visits to York from Durham. Early this summer two buses filled with children from a school in York and accompanied by a mistress and master came specially to visit the church. It is unusual for schools to visit us, and it was a great joy to the Rector to con-duct such interested and well-behaved young folk round the church. They were thrilled to think the pulpit had been there since the reign of Charles I and that some of his cavaliers, in their satin jackets with real lace ruffles, knee breeches and long curled wigs, sat in the not too comfortable Jacobean pews, and that later Cromwell's soldiers with their close-cropped heads and severe uniforms also marched down the stone-flagged aisle, over the graves of a husband aged 18 and his wife 16 years old. The long clock pendulum is one of the longest in Europe – as it swung slowly to and fro we all stood far away from the great Roman millstone which acts as a weight.

To let interested people know how our target of £6,000 is progressing a framed picture of St Cuthbert climbing a long flight of steps is fixed to the outside wall. There are several turns in the flight, and each represents a thousand pounds. One step represents a hundred pounds. It was painted for the appeal by a Polish refugee, and he called it 'St Cuthbert's Progress'. It is sad to think that the young artist died this year, before the target was reached, and after so short a time of peace and freedom in his young life . . .

... *A Change We Expect* is the tendency for more people from the village to commute out to work in town.

A Change We Fear is that children from the outskirts of the village travelling by bus to the large schools will miss much of nature's wonders.

A Change We Hope For is that every child should be assured of a happy home.

A Change I Should Like: speed limit through the village; street lighting; great pride in keeping our village tidy and attractive.

Change I Hope For: that the Church of England and the Wesleyan Church will unite.

*

In the days when the churches were being built and the villages were growing up round them life was not divided, as it is now, into sharply differentiated periods of 'work' and 'leisure', the latter filled with highly organized and special hobbies. Both the modern specialization of work and the countless sectional interests with which modern man fills his time are mirrored in this truly kaleidoscopic list of periodicals read in *Grampound, Cornwall* – 170 households, 287 people:

Countryman, Homes and Gardens, Expository Times, Which? Illustrated London News, Farmers' Weekly, Woman's Own, Woman's Journal, Woman, Listener, Châtelaine, Good Housekeeping, Motor Cycle, Drapers' Record, Horse and Hound, History Today, Amateur Photographer, Ecumenical Press Service, Church Times, Parson and People, People's Friend, Farmer and Stockbreeder, Poultry Farmer, Farming Express, New Musical Express, Do It Yourself, Cornish Magazine, Motor-Cycle Mechanic, Yachting and Boating, Autocar, Punch, Leica Magazine, National Geographic, Motor Sport, Woman and Home, My Home, Mother, Stitchcraft, Pig Farming, Hi Fi News, Tit-Bits, Woman's Weekly, Mirabelle, Country Life, Shooting Times,

Home and Country, Spectator, Blackwood's, Bunty, Woman's Realm, June, Wham, Eagle, Hotspur, Topper, Lion, Robin, Judy, Liberal News, Sporting Life, Field, Where?, Reader's Digest, Riding.

*

Where the church hall is the main centre for gatherings its position is taken for granted; so, in an increasing number of villages, is the hall, with its well-equipped stage and modern lighting, of the new primary or secondary modern school, used in the evening for adult drama or education. The third class of hall, built by public appeal, energetic local fund collection, helped with grants, seems to differ from the others as the American Constitution differs from the British; it needs written terms, a definite formulation of aims:

Site bought and village hall opened in 1951. Trust Deed ... 'for purposes of physical and mental training, and social and moral and intellectual development through the medium of reading and recreation rooms, library, lectures, classes, recreations and entertainments or otherwise as shall be expedient for the benefit of the inhabitants and residents of the Parish of Willoughby in the County of Lincoln and its immediate vicinity without distinctions of sex or of political, religious or other opinion.' Since the advent of television participation in such events and inclination to organize them has declined, until at the present time and in common with many village halls there is a real danger that they may have to close through lack of funds and bookings.

(*Willoughby*)

There used to be some very good operas performed under the conductorship of the late Mr E. V. Williams and there was a keen drama group, but it is now disbanded. The number of functions in the hall since television has decreased, and the whist

227

drives, particularly, have not had the same patronage as in former years.

(Laugharne, Carms.)

The Memorial Halls which were erected in so many villages after the 14–18 War have done a great deal towards enriching village life. There is surely no better way of commemorating those who died for their country than by making that country a better place to live in, and the Memorial Halls have helped in no small way to do this. Bramcote's is constantly booked; badminton clubs, Pathfinders, W I, handicrafts, children's dancing class, socials and youth dances, school meals service, produce shows and Christmas fairs, not to mention the baby clinic run by the Welfare State every fortnight in the hall.

(Bramcote, Notts.)

At Bramcote the Community Association, among many other activities, 'Purchased a 3-length extending ladder, 3 decorating and pasting tables and a blowlamp; these are on hire at a very nominal charge to members'. Bramcote apparently has no difficulty in finding uses for its hall, even though there are now first-rate modern rivals (see page 35).

Each Wednesday night a few of us
Unravel ourselves from the cocoon of our everyday lives
Into a world of make-believe
Rehearsing, painting, building sets
And characters
Breathing life into a poet's imagery
And, eluding our own personalities,
Finding them.
Once in a year, or maybe twice
We shed our inhibitions like a chrysalis
And, transformed into new beings by greasepaint

And our other selves
Emerge into a blinding glare of light
With fluttering hearts
Hoping to move our audiences to laughter
Or to tears
Culminating in the joyful music of applause.

It is noticeable that the scrapbooks of several places like Bramcote, where a councillor in a signing-off piece notes that

a stranger passing through could never imagine that it is a ward of one of the largest urban districts in the country, the population of the urban area being 58,000 . . . yet one can still say that it has managed to maintain its village atmosphere . . .

do, as far as their village halls, their drama and organized social activities are concerned, often seem more lively than the more traditional and unadulterated villages. Perhaps this is simply an example of Toynbee's 'challenge and response'. If it is true that the great civilizations have very often arisen from unpromising physical surroundings – Attica with her light and stony soil, Chinese civilization growing in the flood-and-ice valley of the Yellow River rather than the easier one of the Yangtse – might not the stark rows of new bungalows, in a minor and domestic version of the same process, produce a determination not to relapse into suburbanism viewed as the total isolation of household from household, but indeed by their inhabitants' own initiative to create from scratch a social and cultural life which older villages are only assumed to have? Bramcote, to look at, is very much like Fairlands, whose thriving community life we have seen (pp. 152–5); with all due respect to the councillor, *this* stranger could very well 'imagine that it was a ward of one of the largest urban districts in the country', having come down from rolling high land to the flat Nottingham strip, with its immense power-station blocks, cables and transformers, evening rush of workers in cars and buses, municipally-lit dusk on the outskirts of a large city – and having been surprised and delighted to find underneath all this the older village structure.

It would be as absurd to generalize in this as in any other field, of course. Sometimes social activities start from below, as it were, simply because a lot of people get together through all having felt, for whatever reason, the same need; sometimes there just happens to be one remarkable individual:

Few villages are as fortunate as Dalston in possessing such a wide variety of talent in all age groups. Some of this young talent has been fostered and encouraged by Miss Farbridge, who entirely voluntarily runs a small orchestra for the youth of this village. These children are all very keen musicians, and are only too pleased to spend hours of their spare time practising and developing their skills. The orchestra of 20 includes recorder, (descant, treble and tenor), cello, piano, violin and guitar players, who every Monday evening spend a very happy hour together playing tunes of every description, from carols and folk music to excerpts from all the classical composers. They give a very polished performance, but are unable to enter any musical festivals because there is no class for them. But they gain great pleasure from playing at social functions in the village, special church services and giving short recitals for parents and friends.

Air from the Water Music	Handel
Song of Victory (King Arthur)	Purcell
The Old Woman and the Pedlar	(Folk Song)
Larghetto from Alcina	Handel
Les Jongleurs	Couperin
O Lovely Peace	Handel

Largo from *New World Symphony*	Dvorak
Slave's Dance (*Magic Flute*)	Mozart
Winter	(Folk Song)
Fear No Danger To Ensue (Dido & Aeneas)	Purcell

(*Dalston, Cumberland*)

*

A stranger might think that the remoter villages of the Plain of Holderness, the part of Yorkshire between the north bank of the Humber and the sea, would convey a slight sense of having been by-passed by the main stream of life. After Hull, the cranes and masts and tank farms can no longer be seen across the flat fields, and this is not the grander rural Yorkshire of sweeping dale and moor and fine stone towns either; it is one of the places where England dwindles to a point among clays and muds – *Sunk Sand, Skeffling Clays, Kilnsea* – where, as the *Hollym* book says,

Annual average rate of recession of cliffs is estimated at between four and seven feet; despite low rainfall, generally under 25" for the year, the cliffs dry out at the surface only during the summer months. In winter the cliffs are very wet, and extensive 'mud flows' develop on the cliff face itself.

On a dry summer day the wind rustling the few trees has a hint of sea mist in it. Far off across the flat fields a lighthouse stands like a great white sail. Gardens shelter behind windbreaks. There are derelict windmills. Outside one village, a huge pile of old fairground machinery.

Recent floods have turned vast areas of land into a huge lake, the like of which has not been seen for forty years. Mr Walter Smith of Fir Tree Farm, Winstead, whose land is under water, saw thirty-seven swans flying in a V-shaped formation, with necks outstretched. He said it was one of the most wonderful pictures he had ever seen, especially when the sun came out and gave the water a beautiful silver gleam.

I spoke to an old man of 93, gently moving about with a rake; across the road, his tight, faintly Dutch-looking little house, called Vera Dene. Nothing else would happen, one thought, looking at those bricks; it was all in the past. The old man, who was called Mr Bosman, spoke of his early days on £35 a year, without bitterness. 'Aye, I've got two good dowters,' he said. He had never been farther afield than Leeds in his life. He seemed as natural and happy a part of his environment as a frail-tough flower growing on an old wall.

Albert Bosman, 93, is often a worry to the neighbours. He was found this summer high on a stack of bales rescuing a self-hatched brood of chicks, and during a severe autumn gale on top of a ladder, fixing a spout, and proudly explaining that he had been twice blown over. He is often to be seen cycling in the village. He is also a regular attender at the Methodist Chapel and a highly respected member.

But there is nothing about a falling-off of village hall activities in Hollym's book:

The village Hall Committee, which already had £1,200, raised another £800. It has a maple floor, costing £250, and air-conditioning in the roof. It is occupied five or six nights a week.

There is a very jolly colour photograph of the Hollym Follies, a lot of ladies dressed somewhere between the can-can and a pierrot show and obviously having the time of their lives – and, according to a cutting from the local press (not automatically laudatory, as many amateur producers know) wowing their audience.

However, villages in Britain, as we have seen, are one and one; it is perfectly possible to have a thriving dramatic (for instance) society in the same place that there is fierce opposition to a new village hall. Perhaps *Banstead* is not everyone's idea of a village; one comes on it from the South through tangled, steep, wooded Surrey hills, along thin roads where, suddenly, there are London buses which one can never pass; on the day I went thunder brooded over the blocks of flats with their views over to Epsom and the bungalow roads being hacked into hillsides. It is an urban district of 12,000, but Banstead *village* (about 7,000, never mind about the 4,000 rule), is one of the places where London smells the open south and the sea, and has a church much of which is twelfth century; and *its* dramatic society does things like *Figure of Fun*, by André Roussin, and *Amphitryon 38*, by Giraudoux (in a Little Theatre); and, says a press cutting,

the tone of the petition by residents in the Park Road area, in its references to the Centre as 'a luxury amenity excessively large and lavish for the needs of a small village community' suggests that the residents who have signed it are completely out of touch, and out of sympathy with the needs and aspirations of the community in which they live.

In any case it is possible to get too intense about the village hall as a *cultural* centre. There's nothing very cultural about drinking coffee, but let *Riding Mill* (Northumberland) have the last word about its social importance:

Of all the activities at the Parish Hall none is more popular than the Saturday morning coffee, at which young and old gather to gossip.

A photograph shows at least sixty people all happily doing just that. It seems just as important as

... very active drama club, badminton club with a membership of 18. The Choral Society did a concert version of *Ruddigore* and *Trial by Jury* in costume, and at the Tynedale Musical Festival they won the trophy for the best senior choir of the Festival.

Riding Mill has 623 inhabitants and 237 households, and a skiffle group (if that word, let alone the group, still exists!) called The Konkords, 'available for dances, parties, cabaret etc.'.

The Chamber of Feoffees, founded in 1546, meets on the second Tuesday of every month to discuss matters concerning the letting and maintenance of their Town Hall, to pass the accounts, and to consider any charitable appeal. In January they received from the East Devon Water Board £7,289 for the compulsory sale of their water undertaking, which they have maintained since the year 1641. . . . Hire charges: whist drives, up to 20 tables, £2, 20 to 30, £2/15/–, over 30, £3/5/–; dinners and dances, £5; meetings, Colytonians £1/15/–, others £3/3/–, political, £5/5/–, badminton, 14/–.

(*Colyton, Devon*)

*

In London and other big cities you can study practically anything in evening classes, from playing the flute to Chinese, from linear programming to wine-making. In the country there do exist, naturally, specifically rural forms of vocational training:

Riseholme Farm Institute gives day-release classes in crop

husbandry, animal husbandry and farm machinery, and there are adult farmers' evening classes in welding.

(*Wrawby, Lincs.*)

But the main stream of subjects offered is very much the same as in towns; and the admirable WEA seems to come in for almost as much mention as the local authorities.

There are a dozen WEA students for a course on 'The Study of History'. The reasons for studying history, its value in explaining the past or present, the reality of historical laws, are some of the subjects that can be usefully discussed. Wider conceptions, such as the nature of historical truth and historical evidence, will be examined, and we might also discuss the changes in attitude towards history in different eras, the idea of 'progress' and the possibility of teaching history without bias. Finally we shall look at the charms and perils of local history, and the most profitable method of studying it . . .

Evening classes: Scottish country dancing, 33 students; car maintenance 12; football coaching 12; golf coaching 18; dressmaking 15; embroidery 10; stick dressing 9; art 14; cricket 10; metalwork 28; soft furnishing 9; cake-icing 11.

(*Bellingham, Northumberland*)

(Stick-dressing, incidentally, is the making of shepherds' crooks. A stick is dressed down, a ram's horn is put on the top and the whole thing is polished.) For a place with a population of 1,000 it seems a pretty impressive list of activities.

It is obviously more possible to have striking contrasts in a short list than in a long one, and perhaps the evening class subjects in *Harden* (*Yorks.*) show this as well as any; they are French, German, soft furnishing, drama, and flower arrangement. But it should be remembered that Harden is only five miles from Bingley and twelve from Bradford, with an enormous range of subjects available.

In the adult education and evening class field, although people may snort at the idea of soft furnishing being promoted to the same academic dignity as French and German (and as I write this my local newspaper has a photograph of a young man described as a 'second-year hairdressing student'), there is a curious reminder that the word *scholar* is derived from σχολή, the Greek for leisure. The automation of housework has meant that many women, especially childless wives or those whose children have grown up, are faced with the problem of empty time (a platitude which has been dressed up with more sociological guff than almost any other, which is saying something):

My husband prefers me to stay at home, so that in the evenings I can relax with him instead of doing the household chores. In the winter we enjoy doing crosswords and reading. I like cooking and gardening. I can try out new recipes and grow more unusual flowers, things which I could not do if I went out to work. My sons come home at irregular hours and I consider it a duty and a pleasure to have a warm house and a meal ready for them and my husband, and I know they appreciate it. I also have time to talk with my neighbours and friends, besides taking part in village affairs . . .

. . . When our children were all at school I resumed my own career, with my husband's full support. I enjoy my work, the responsibility, meeting other people, conversations on a professional basis. The extra money helps to provide domestic help, another car, lessons in music, dancing, elocution and riding which we want the children to have, and holidays abroad. Sometimes I feel that my life is over-organized, but when I get back home I think I can contribute more as a wife and mother. We appreciate all the more our family time together, the evening meal, the garden, going for walks, joining in village life.

(*Woodmancote, Glos.*)

Perhaps it is significant that neither woman mentions 'subjects' or 'lessons' except in the traditional sense, as applying to children. The country itself, and the business of living in it, seem to soak up living-time very agreeably. All the same, if it is subjects people want, on the evidence of the scrapbooks they are readily available.

*

Town-dwellers asked to say what they thought was the characteristic summer function of the English village if they did not say 'village green cricket' would probably say 'the village flower show'; and certainly this seems to be one thing on which television has had no effect whatever. Year after year they go on, with ever whiter and straighter turnips, dazzling dahlias, flawless lilies, flower arrangements either opulent or of restrained Zen asceticism, judged by mysterious men in pullovers who appear from three villages away, applying their secret, arbitrary, technical criteria to every entry from lupins to Children's Handwriting or A Raspberry Flan, in the morning, in the green twilight of the marquee, before the minor character from the TV serial comes in the afternoon to open it and the people are let in. Let *Bellingham* (again!) stand for all:

Bellingham and District Leek Club members held their annual show – the 32nd show of flowers, vegetables and also bread – in the Town Hall, Bellingham on Saturday, 9th October 1965. Two challenge cups are awarded for the best stand of leeks and onions in the show. It was open to the public from 2 o'clock till 6.55 p.m. Total membership for the year stood at 55. An extra attraction was an Open Quoits Competition during the day. A dance was held, commencing at 9.30 p.m., with music by the *Shades of Blue* beat group, admission 3/–. Every September, a week before Bellingham show, a fair comes, with dodgem cars. Usually a large crowd collects on the fairground, known as 'The

Hoppings' by the local children, on the Saturday afternoon and evening of the Bellingham Show. Unfortunately wet weather often spoils the ground, leaving everything in a quagmire.

There are still regional sports, like the quoits mentioned above; although, according to *Fylingdales*, they are declining:

At one time they played this masculine Quoits across a wide area of the north-east. There was even a North of England championship, competed for every year by teams of miners from the Northumberland and Durham coalfield, shipbuilders from the Tees-Tyne and Wear, and sun-burned farm workers from the North Riding, but all that has gone now. Of the great network of local leagues, each with its heroes and its champions, only two remain; the Dales League and the Hawsker and District. Between them they muster only a handful of teams. It is an end-to-end game. The player, his iron quoit in his hand, stands alongside a three-inch-high iron peg called the hob. The hob is set in a square yard of moistened clay; the player takes two steps down a wooden platform which surrounds the clay and then with a flick of the wrist dispatches his 5¼ lb. quoit towards another hob set in another square yard of clay 11 yards away. After he and his opponent have each thrown two quoits they go to the other end and continue their game by throwing in the opposite direction. As a quoits ground usually has two parallel pitches the air continually appears to be full of flying iron, a hazard more apparent than real, because injuries are rare. One Hawsker veteran ran apart grizzled hair to show a scar acquired at a tender age, but he was the exception rather than the rule. Scoring is simple; you get two points for a quoit over the peg, one if your best shot is nearer to the hob than that of your opponent. The first to 21 wins. It sounds easy, but in fact a quoits game is a testing battle of tactics, skill, guile and strength of arm. The uninitiated might think, for instance, that it would be sufficient to land the quoit on the hob every time to win a handsome victory. It would be a useful accomplishment certainly, but the successful player needs other skills. A quoit landing on a peg nullifies the score of any quoit already there. If all four go on (and that has happened), the score is two points to the last player. The second factor is the clay. It is the clay that injects much of the skill into the game. Its effect is that the quoits don't bounce unless they land on another quoit. They thunk down into the clay, embedding themselves firmly and making it possible for a skilled tactician to dictate not only where they are going to land but, with an uncanny degree of certainty, how – upright, at an angle, or flat. The most admired shot of all, the quoiting equivalent of the immaculate cover-drive, is the *gater*. It is so called because it effectively 'gates' the hob against encirclement by an opponent. The best *gater* of all, the *hill-gater*, is achieved by landing the quoit so that its top rests on the top of the hob and the bottom is firmly rooted in the clay at the base of the hob. An opponent faced with this master-stroke can barely see the hob, much less ring it. It is occasion-ally beaten, but only by a chancey shot known somewhat dis-dainfully in quoiting circles as a *lucky back pot*. The game has a language of its own. There's the *Frenchman*, the *flat*, the *ringer*, the *hill-gater*, the *whole-gater* and, an omnibus term for un-likely ones, the *nonsucher*.

The quoits used to be made by a village blacksmith. Nine players are needed for a team, and owing to declining interest in the game it has only just been possible to get enough playing members to keep the team at full strength.

Down at the other end of the country, another regional game:

Another side of life in our two villages is the stoolball club, a real Sussex game, has become very popular. We play in the fields that look towards Patching Pond, a wonderful setting. Monday and Wednesday evenings we play. Some have been in the club some years, and we have some young girls in their first season, and they are playing jolly good, we find married women enjoy the evenings, a change from the house, some are WI members, and we are proud to have a WI member (Mrs Cooper) as our President. Our scorer, Mrs Fields, has been with us years, the young schoolgirls, we feel it keeps them interested in village life.

The game of stoolball itself is very much on cricket rules, except a much quicker game, eleven players, umpire, round flat bats, small ball, little bigger than a rounders ball. In May or June we hold a tournament in the field. About twelve teams enter, and we present a cup to the winning team, and one cup for the Runners-up. A wonderful sight, with all the players in red, blue, yellow, orange cardigans and white shorts, we give a lovely tea, all the girls helping and plenty of children playing in the field. A wonderful day.

This last season our club did very well, we went to Toddington to their tournament, and won the cup, the girls were so proud, we also won the cup (Adam and Eve) at our village flower show, funny thing, we did not play Stoolball but Croquet.

We have the funny side, people asking what game it is, or like one evening waiting down the field for the team to come and play, sat there till eight o'clock, then found that we should have gone away to play. Once our only transport was an open van to take us to Petworth, most of the way it poured with rain. It's great sport, and we feel part of the village life. Clapham and Patching have had a stoolball club for forty or fifty years, so that's what village life feels.

(Clapham and Patching, Sussex)

Another local enthusiasm, fireworks, is described in the same vivid, Mr Jingle style:

Clapham and Patching Bonfire Club. From January to September there may not be a club, it just sleeps. Four weeks to Bonfire Night – meetings – ideas, discussions – and – work? Target six hundred torches, another society coming – eight hundred needed. Fireworks arrive – rockets, bangers, cascades, and six gross to be made into intricate design, fused together.

It is top secret till the night. November 6th, all is set and a fine day. Trailers convey matted gunpowder to the field, the effigy of Guy Fawkes awaits a lighted match. Darkness falls, with cowboys, Indians, witches, guys, dolls of every kind stir in the streets, and the spectators mount in number. The celebrations start – torches flaming, costumes swaying, the band plays, through the streets, to the bonfire, soon to be billowing flames. Guy Fawkes went with a bang, Rockets too, and it's Tiger in the Tank, with car, revolving lighthouse, motor boat and surf rider in motion, Bangers and flares, lighting up hundreds of faces, then good night, it's all over. The response is most appreciated, we hope the collection will be as good, for it's to next year we look now. The weather was kind – but it is just starting to rain. Within half an hour, our streets nearly back to normal for another year.

This village is in what used to be good Pope-burning country on Guy Fawkes Night; near to Lewes. But now

The Bonfire Club also organize an annual carol concert on Christmas Eve. People in cars and on foot wend their way up the narrow track through the woods for the midnight Communion Service at Clapham Church. Of late years this has become a great feature of village life. The church is always crowded. Every available nook and cranny is decorated with flowers, holly and ivy, which seem to glow in the light brighter and more concentrated without the competition of daylight ...

Young Farmers: what we read. Ian Fleming, Nevil Shute, Monica Dickens, Margaret Drabble, Elizabeth Longford. We had a minority vote of 2 for Marcel Proust, and 1 for Charles Dickens. The *Mirror* and the *Express* take the first place with 80 or so copies closely followed by the *Daily Mail* and the *Telegraph*. *Times* and *Sketch* numbers dwindled to 16 and 18. The *Sun* gets the support of 4 only and the *Guardian* 2.

(*Smarden, Kent*)

The *Eastern Daily Press* sells three times as many as all the rest.

(Hickling, Norfolk)

Several farmers have told Mr Reynolds, the librarian, that they often felt an urge to 'venture' into the Lampeter and Tregaron libraries but could not bring themselves to do so. But with a van on its premises every farmer could have as many books as he pleased.

(Llanilar, Cardigan)

Books enjoyed by the village are again very varied, from the light romantic novels of Barbara Cartland, Netta Muskett and Marie Corelli to thrillers by Raymond Chandler, Georges Simenon, Ian Fleming, D. K. Broster, Agatha Christie and Bruce Marshall, and the deeper books of Norman Collins, J. B. Priestley, Louis Golding, Richard Llewellyn and the wonderful historical novels of Doris Leslie and Hilda Vaughan.

(Wrawby, Lincs.)

In most of the homes can be found well-read books of the hobbies they are interested in; e.g. anyone wanting to borrow a book on sheepdog training or pedigree Friesians could go to Uzmaston Farm, sheepdog training being a hobby of Mr Davis; anyone wanting to borrow a book on gardening, smaller breeds of pedigree dogs or birds could go to Cedar House ...

(Uzmaston, Pembs.)

... a mobile library of about 2,000 books. Brief reviews are provided, e.g. *This Side of Hell* (26th December). 'In the violent wasteland of Katanga, with a bullet-sprayed ambulance containing five seriously injured men and one hysterical nurse in his care, Corporal David Canning faces heat, dust, thirst and hunger to bring his charges to safety.'

(Bellingham, Northumberland)

*

To live in the country at all is to be compelled to have an ambivalent attitude to animals. Hunting, which began as a way of keeping alive and ended as a sport, an art-form, an unquestioned life-style which is now *being* questioned, does not appear in these scrapbooks in quite the way the urban inquirer would expect:

Farmers shoot foxes on sight, but they are cunning creatures and rarely seen. Hunting is done in the hilly parts on foot, as the foxes get higher up among the crags. The farmer welcomes the foxhounds in his district. It means less damage to his flocks of sheep, less raids on his poultry, all the more important because the decrease in the rabbit population has meant a rapid increase in raids by the fox.

(*Outgate, Westmorland*)

Fifty farmers and expert shots from the district took part in a hunt which resulted in twelve foxes being killed. Their intention was to kill off as many foxes as possible before they could do any damage, after several lambs had been attacked.

(*Hollym, Yorks.*)

There doesn't seem to be quite so much time for the ceremonial kind of hunt (and so they *do* shoot them, after all!); in the only extended account, which comes from *Smarden*, there is a combination of the new ambivalence about hunting with some very acute nature observations:

This village lies at the centre of a favourite stretch of the Ashford Valley Foxhounds country. A run from Smarden to Headcorn or on to Bethersden is over beautiful fences, and although there are more 'spiles' now than formerly the good hedges are still there and the wire is not too great a problem. Local farmers always preferred the Mid-Kent Staghounds, partly because the runs are faster and longer, and also because the stag,

243

once uncarted, would go right away. A fox found on your farm, on the other hand, might keep hounds and horses going round in the circle stodging up the clay. The Mid-Kent, however, came to an end a few years ago, and the only sign left in January 1965 was the presence of four hinds lying up in Smarden Woods, to which many of them have been in the habit of escaping over the years. No longer can farmers ring up the Hunt to come and take them away when they are seen eating young fruit trees or feeding with the sheep on snowy mornings. Temperaments differ. One small farmer shyly admits that he feeds them in hard weather; but the more prosperous shoot them, and now at the end of the year there are only two left.

The season, which used to last right on through March, now finishes at the end of February. This is because lambing is earlier taking place. Hoof marks in February cannot be criticized, because excessive moisture in the ground adequately fills them up with silt, whereas holes made in March dry out quickly and remain hard all the summer.

There is a good earth in Dead Man's Wood, but the best one is in Mainey Wood. When the latter is being drawn the Hunt and onlookers line the railway, recently electrified, to make sure that the fox and hounds do not cross it. One consequence is that Smarden Woods, which border the northern side of the line, are avoided because of the new danger, and consequently are full of foxes. No hounds have yet been killed. It has been noted that rabbits jump over the live rail, whereas hares, it is reported, have been seen to place their front paws on it and are killed in greater numbers.

Two badgers, at least, have been found dead on the line, and so another hazard is added to the lives of these mysterious, persecuted and harmless animals.

Kimcote and Walton Racing Pigeon Club. Old Bird Races are flown from May to July, and the Young Bird Races from July 31st to September 18th. The birds are sent in baskets on Friday evenings by car to Hinckley, where they are then transferred to a Road Transport and taken to the race point. On an average 4,000 birds from Warwickshire and district are liberated together on Saturdays.

(*Kimcote and Walton, Leics.*)

I only managed to meet pigeon-fanciers' *wives* the whole time I was gathering the material for this book. There was an apple-cheeked old lady in Yorkshire. 'My husband will be that sorry he missed you, he's gone off to Doncaster today to train.' Through a long house with scullery, out through long garden to small paddock with two neat lofts. 'Of course it's difficult in the Spring; they've got the young ones on them, so they can't race. He took it up for something to do when he retired. But there's lots of young lads in the Club too.' In the crowded neat front parlour, smelling of linoleum polish and old armchairs, a framed photograph of a cup. 'When you lose it you have to give it up to the man who wins it next year, and he didn't like to give it up. Of course, we've given a cup to the club ourselves now. His niece gave him this.' It was a china pigeon. 'She took the trouble to bring it from up North. She said he'll always have a pigeon in the house now.'

*

Photographic Society, Ciné Club, Art Society, Coin Club, Gardens and Allotments Association (profit made during the year was £37/16/–); membership rose during the year by 23, making 225. In February a dinner was held; 55 members were present. Entertainment was provided by a ventriloquist from Grimsby. A Prize Silver Band, Toc H (men and women), WEA Archaeological Society (Horncastle was a Roman site), Pram Race to Woodhall Spa (6 miles), Young Farmers Club. Horncastle Playing Fields Association; cash in hand at the moment is £3,300, raised by bingo drives, garden fêtes, Christmas draws and professional wrestling. The first phase is to provide a bowling green, tennis courts and putting green; the second is to build a hall large enough to hold all kinds of indoor sports (held up by the Squeeze). Badminton Club, Angling Club, Bridge Club (31 members), Bowls Club, Chess Club, Darts Club, Motor-cycle Club, Football Club, Rifle Club. Horncastle Invitation Flying Club; headquarters, Kirkstead Railway. The Club has 18 members and is in the Peterborough Federation. This Federation is the largest in the country, and each year £30,000 in prize money is competed for in races from such places as Goole to Lerwick in the Shetland Isles. Tennis Club, Swimming Club. The 'Castle Tones' pop group, deriving its name from the town, was formed in July 1965 by three local lads. The Group considers itself non-commercialized, not only playing music in the modern style for the teenagers but also music for older people, i.e. waltzes etc., and great standards in modern music, such as *Somewhere over the Rainbow* and similar tunes.

(*Horncastle, Lincs.*)

This is the most comprehensive single list in any of the scrapbooks I have seen, and seems to implement the visual impression one has of Horncastle. I came down from the wolds on one of those days when there are three different thunderstorms hovering over the huge landscape, waiting to see which way one is going and joining up across one's path, suddenly turning comfortable England into an ambush by really quite bloodyminded and powerful demiurges of atmosphere, water and electricity, leaning blackly over low hills, striking at random; so that the sight of a lorry looming out of the absurd curtain of grey water is a comforting reminder that other people are about too, life is going on. Horncastle was all peace after the storm, distant growlings as in the Pastoral Symphony, rainy roofs in the sun, the glittering lime trees in the market place seen against the light, a comfortable huddle in a cleft in the wolds, in an obvious site for a community of 3,900. One could well imagine how the market square bursts at the seams on Saturdays, when farmers from the wolds bring their families to buy and sell at the weekly market.

But in fact the list of activities is a good example of how over the years one kind of community, oil-in-the-beard-of-Aaron feeling, of a perhaps more inherited, traditional, unself-conscious way of life, has given place to other more particularized forms of association. For the account goes on

I think in some respects it has retrogressed in the last thirty years, for then there was work in plenty for the male population of the town. There were three malt kilns, a chemical manure factory, leather works, gasworks, three thriving corn merchants and a railway station with 26 employees. At the present time busloads of men go to work away from the town each morning and upon leaving school a large number of young people leave Horncastle altogether, and work and make their homes elsewhere. The markets have diminished. Thirty to forty years ago Horncastle sheep fairs were among the largest in the country, bringing buyers from all parts of England for sheep, and for the wool. The horse fair, as it was in my childhood, was second only in size and importance to the one held at Leipzig in Germany. Consequently hotels and inns prospered, and the town had a robust, Elizabethan quality which did not seem to belong to the twentieth century. The churches and chapels were lively institutions. The vicar of Horncastle always had, and needed, a curate, and Mattins and Evensong were sung regularly in both Holy Trinity and St Mary's churches. The Wesleyan chapel and Primitive Methodist chapel had large congregations. Today the malt kilns, chemical manure factory, leather works, brewery, gasworks, horse fairs and Primitive Methodist chapel are no more, the sheep fairs and railway a shadow of their former selves, and neither parson nor publican can be overworked. The local shopkeepers fight for existence against the ever-increasing numbers of multiple and cut-price stores, unknown fifty years ago. The narrow streets of Horncastle from Easter until September are filled with an ever-moving stream of traffic to the coast, and I am filled with a nostalgia for those quiet Sunday mornings when the only sound was the pealing of church bells and the Salvation Army holding a service at the end of our street, standing round the drum in the middle of the road.

*

Certainly, that silence has gone for ever. It could almost be said that the only undeniable identity a village now retains is the identity of place. All those other traditional parts of its identity – its interlinked and rooted families, its dialects, its local materials and architecture, and the other qualities that go into its uniqueness – cannot be thought of any more as *fastened* to a place. They can be uprooted, they can die or be universalized out of reality; it is as though the medium in which they existed had itself become mobile; as though each village were once a rooted growth of seaweed in a still, living, pregnant ocean which is now no longer still, so that the separate growths were mingled and tossed into one general, undifferentiated growth.

There are few places beyond the sound of gear-changing; none beyond the sound of the aircraft and the transistor. To the motorist in all of us one place is the same as another.

Yet there are moments when that ocean does stop roaring and moving, when for a moment no car can be heard, when *these* rooks in *these* trees are unique. Or even, merely, this dish is unique. Wittenham Pudding, for instance:

Well grease a pie dish. Then coat bottom of dish with golden syrup. Sprinkle thickly with dried fruits, currants, sultanas etc., make suet crust, adding more liquid than usual to make dropping consistency. Spread on to the fruit. Bake in a moderate oven three-quarters of an hour, turn out and serve hot, with custard.

(*Long Wittenham, Berks.*)

After all, there are as many ways of mixing, preparing and cooking the fruits of the earth as there are particular spots on the earth; if 'local culture' is to mean anything it should certainly include local cooking. The two cookery books most used in my own household are (about once a year, when we've got the time and the money), the great big Robert Carrier (which I, along with six hundred other journalists, got as a going-away present at an extraordinary dinner that Lord Thomson gave for Lord Beaverbrook) – and, about once a week, *Farmhouse Fare*, a collection of recipes sent in to the *Farmers' Weekly*, which soon makes one realize that it isn't only the French who have *spécialités du pays*; Old Norfolk Partridge Stew, Old Devonshire Brawn, Somerset Rabbit, Cornish Potato Cake, Quorn Bacon Roll, Huntingdon Fidget Pie, Buckinghamshire Dumplings, Balmoral Tripe, Little Billingham Pudding, Oldbury Tarts, Wiltshire Lardy Cakes, even (who would have thought it?) *Wimbledon* Cake, to say nothing of Fish Ramekins, Colcannon, Skirlie-Mirlie, Pineapple Upside-down Pudding, Emergency Marmalade and Yorkshire Old Wives' Sod.

Yet the mere fact that all these should have been published, for anyone to read, is part of the seemingly irresistible trend towards what one might call, the Cafeteria Culture. This is a term which could be applied in the context not merely of food, but of all culture. In the Cafeteria Culture it is possible for many people to have, for instance, a cafeteria religion, saying as they walk past the chromium rails of life, I'll have a spot of Eastern Non-violence, and some of this Greek dish *Koinonia*, it looks very tasty, it says

Fellowship in small print under it, I don't think I want any Chastity today, looks as if it's gone off a bit, and I say, here's something new, they've made a special display, look at this card, MEDITATION, FRESH TODAY, I'll have some of that to finish off with. There are cafeteria politics, cafeteria literature. . . .

People in (say) Islington making Huntingdon Fidget Pie, or even what they think of as Yorkshire Pudding, are demonstrating in a very dilute form the tendency of which the extreme example is the rich tourist, from a highly-developed industrial country full of machines capable of making absolutely anything, who, endlessly trying to outdistance the poorer tourists following him, goes in ever costlier aircraft to ever more primitive countries where he can buy ever more primitive jugs and little straw things.

Real life only begins when you stop being a tourist, when you get out of the car; whether what you then do is ride off on a white horse into the dawn, play the violin, make war, or pay the first instalment on a mortgage is another matter. What is certain is that in the end you have to stop moving about, you have to be in one place. Villages are the fine flower of what can be produced by many generations being in one place, and there are still a lot of people living in villages who are tying things down and hope to be left quite a lot when the gale of change dies down a bit and we can hear ourselves speak.

To return to the question of Yorkshire Pudding, which is more important in this connection than string quartets, it is clear that somewhere in Yorkshire there does exist the absolute, the pure Platonic Form of Yorkshire Pudding, a perfection which all actual puddings mirror more, or less, dimly. This reality is not something capable of reduction to abstract formulae, a mere sophists' juggling of words, something that any colour-supplement fool can understand.

When one reads of it in the *Askrigg* and other Yorkshire books one soon realizes that the one, true, sacred recipe *cannot be written down*. The ones we read, all differing slightly from one another, all doubtless productive of very good puddings, convey cumulatively, with their surprising individual details — snow, mustard, Tupperware — a strong sense that this, and many other things, will be preserved against that gale of change:

S. Trotter

4 tablespoonfuls pea flour, 1 egg, pinch of salt, ¼ pint of milk and water. Put flour and salt into Tupperware shaker, add egg and liquid and shake five minutes. Leave to stand one hour. Put a knob of dripping into each patty tin. Place in hot oven until fat is smoking. Shake the batter again and quickly pour into the tins. Place at the top of oven at 425°F for twenty to thirty minutes. If only half the batter is used the remainder can be left in the shaker and used another day.

Mrs Jack Percival

One egg, one teaspoon salt, four ounces of flour, half-pint milk. Method: break egg into the flour and salt, previously mixed in a basin. Add enough liquid to make a beating consistency. Beat well, and leave to stand for half an hour. Heat the oven to 450°F, bake for fifteen to twenty minutes.

Mrs Hopper

makes Pudding with the proportions of one egg for every three tablespoonfuls of flour. (1) After beating well does not leave to stand but puts in oven right away. (2) Grease tins cold, with cold lard, dripping or marge. (3) Just before pouring into tin 'dash in a little of the coldest water I can find; snow if possible'.

Rita Craske

2 tablespoonfools of flour, 1 egg, pinch of salt, ½ teaspoonful of mustard, ¼ pint of milk, 1 tablespoonful cold water. Put dry

ingredients into basin, add egg whole, beat with added milk
until smooth. Stand for quarter of an hour, then beat again.
Finally, add water before pouring batter into tins containing a
little very hot fat. Temperature 450°F. Ten minutes.

Mary Hartley

1 egg, 3 oz. flour, ½ pint milk, 1 level teaspoonful salt. Keep 8-
inch square tin specially for it and never use small bun tins.
Whisk briskly the egg in good size basin. Add a little milk, work
in flour, beat well with a spoon with holes in it. Add rest of
milk. The consistency is thin. Leave for at least one hour. Heat
in knob of fat to blue heat and pour in the mixture. Bake at
450°F at top of oven for about half an hour. Serve with raspberry vinegar, and eat as a first course by itself.

*

A corollary of this primary tension of today, between
motion and stability, question and answer, motorist and in-
habitant, is the faintly absurd position of people who actually *live* in the beautiful places. From childhood seaside
holidays there remains at the back of the mind, never quite
solved, the problematic notion of these people having holidays, too. Where could they possibly go, they already live
in a holiday place? To admit that they're just like us is part
of the admission that the place isn't magic after all, that we
have got out of the car. Surely, we think vaguely, surveying
the mountains mirrored in the blue lake, I could write the
Great Novel, or the Great Play, or at any rate be a more
clear-souled, shining-eyed, happy and good person if I lived
here instead of 24, Boring Road, Drabsville. We look for
signs of this in the inhabitants, but either they try to sell us
little straw things or stay in their houses. There are, it is true,
'writers' colonies' in places like Alicante and Majorca; but
they never write anything, and meanwhile someone in a
bed-sitter off Earl's Court Road with a view of seven lava-

tory outlets and a white brick wall is writing the next Great Novel. Well, writing *something*.

To some extent all country dwellers are in this position *vis-à-vis* town dwellers. The visitor to Norfolk, coming from the west, for the first time, may well have an extraordinary sense of being somewhere *other*. The very light changes, as it does when you enter Provence from the north. Church towers and windmills, with or without sails, stand out across the fens in the clear air with the clarity of dreams; many obscurely exciting wooden contraptions and unexpected bridges deal with the interpenetration of this wide but secret land by water; life is passed among birds, clouds, the rustling of reeds, comfortable farming – *and* they have these huge stretches of pleasure water, full of pleasure boats with people in pleasure clothes, spilling outside the pleasure pubs on warm summer evenings. Is it not absurd for people lucky enough to live here to be thinking of holidays?

Of course it isn't. The people of *Hickling* are just as varied and real as anyone else. They vary, for instance, in their attitude to their summer visitors:

The Pleasure Boat Inn, inevitably, is much engrossed from the small inn of not so many years ago ... out of season much of the new part is cut off, so that once again it is a village house, anything up to 200 years old or more. The house has three letting bedrooms of which all are filled practically all the year round. Throughout the summer the whole place is taken over by visitors. The locals quite enjoy their company but look forward to the winter months for their games of crib, darts and dominoes.

Hickling Post Office. Mrs Gotts laughingly says she feels one of the family now and knows just about everyone, including all the newcomers, which is more than most of the older inhabitants can say ... Osborne, Groceries and Provisions; come October, and except for a few fishermen, Mrs Osborne misses all the visitors who are coming in increasing numbers, and some are now real friends.

... pacing up and down, he went on to say that a different type of person came to the Broads these days. At one time it was all the sailing families, who enjoyed a real sailing holiday. Now it is the factory workers from the Midlands, who only like to take their holiday on a cruiser, and whose idea of a good time is a glorified pub-crawl.

People from Hickling, obviously, want *their* version of that concentrated, formalized search for the mysterious place where everything is magically different and will magically change us, which we call a holiday, to be in very unflat parts of the world; and in their list of places visited on holiday, in addition to places like Wales and the Lake District, they also have plenty which, like every list in the scrapbooks, demonstrate how everyone now goes everywhere. Hickling is a small place, but people from it in 1965 visited Tenerife, Mexico, Lebanon, Majorca, Jerusalem, Rhodes and Istanbul.

Such fabulous roll-calls are a commonplace. Someone from *Kirklington* (*Yorks.*) went to New Zealand. Does not the mind instantly begin to move out; the ship drumming down into warmer waters, the first sight of the Spanish coast, through the Pillars of Hercules into the Mediterranean, white towns, olive trees, down through the steaming Red Sea, *All you Big Steamers*, the fabulous lands, brown men, fainting tropical breezes, spices, drums ...? But on that envied and fortunate boat, what are they doing, how do they pass this magical time out of life?

P and O Orient Lines

Time
10 a.m.   News Broadcast, Riverina Room.

10 a.m.	Keep Fit Class, Gentlemen, Sun Deck.
10.15 a.m.	Keep Fit Class, Ladies, Ballroom. (Battle of the Bulge).
10.30 a.m.	Gents. Doubles, Deck Tennis, Sun Deck.
10.30 a.m.	Ladies Doubles, Deck Quoits, Arena (Stad. Deck).
11 a.m. to noon	Light music by the orchestra, Riverina Room.
11 a.m.–11.55 a.m.	Daily Tote and Sale of Progressive Bingo Tickets.
Noon	Daily mileage announcement and interest talk, Lloyd's Register of Shipping, Golden Harp Room.
2.30 p.m.	Travel and Interest Films, second showing, cinema.
2.30 p.m.	Deck Cricket practice, Stadium Deck.
3.15–3.30 p.m.	Flinders Restaurant first sitting, visit to the Galley.
4.45 p.m.	Film 'Behold a Pale Horse', cinema.
5 p.m.	Classical Music, Riverina Room.
5 p.m.	Old Time Dancing with Orchestra, Ballroom.
6 p.m.	News broadcast, Riverina Room.
6.30 p.m.	Light Recorded Music, Riverina Room and Golden Harp Room.
7.30 p.m.–8 p.m.	Cocktail Music by the Orchestra, Golden Harp Room.
8 p.m.	Bingo, Riverina Room.
9 p.m.	Dancing to the Ship's Orchestra, Ballroom.
9.15 p.m.	Whist Drive (progressive), D Deck, Library.
9.15 p.m.	Sing-song for Dutch passengers, Golden Harp Room.
9.15 p.m.	Aquatic Sports and Beach Night, followed by dancing, Swimming Pool, A Deck, and A Deck aft of Pool.

| 9.15 p.m. | Bible Study, Play Room, A Deck starboard. |
| 9.30 p.m. | Film, 'Behold a Pale Horse', cinema. |

It must have seemed a long day. And Kirklington, that place few people have ever heard of, with its solid and unassuming houses round a long green, its church on the edge of the fields, its sheltering trees, must have seemed very real, and a special place to live in, after all.

The Ecchoing Green

It would be very easy to make the romantic assumption that young children in rural areas have a specially poetic vision of the world. An old church is more poetic than a fish-and-chip shop and church bells are a more poetic sound than the dreadful hoarse tintinnabulations, as though a giant were banging a dulcimer, which herald the urban ice cream van, whether or not it is actually snowing (come to that, all too often they herald the rural ice-cream van as well nowadays). But there is a sublime matter-of-factness about children's vision, wherever they live. It's poetic all right, but not in the original sense of a self-conscious *making* (which is what the word means). Church bells mean one thing to Gray or Betjeman; to a child in *Dalston, Cumberland* –

Last night Rodert and David Beatty and I went to the square and they were putting the church bells up, and the men were just testing the bells and they gave me a headache and I said good-bye to David and Rodert and I ran home and got an alka-seltzer.

The children in *Stonham Aspal* wrote an essay about Space (which one might almost say is the *opposite* of a village; a lot of generalized nothing, instead of a highly particularized something):

1. Once a girl who lived in a Town her father made space ships One day the girl asked me to come and stay with her and when I was asleep I sleepwalked and got into a space ship and

my friend came after me and got in the space ship and she was asleep and I started it up and we went in to the moon. Just as we landed on the Moon I woke up and my friend was asleep and I thought that I was still dreaming but just then my friend Jane woke up, she said how did I come. I said let us get out and look round. I got out and we found a cave it had a table it was laid for two. I thought it could not be breakfast because it was still night. We sat down on a chair and fell asleep. Then the next morning we found ourselves in a bed a lady came up to us and gave us a cup of tea she gave us funny clothes we had breakfast but it was not like the food we eat it was ice with some sort of sauce. The tea was not like our tea we had day and went home. Every Saturday we went up to see the lady. One day when we went up she was dead. She had died of a heart attack.

2. One night I set off in a rocket to Venus, it took me two days to get there. When I got there I found holes all over the place, then all of a sudden a little man popped up a hole, and another another and another. Until there were thousands of them they were only about one foot tall, but they looked very strong. My dog called Judy barked at them she was an Alsatian she was three years old. The little men all stood staring at me then all of a sudden they jumped at me and grabbed my skirt and pulled me down a hole and in a mysterious room. It had got on one side of the wall a little door. After a little while I just could not stand it any longer so I crawed over to the little door and opened it thought it was locked but it was not and out came a dragon. I do not know what happened then because I think the dragon ate me.

3. I landed on the moon. The moon is cheese. I ate the moon it was dark I went up to the moon when I got to it I got out and the next day I went down. I did not like it up there so I came down from space.

4. Once a man went into space in fireball XL5 and suddenly he saw a light coming toward him. He turned and headed for earth to tell the rest. He landed on a field next to Cape Canaveral. He

walked across the field and told them about the light they all crowed into fireball XL5. And went right to the light and saw it was a planet. It was Mars. They landed on mars and the got out. Rabbits were running about everywhere. There were tree stumps around and they went and explored more.

Entertaining, like all children's essays, though these are (I particularly like those awful little men only about one foot tall *but they looked very strong*) they do not seem particularly different from what town children would write; the matter-of-fact yet violently arbitrary way in which redundant characters are got rid of (the lady with the heart attack) or endings arrived at ('I think the dragon ate me') reflect that ability to be simultaneously inside a fantasy and outside it which *is* childhood. Or is there a difference after all? Is it more than a coincidence that in (1) it is a Town girl whose father provides the entrée to this rather exotic place where they wear funny clothes and eat ice with some sort of sauce, that in (2) the comfortable family Alsatian is there to counterbalance the general creepiness, in (3) space is no substitute for a Suffolk village and in (4) it is just *like* Suffolk, with tree stumps and rabbits all over the place?

As has already been seen, East Anglia is, or was until very recently, one of the most inward, self-contained and stably unchanging parts of the country; there is something charmingly characteristic about *Stonham's*

although increase in prosperity enables people to dress well, fashions are 'out' for the older folk. The women wear good long skirts and have a tendency to remain faithful to one style in hats. A pair of stout shoes completes the outfit. In the course of time the garments of men and women take on the character of their owner, which greatly adds to their charm.

Nevertheless, here as in the rest of the country, the total stability of the village background as represented by the school had been affected by the change whereby, even if there is a primary school, it only takes children up to 11 years of age. As a matter of fact, in Stonham

the Old Pupils' Club was formed by the late Mr Robert Spall in 1930 for young people who had left school. It meets during the winter months in the village hall for darts, table tennis and card games, playing pop music, on Wednesday evenings. Subscription 6d per evening.

It may very well survive; but there is something significant about the date of its foundation. Obviously it would be easier to form a cohesive body from those who had been together until they were fourteen than from those children, today, who attend the same large secondary school and just happen to live in the same village.

Nevertheless, the primary school is pretty formative, and is likely to be most so, most like the old kind of village school, in the kind of village large enough not to have had its primary school closed (for many large new primary schools, as well as secondaries, now serve large catchment areas), but for various tactical reasons not chosen as the site for a big new primary. Such a school will very often have as nucleus a building which didn't cost much, even by nineteenth-century standards –

... built at a cost of £504/16/10 in the late 19th century. It was then the National School.

(*Askrigg, Yorks.*)

And while we're at Askrigg again –

WINTERTIME

When the wintertime is here
Everything from far and near

Is as white as white can be
And an icicle
Hangs from a small boy's bicycle
Then it snows
And the wind blows
And we get drifts.

— Richard Brisbane (8)

The schoolhouse was built in 1855 and cost £700. It was re-modelled in 1912 and brought up to date in 1964, which cost £18,000. When compulsory education began in 1870 there were over 100 scholars from Radwinter only, who were compelled to walk to school in all weathers. Today there are 70 children from Hempstead and Radwinter. The headmistresses of 24 schools in this area, including our own, were asked to attend a two-day meeting in Chelmsford to study a pilot scheme for mathematics. The aim is to introduce the children to a modern approach in mathematics, and will include work on Sets, Transformations and Number Bases. Miss Bruton will have to attend follow-up meetings every other Thursday till December.

(*Radwinter, Essex*)

At the time the Radwinter scrapbook was being com-piled

the school is being run by a master while the permanent head-mistress, Miss Bruton, is taking a course in Cambridge for the Associateship and Diploma in Primary Education. The subjects she studies are psychology, sociology and philosophy

and women teachers play perhaps an even more important part than men at village primary level (see, for example, *Appley Bridge*, p. 115). Any good teacher is of course a basic village figure:

Mr McGregor, headmaster of Little Houghton C of E Primary

School for the last ten years, has achieved a wonderful record of eleven-plus examination successes. In addition to this he has educated the children to a much wider knowledge of life than is usual at primary schools, and many children after leaving his school often say 'well, Greg taught me that years ago.'

(*Little Houghton, Northants.*)

'Going on a course' is a pretty familiar phrase in the fast-changing modern world, and the teaching profession is no exception. Sometimes the latest methods have to be absorbed in this way, as in the case of Radwinter. Sometimes the scrapbooks present them as simply being already in existence:

. . . primary school to eleven years. Children are introduced to number work by using Cuisenaire Rods. Each child has a box of ten compartments with wooden rods of different colours and lengths. Each colour stands for a number of units, and the rods increase in length from one unit to ten units. At first the five-year-olds play with the rods, learning the colours, making patterns, and gradually connecting the colour with its own number, and building a staircase from one to ten. Music is very much enjoyed. Teaching is based on the Carl Orff system, which plans to evoke the musicianship which he claims is in every child. Children accompany their class singing with pitch percussion instruments – glockenspiels, xylophones etc. – and are led to compose their own tunes.

(*Pembury, Kent*)

It doesn't seem to have turned the Pembury children into tiny intellectuals; they still have some pretty trad game-rhymes:

BALL-CATCHING RHYMES

Plainsy to America, plainsy to Japan,
Plainsy to Old England and plainsy back to land.

Plainsy hullabaloo, plainsy hullabaloo,
Plainsy plainsy, plainsy plainsy, plainsy hullabaloo

BALL BOUNCE AND CATCH

Little Mrs Fluffy Ball
Went to see a waterfall
Fell in, couldn't swim,
Little Mrs Fluffy Ball.

(over, up, dropsy bounce, salute, one hand, the other hand, curtsey, bow, one leg, the other leg).

SKIPPING

Donald Duck
Washing up
Broke a saucer
And a cup

CLAPPING RHYME

Did you ever ever ever in your long-legged life
See a long-legged sailor with a long-legged wife?
(2nd verse 'bow-legged', 3rd 'knock-kneed', 4th 'bald-headed')

All the same the move from the old one-and-one system into the integrated national system – like a move from thousands of different step-ladders, all the same size but differently painted, some beautiful, some clumsy, some practical, on to one smooth national escalator – is not made without stress and disruption:

We in primary schools feel we are at the cross-roads. The eleven-plus examination is about to be abolished, comprehensive education is about to come to Caistor within the next decade.

263

Reorganization might mean three schools in the following groups: (1) 5 to 8 years, (2) 9 to 14 years, (3) 15 to 18 years. If such reorganization occurs, then many village schools will close. No doubt this will emerge as a primary or infant school feeding the children to a middle school at Caistor.

We are being asked to teach or incorporate many new subjects, such as science, French, 'new' mathematics, and the old maxim applies; if we teach these, then something else has to go. Many of the older generation of teachers are not prepared to change their old ways. These new methods are being introduced with great publicity. The Initial Teaching Alphabet by Pitman has been forwarded as the answer to every infant teacher's prayers. I am not prepared to accept their thesis to date. Much more investigation is required before it is universally adopted.

I think from the above that it will be seen that primary education is in a state of flux. This is considered by 'educationists' to be a sign of virility. It is to be hoped that by the time this report is read in twenty-five years' time thoughts and actions will have crystallized. Secondly, I hope the teaching profession will be held in greater esteem by the populace, especially where payment for services is concerned.

... the headmaster came three years ago, started a Parents' Association, and with generous village friends raised money for a fine Purley swimming pool. Some of the children swim very well, and heartily enjoy a lesson even in the rain. Their happy shouting can be heard most afternoons in the summer.

(*North Kelsey, Lincs.*)

As already noted, the swimming-pool story is the one that occurs over and over again in the scrapbooks. Water, after all, is not only one of Jung's symbols for the Unconscious, it is also totally non-controversial. In many villages the swimming pool seems to have been the main reason for forming a PTA, and everywhere it has been the means of bringing together into a collective enterprise people many of whom might never have met each other.

The school built its swimming pool by local effort. 40 ft by 20, 2′6″ to 3′6″, filter and re-circulating plant; 3 inch concrete blocks, cavity wall, cavity filled with waterpoof concrete; topped with coping stones, cement rendered and painted blue.

... Construction of the pool is to be by voluntary labour and will start next Saturday afternoon. If you are free to help us with the construction please inform the collector or me, then we can arrange for the times of work. Fund-raising activities: a skittle weekend, sales of work. ...

(*Bradford Abbas, Dorset*)

Boroughbridge County Primary School; the highlight of the school is an open-air heated bathing pool built in the quadrangle. Here the children are taught to swim by Mr Lousley. After school on a summer's afternoon the quadrangle looks like a seaside beach, with gaily-coloured towels on the grass, and mothers and babies in prams watching their 5- to 7-year-olds splashing about in the water. A Swimming Gala was held in the evening of July 21st. Parents who had attended the evening swimming classes paraded in comic costumes. The York City Police Sub-Aqua Team showed the training of frogmen and the clothing they wear. The Parent-Teachers' Association were busy making hot dogs and selling crisps and lemonade to swell the school funds.

(*Aldborough, Yorks.*)

The meteorological forecast said thunderstorms, and it was right. All through the day there were torrential downpours of rain, but occasionally the sun peeped out. This was the day which the Stonham Aspal Parent Teacher Association had worked for during the past two and a half years; our school swimming pool was going to be officially opened. The £600 was raised by various PTA activities. 40 feet by 20, 2 feet deep sloping down to 4 feet at the deep end. Two dressing rooms and the engine house were built by some of the dads during the winter months, with the aid of some photographer's lights, tarpaulins

265

to keep out the east winds and plenty of tea for inner warmth.
(Stonham Aspal, Suffolk)

The school swimming pool is the outcome of a really successful community effort and we are proud of it. In 1961 a meeting
of parents resolved to raise the money needed and in eighteen
months over £300 was collected to purchase and instal a Purley
plastic-lined pool. Since then it has given great pleasure and
many children have learnt to swim. In the past two years every
child leaving for secondary education has been able to swim at
least ten yards. The school is also well equipped with many of
the useful aids to modern teaching, including radio, tape recorder, filmstrip and slide projector, spirit duplicator, Baby Bell-
ing cooker and P E apparatus.

(Beckey, Oxon.)

New C of E school, 59 children. This entitled us to two
teachers only, so unfortunately our nice new school's advantages were diminished. The rooms are designed to accommodate
22 children and the necessary furniture. In one room 35
juniors, with ages ranging from 7 to 11 were herded together,
with Mrs K. Morris, headmistress, as teacher; 24 infants were
taught by Mrs Dunn in the second room. The third room was
empty, and almost bare of furniture ... after Easter two more
children were admitted, bringing our numbers up to 61. This is
the magic number which entitles the school to three teachers.
Application was made, and the Authority granted us a supply
teacher to start duty the following week ...

DISLIKES
(aged 11 yrs)

I dislike spaghetti. I don't like its looks and I loath its taste. I
hate —— because he takes our pigeons without permission. He is
fat and has little piggy eyes and hardly ever does as he is told. I
don't like riding in cars or buses on a hot day because I get a
terrific headache. I dislike winter because it is too cold and mis-
erable. I don't like my great aunt —— and Uncle —— because
they are nosey-parkers.

(age 9 yrs)

I dislike going to bed at night. I don't like it because there are some good programmes on television. When I am in bed I feel as though I would like to get up and switch on the television. I would like to stay up till about ten o'clock. When I go to bed I do not go to sleep. I dislike beetroot because of the vinegar. I do not like onions. They make me feel all funny. I dislike being all alone in the dark. It gives me the creeps.

(age 8 yrs)

I do not like it when my sister Maria is getting some new teeth. She keeps me a wake at night. I feel as if a Snake is going to creep into my bed and sting me. I do not like cheese because it has a bad taste. Cheese has a sting taste. It makes me feel sick. Another thing I do not like is when I have to play with Caroline, because she wants me to play baby games and I hate it. When I go out my mummy say 'don't do this, do that'. It makes me feel as if I could get a bucket of water and throw it at her.

(Fylingdales, Yorks.)

COUNTING-OUT GAMES

Dip dip dip
Your blue ship
Sailing on the water
Like a cup and saucer
Dip dip dip
You're not it.

My little red ball
Went over the wall
I told my mum
She smacked my bum
Until it was red
And sent me to bed

(Bransgore, Hants.)

*

The best teachers (and, for that matter, the best parents) are those who can preserve an adult equivalent of that children's double life, easily straddling fantasy and what we are pleased to call actuality; who retain some sympathy with the capriciousness of attention which can stray from the undeniable path of reality into areas of free association and untroubled awareness of being which for us now are only magical glimpses. It is fine that there should be, for instance, music – indeed it is one of the complex adult ways for getting back into the magical garden. To some extent music may be said to be an urban art; if a talent for aught of oaten stop or pastoral song shows itself, there is the huge apparatus and formal discipline of concert halls, cathedrals, opera houses, academies and conservatories, all city expressions, calling to it to come and be developed – and absorbed. To this extent a country children's music festival is an urban reaching-out into the country, a collecting, a concentration; another *subject*, something to be organized and adjudicated, not thought about except in terms of itself, its end and aims. But read a child's account of it, and the music is diffused among meals, windows, coach seats, briefly-appearing grown-ups, whose vague praise is accepted with equanimity. . . .

On Monday, May 31st at 9.15 Mr Neave's coach came and took us to Stalham for the Stalham Area Music Festival, which is held every year at Stalham. There were eight schools there, Barton Turf, Hickling, Smallborough, Ludham, Happisburgh, Lessingham, Stalham Primary and Stalham Secondary. I sat with Steven on the coach. We got there about 9.40. We shared the room with Smallborough. We had the geography room. Mr Coombes played the piano and Mr Mallaband was the conductor. Our first break was at 11 o'clock and we came in at 11.15. For dinner we had potatoes, lettuce, tomatoes, cucumber, crust fingers and some cheese. For second course we had apple crumble and custard. In the concert in the afternoon Peter's mother came and heard us. Barton Turf only had five children there, last year there were six. Ludham played a rondo and sang a song with chime bars. We did a rondo and sang a song called Wishes, and Rita and I played a recorder solo. The coach came about 3.10. We got back about 3.35. Mr Kemp gave us a half-bar of chocolate each, and then we went home. The adjudicator said 'a delightful Performance'.

(*Hickling, Norfolk*)

*

It is obvious that such differences as exist between rural and urban schools will tend to disappear as the ladder of education is mounted. A rural university would be a contradiction in terms (although there are 'village colleges', of which Impington in Cambridgeshire is a pioneer example; but these are a very different matter, a combination of adult education and social centre). Technical and grammar schools, too, are concerned with disciplines which can be, and usually are, taught as well or better in the middle of Manchester.

It is slightly different with the secondary moderns. Many of these actually are in villages or in small towns; we have already seen (pp. 211–13) what can be achieved by a school specifically geared to teach courses of urban children about the country, but there are plenty of good secondary moderns that do this for their own children. From Northumberland comes a refreshing reminder that for 11-plus passers, too, life is not all algebra and abstraction. Brownriggs Secondary Boarding School used to be called a 'Camp' School; this title has now been dropped, and it is used as an ordinary secondary boarding school for intake of 11-plus children but still, during the summer holidays, opens its doors and holds an International Camp (these are mentioned in several scrapbooks) where boys and girls of all countries meet:

They have their own car, pony club, rabbitry, dramatic society, stables, hen-houses (litter and free-range) and pigsties.

The modern secondary school has 6½ acres of sports grounds. If not GCE or secondary education, there is a course of commercial studies, a course with a nursing bias, a course with an engineering bias and a course with a rural studies bias.

(*Cherry Willingham, Lincs.*)

One of the claims made for the comprehensive system is that it is flexible enough to allow the considerable number of children who for various reasons cannot show their real potential at the age of eleven. For obvious reasons the country child is not likely to have the range of option of a town child; nevertheless the scrapbooks provide several examples of a big secondary modern making the most of its facilities:

More than 85% of the children in the secondary modern school in Dalston come from outside the village, as it serves a catchment area of 100 square miles. Extended course pupils, who are all fourteen or over, come from as far afield as Millom and Grisland, Longtown and Maryport, some of them boarding locally during the week. All these pupils, totalling about 60% each year, are staying at school beyond the statutory leaving age as they realize the value of further education. The majority of them obtain some qualification through external examinations before they leave at 16 or 17. For example, of the pupils who left Caldew in July this year four are now in sixth forms at grammar schools working for 'A' levels after obtaining 5 to 8 'O' level GCE passes at Caldew. 8 boys are apprentices of world-famous firms in various parts of the country.

(*Dalston, Cumberland*)

The new school architecture has a horizontal rhythm.

Travelling through the country one is constantly aware of the new shapes; low, efficient, well lighted, uniform, surrounded by playing fields made flat by mechanical graders, sown with seed. Under a few well-placed trees throngs or groups of children walk, loiter, or run and shout across the evening air; from behind the car windows they seem like figures in an architect's drawing. These slightly abstract shapes, with their air of having been put down on the land from above, altering it, infiltrating it, occupying it, these long premises that mean business, are a repeated expression of some kind of national, or even international norm; an expression simply of the twentieth century. Something *spreading*. The rhythm of the old village school, on the other hand, is vertical; tall windows under a steeply-pitched roof, usually signs of Gothic. The whole thing is a tight, once-only pyramid, from the base of the little asphalt playground to the apex of the roof or the chimney pot which once served a coal fire or coke stove; although of course visited by shadowy HM Inspectors from county authorities, as much an individual, local growth of the village as its church, its pub, its particular cluster of elms.

The children are growing into both these worlds.

Before They Leave the Nest

Although modern mobility has brought about all these immense changes in country life, the effect on the average village where it is possible for a car-borne commuter to live has been overwhelmingly an influx of *residents*, rather than a wholesale 'modern' decentralization of industry. Incidentally, of all the villages mentioned in this book the one that looked least likely to harbour car-borne commuters was *Dunsop Bridge (Lancs.)*. Surely here, where the great sweeping Fells softened down to a snug river-crossing, a compact village, a trout farm with many stepped, gravity-fed pools containing ever larger fish leaping spectacularly out in hundreds to catch food pellets made in Sweden, and where to take an evening stroll is to hear television quacking quietly behind curtains as a sound embroidered on blissful silence, no one would commute? But Blackburn, unbelievably, is less than 20 miles away, and

one farmer has a daughter aged 22, who is a secretary at the Mullard factory at Blackburn. She travels in each day by car, a journey of about fifteen miles.

All villages can be reached. A very high proportion of the new residents are families with children. If they are in council houses they are quite likely to have been high on the waiting list because they had children; if they are buying a house on the new estate they are quite likely to have moved out from denser urban pressures to somewhere where there is room for the children to grow up.

Obviously neither they nor the native inhabitants move from property to property as does the bed-sit or even the flat dweller. Most moves to, or in, the country are *settling-down* moves, by families. The movement away from the country by young people 'because there is nothing for them to do' may doubtless occur in later adolescence, but it is all the time being counter-balanced by this strong growing-family element. In any case surely the complaint that there is nothing to do is one that ignores modern mobility; by the time young people begin to find village life constricting they can usually manage at least a motor-scooter. For occupation, as well as social life, the example of the young lady from Dunsop Bridge is a reminder that it is not necessary to have a factory with x guaranteed jobs in every village to 'keep the young people from going away'.

The actual reduction of the specifically agricultural work force (see p. 88) is of course a separate matter, largely stemming from the mechanizing and amalgamating tendency in farming. Young people leave the nest anyway, whether it's urban or rural.

1. My teenage son Robert is now in his fourteenth year; only two years as a teenager but I realize he is now growing up. Before a child becomes a teenager he has to be taught right from wrong, and once he reaches that certain age he begins to think for himself and could easily start to want things which are not good for him. For instance when a visit to the barber was indicated I was told 'my hair isn't long in comparison with some of the boys at school.' I pointed out that these boys were in the minority and he wasn't joining them. When 13 he wanted pointed shoes I compromised by buying a sensible square-toed type of shoe and he has been content to wear this type ever

since, and thank goodness that is the nearest I have got to the newest trend in fashions. It could have been jack-boots he wanted.

On the whole I feel I have no need to fear my son will be a Mod or Rocker, as they call themselves these days. He is quite a sensible boy, interested in his studies, games and hobbies. He is a keen philatelist and has quite a selection of stamps and spends some of his pocket money each month buying stamps from a stamp club he has joined.

When Robert reached the age of 14, he was old enough to join the ATC and attends 1465 Squadron Headquarters at Menai Bridge on Thursday evenings. Since the age of eleven he has wanted to go to Cranwell, the RAF college, but now he has second thoughts on this subject and is thinking more in technical terms and would like to enter the RAF Technical College, Henlow, and study electronic engineering. When I found his thoughts and ambitions were in this direction I decided to buy Robert and my younger son, who is within eighteen months of being a teenager, two sets of electronic engineering kits. Between them they have made a transistor radio, an electronic organ (this sounded like bagpipes), an intercom radio and a burglar alarm. Last year he wanted a microscope, and we gave him an Optikit. With this he made a microscope, telescope, kaleidoscope and miniature projector. I find it more profitable to buy something to occupy a boy's mind; it gives hours of peace and contentment.

Like all teenagers he enjoys his pop records, and I tolerate these little sessions as they are not very frequent; because so much of his time is spent doing homework I feel I cannot begrudge a little relaxation. Ask me again in roughly five and half years' time what it has been like being a teenager's mother and I know I'll say it's been a pleasure.

2. *My teenage daughter Rosemary*. I suppose I should go back to her first teen year. At that age Rosemary was a pupil at a grammar school and just beginning to realize that life was not just meant to be spent listening to pop music, etc. After serious thinking she decided to enrol with St John's Ambulance Brigade

as a cadet, giving her an outside interest and also a rewarding one. Her pocket money was 3/6 weekly but we paid for any school excursions etc. Her clothes requirements were not very great at this stage, having to wear school uniform daily and usually changing into jeans and sweaters for the evenings. She was also a member of the Parish Church and took an active interest in the Youth Club, preferring to have a group of friends as opposed to one particular friend.

At 15 years Rosemary sat for and passed her examination for Home Nursing in the St John's Ambulance Brigade. Unfortunately homework was now taking up a lot of her time and she was unable to attend classes regularly, as she had been used to doing in the past. At this stage her clothing requirements were much greater, having grown out of many of her clothes, and we found it necessary to replenish quite a lot. Fashions were changing so rapidly that we found she was quite happy with cheaper dresses which we were able to buy more of, than maybe one or two good dresses which very soon, according to the average teenager, were out of date after a few weeks' wear. We also increased her pocket money to 7/6 a week. Rosemary was still interested in her church Youth Club and went on many rambles with them. She also took an active interest in school sports, being in the senior hockey team and also taking part in school plays.

We found as she got older she wanted to make more use of Saturdays and also wanted to be a little more independent financially. She was eventually successful in obtaining a job as sales-girl, for Saturdays only, as with many of her friends, in Woolworth's. They paid her 16/- for the day. Taking off her bus fares, and money for breaks and lunch, she was left with 10/- to call her own. She saved this until she saw something she really needed, very rarely wasting it. She was working Saturdays until leaving school this year.

Rosemary is now 17½ and is an auxiliary nurse at St David's Hospital, Bangor, but in October 1966 she joins QAIMNS at the Naval Hospital, Haslar. Thus culminates a lifelong ambition of combining nursing and travel. The one thing she is particularly pleased about is that she has been able to arrange to have her own banking account and cheque book, although I suspect she probably only has one pound left at the end of the month. But I think it shows a good sign of thrift and achievement. Generally speaking we feel a certain amount of pride in our 'teenager'.

(*Llanedwen, Anglesey*)

Not all children, even rural children, are so right at the centre of a system of handed-on values, with an upbringing that takes no notice of

> *Falling towers*
> *Jerusalem Athens Alexandria*
> *Vienna London*
> *Unreal*

or of what the Secretary of the National Union of Students, in a letter to *The Times* about student violence, called 'the general climate of despair in Britain today', in as casual a manner as if he were speaking of the weather, as though of course we all took *that* for granted. The two quoted above, and their parents, are in the grammar-school tradition, and it simply doesn't occur to them to question what it is that they and the grammar school have to hand on. And of course they never get into the news. But one can well imagine them saying, '*What* general climate of despair?'

However, in the sense they convey of a peaceful, effortless, continuous handing on of ideals from generation to generation (and I believe they are merely articulating what the vast majority of ordinary families still feel: but nothing is perfect, both these careers are in some way connected with arms, force, death; and other reservations all to do with the fact that nothing is perfect) both teenagers undoubtedly are at the other end of the scale from the kind of youth which obsesses colour supplements and television documentaries – and can be seen just as much in the country as in the towns.

In a West Country village I found an extraordinary sort of unofficial youth club which had met the problem head on – with, it seemed to me, considerable success. Mr and Mrs A. had taken over a village store, and to this was attached a café, at first intended primarily for tourists (it was in beautiful holiday country). But from the first it attracted the black-jacketed motor-cyclists and their girls; not, as may be imagined, to the general pleasure of the residents.

I sat in the kitchen behind the serving hatch of the little sweet-and-cigarette and tea-and-coffee store. The main shop had been sold because, Mr A. said 'We were just as happy with the smaller profit from the café as the bigger but more doubtful one of the shop where everything is done on credit. And anyway we came to feel responsible for these kids. No one else is.' The beautiful and well-spoken children of the A.'s kept coming in and out of an inner room where they were watching television with Mrs A.'s mother. Mr A. was in paint-splashed overalls, this being a do-it-yourself Saturday afternoon. I should say the A.s were in their thirties.

This being the afternoon, there were not many teenagers in. But every now and again a hatch bell would ring and Mrs A. would serve a coffee or an ice-cream; and she would be addressed as *Mum*. 'They all call us *Mum* and *Dad*,' she said. 'The average youth club you get in a village, well, it's academic, they have to *do* things, if it's only play ping pong. But these ones don't want to do things. They just want a place to *be*. We tried snacks and that, but they're not really very interested. When they really started coming here in crowds we did try to start an actual club, it was called "The 50 Club", but they weren't interested in that either. So there's no formal organization. When we had the place done up we asked the kids what decor they wanted, so it's all their choice.' (The general impression was of a dark cave; the very deepest midnight blue, little modern pinpoint lamps.)

'We got pin-tables in, and they loved that, also a one-armed bandit. The pub's just up the road, but they're not interested. Sometimes after closing time a party of older people come in and their language is shocking, much worse than the kids. They come from miles round. We're closed on Sundays, and one Sunday some of them hired a taxi and came out from the town and sat on the doorstep all day playing cards.'

I asked if there was ever trouble, and what Mrs A., who is about five feet four, did if there was. 'If there is a fight, the best thing is to ignore it if possible. Don't say "don't do such a childish thing." This is the worst insult you can offer them. Once the kids all came in here, they were terrified, they said "there's a gang coming." It turned out to be some lads who'd been here last summer. I said "hello, nice to see you again" and they sort of just collapsed, everyone got on fine. Sometimes I spend hours playing games, like knockout whist, with them. I didn't know it, but they taught me. Or with a glass, like a planchette, till midnight. I say "I love your company but I hate your hours." Once, on a Thursday night, they had no money, I was playing *I-Spy* with these enormous lads in black leather; the kind of games I used to play with my parents when I was a child. Of course, people don't like them. I had two here one night, they'd been turned away from a harvest supper at the chapel. The man at the door wouldn't let them in. And they could see the father of one of them inside.

'A café-owner in the town said "How do you manage it? They cut up my chairs, they write all over the place." Well, in a café, a person comes in and *what do you want?* They have to order something. But here they don't, and they're not watched; they're on their honour.

'They discuss absolutely hair-raising problems with us. I suppose that's one reason why they come. It all starts with the wife working. She ceases to be a mother as we knew it. They can't communicate with their parents about these things.'

I made conventional noises about hearts in the right place, youth settling down. A troubled, serious look came into Mr A.'s face, in that warm kitchen with its contemporary wallpaper, the big commercial fridge, the domestic sounds from the inner room.

'I'm not sure,' he said. 'Families are brought up by the force of example; and now there's, like, a vacuum. I think Communism, or anything, could fill it now. Half the time, the parents give them money to be rid of them. I'd like to do work in the youth line. I'd like to do it at Club level. But I've got to earn my living.'

I left them. Later that evening, when I was being entertained to very pleasant drinks in a household whose children would very likely have careers even more purposeful and rewarding than the Llanedwen teenagers, there was a very loud knock on the door. It was a dark night. Outside was a police car, and the driver was asking his way to the village (the house was down a narrow, twisting lane, heaven knows how he had got there). There had been a call from Mrs A. One of her rare ones. As I drove back there was still a crowd, police were talking to a lad by their car. I gathered afterwards it had been nothing serious; a threatened fight. I turned my VW caravan into a windy field from which land sloped down to distant lights, then the sea, and started to cook sausages. On the radio was the Last Prom, with Colin Davis inheriting the mantle of Sargent; an Atlantic wind buffeted the windows while four thousand young voices sang, with tremendous vigour, *Rule Britannia*.

*

For most young people growing up in most villages life is nearer Llanedwen (though not always as well organized as that) than Mrs A.'s café. It would be a great mistake to think of the ideal as being actual youth club premises, in every village, open every night, like tiny Mechanics' Institutes. Doubtless the two hours one evening a week in a church hall which is all that some villages have to offer goes too far the other way, and *is* inadequate. But all such activities require some form of adult initiating or leadership – and in any case 'youth', however clear a term this may be to the middle-aged, is in fact increasingly subdivided into separate age-groups; what interests one will repel another. We have not yet got as far as America, where there are not only *teeny-boppers* (thirteen to sixteen) but *micro-boppers* (nine, if you please, to thirteen), and where a fifteen-year-old boy can write in *Esquire* 'we used little slang and most of it Early Sixties, such as "neat" or "cool" in the old, non-intellectual sense ... in junior high school we began going steady. We lost our good humour about sex.' But in the *Harden* (*Yorks.*) book

From the age of about 3 to 14 years, when I still 'played out', I thought Harden was a marvellous place. But then I began to have doubts. The village has no cinema, coffee bar or dance hall where young people can meet and enjoy themselves. Most of the village youth congregate either at the fish shop or on the seat in the centre of the village. Youth clubs have been started by church and chapel, but my experience of the church one was that owing to the small population the age range was too large. It was ruined for me by young 'ten-year-old tearaways'.

You can't have it both ways. In a small village there will never be the adult leadership resources (and should not be the need) for highly particularized age-group organization, especially when, perhaps more than in urban areas, there is still a strong traditional pull towards older-established forms such as scouting, church and school activities and local sport. In the more rooted communities of the countryside there is detectably less of the modern tendency to regard 'youth' as a strange, cut-off Martian race, and more ability to see life as one continuous stream. In the following it would be difficult to say which is the main subject – the cubs or their parents:

Houghton Cubs, dressed in large Scout football shirts of yellow and green, descended on Cogenhoe to play the Cogenhoe Cubs. There was a slight shortage of 'men', so a young brother of five who was standing on the sidelines clutching a rattle was quickly hustled into a shirt (it reached to his knees) and rushed on to the field. Quite a few Dads turned up to support both villages and were frequently heard yelling advice to their sons. One had the feeling that they would have done so much better if they had had the chance to play. It was a good game and we won by one goal, scored in the closing minutes.

The Scout and Cub Parents' Dinner was held at the County Hotel, Northampton. A good meal was provided, though the room itself was a bit small for the games, which were usually of the hearty scout type. I have a feeling that we shall not be welcome there again, as at the beginning of the evening in a relay-type game a mum could not stop; she was going so quickly that she crashed into a window. Fortunately the curtains were drawn so she was not cut, but the window was smashed. When everyone had recovered from the shock we resumed our games, but in a more sedate manner. On the journey home in our private bus we passed the time in singing the Top Ten of our young days.

(*Little Houghton, Northants.*)

With every year that passes the cultural split seems to re-align itself from the old divisions highbrow-middlebrowlowbrow, which cut across all age-groups, to crude battle lines drawn up simply between the Young and the Old (because the old, instead of handing on to the young a strongly-held system of values, face them with a distracted shrug of the shoulders, as if to say 'there's nothing. Make up something yourselves'); and to this extent the young *are* alone today in a way their elders were not. Nevertheless, whatever treasons the clerks commit, however much the very people who should be speaking for the West are those who have most lost faith in it (or in the East for that matter; the fastest-spreading movement in Japan, *Sokagakkai*, means literally 'value-creating society'), if you live in a village with an old church, even purely on the visual level you can't possibly be on your own, a lonely adolescent in the new age. Theories, whether creative or destructive, are made in towns; there is a house-of-cards, let's-start-again quality about them that puts them in a different category of existence from the ordinary practical life of those who bring up families – and in any case there's no time to review the case for and against the existence of God and the nature of moral sanctions every time you find Johnny has pinched sixpence from the sideboard or pulled his sister's hair. This is true anywhere; but perhaps in the country, where crops as well as generations have to be raised, like waves continually and freshly breaking from the great ocean of the past, there is a more instinctive realization that life *must* be continuous, that there is a context in which a teenager is no more alone and separate than anyone else.

A great deal of pop teenage culture is made by city middle-aged gents and hardboiled executive ladies turning out sweaty little papers and magazines and extending merchandising empires and building the organizations which sell worthless records with lyrics that keep on telling the teenagers how separate and lonely they are; but perhaps it is not an accident that the same scrapbook, Little Houghton, should provide a teenager's account of a pop happening which, without at all being detached from it, shows a cool awareness of the *manufactured* element in it which makes the frantic identification of the average trendy middle-aged Sunday reporter look pretty silly:

One cold March night outside the Saville Theatre a car stopped at the traffic lights. To anyone above the tender age of twenty it may have seemed an ordinary car, but to anyone sufficiently interested in the 'pop' world that car contained Herman, of Herman's Group, The Hermits. Immediately thirty screaming teenagers launched themselves on the car and attempted to wrench the doors off. One little twelve-year-old, unnoticed, is scraping some dirt off the back of the car near the mudguard as a souvenir. Herman dives into the theatre and several hysterical teenagers, sobbing and calling out his name in a zombie-like manner, follow him in.

Inside the theatre (the staff having accepted no bribes) from six o'clock to half past six the air was alive with screams from teenagers who were performing dances of frustration and happiness. Frustration because there were over twenty burly attendants trying to stop them getting on stage, and happiness because they can at last see their pop idols in the flesh.

At half past six a voice calls apparently from nowhere 'Welcome to this star package bill. Tonight we present many of your favourite stars. How about a big welcome to your compère....' No big welcome, in fact stony silence! He has the extremely difficult task of quietening the girls before their idols appear and also telling jokes, while the stage is being set with drums, organs and guitars. The audience is not appreciative of the compère's mimickery of Charlie Drake, Yogi Bear etc. Then the big moment has arrived, the star is ready to appear at any moment. Girls hurl themselves at the attendants, who throw them back unmercifully. The twanging of an untuned guitar, and there, in front of all, on the platform is the star of the show – Del Shannon. For those who had queued overnight to get tickets this was their big reward for their agonizing wait in the cold. He launches into his first song without warning, a girl standing in front of us collapses into the gangway. Police officers and men rush to her and carry her out bodily while her friend intent on the show does not notice her disappearance. Girls with sashes bearing his name, girls with 'gonks' and cushions and toys and sweets and clothes try to throw themselves or their toys on to the stage. Somehow a girl rushes on to the stage and throws her arms around Del, and although pushed down he manfully continues his song. She is bundled off as quickly as possible.

The screaming is continuous, and no sound can be heard by anyone, but who cares, everyone is enjoying herself, clutching her friends and racing down the gangway. Whenever there is a lull in the screaming the stars twitch themselves and wriggle and all go off into moods of ecstasy once again. On the final number, Del falls to his knees on the last long note. That provokes absolute bedlam and surgence. Soon all is finished, and a rendering of 'God Save the Queen' sobers down the audience. The day after, peace is restored completely, the manager breathes freely again and the grown-ups feel free to walk that strictly taboo street again.

(*Little Houghton, Northants.*)

In many villages the tale is of fluid, informal, stopping-and-starting ventures rather than continuous clubs in the adult sense:

On Wednesdays there is a weekly 'Youth Squash' for teen-agers in the home of Mr and Mrs R. Watson.

(*Cherry Willingham, Lincs.*)

The Youth Club meets once a week. One room is to be used as a coffee bar and discussion room, whilst the larger room would house most of the indoor games. In addition to the club facilities members are offered week-ends in North Wales at Aberglaslyn

Hall, or pony trekking in Derbyshire run by the local education authority. This authority also runs popular music week-ends, guitar classes etc. at a small fee to any club member.

(*Kimcote and Walton, Leics.*)

Characters in *Birds of a Feather*, by J. O. Francis, a play put on by the Youth Club at Ysgol-y-foel; Twm Tinker, Dicky Bach Owl, Jenkins the Keeper and the Bishop of Mid-Wales.

(*Kilcain, Flint*)

Youth Club members soon felt that what was required was not a regular meeting in a communal hall but a place of their own where they could go as and when they liked; so a room in a cottage was set at their disposal.

(*Hovingham, Yorks.*)

The last example shows the contrary (and certainly not uncommon) tendency, the desire for a place of their own. But youth activities have, all the time, to be considered against the background of family and other links, and in a sense there is something self-cancelling or compensatory, a response to natural laws and pressures, about what actually does get provided. To see this more clearly, let us project to their logical but absurd extremes the tendencies and potentialities in the confused swirl of rural and urban culture, modern and traditional, local and national, family and outside, enthusiasm and boredom, that go to make up life in a village. Imagine an impossible, ideal, Golden Age community, like the one conjured up in the poem from Blake's *Songs of Innocence* which gave the last chapter its title –

> *The Sun does arise,*
> *And make happy the skies;*
> *The merry bells ring*

To welcome the Spring;
The skylark and thrush,
The birds of the bush,
Sing louder around
To the bells' chearful sound,
While our sports shall be seen
On the Ecchoing Green.

Old John, with white hair,
Does laugh away care,
Sitting under the oak,
Among the old folk.
They laugh at our play,
And soon they all say:
'Such, such were the joys
'When we all, girls and boys,
'In our youth time were seen
'On the Ecchoing Green.'

Till the little ones, weary,
No more can be merry;
The sun does descend,
And our sports have an end.
Round the laps of their mothers
Many sisters and brothers,
Like birds in their nest,
Are ready for rest,
And sport no more seen
On the darkening Green.

The sun rises and sinks, the crops come and go, apples fall from the tree, men grow old, but in a place where the laughter of children is as continuous as the wind in the branches. The lamps are lit in the evening, all the ages are together. You feel a Youth Club would be superfluous.

Then imagine (something equally unreal) some hellish and

impersonal city, something like the nightmare metropolis of the future, full of hurrying, utterly unsmiling people, which was so disturbingly shown in Godard's film *Alphaville*. Imagine the kind of Youth Club which the young of such a place, betrayed by faint race memories of the 'Ecchoing Green', on the defensive against the society into which they must grow up, would have, even in premises provided by a not inhuman government ...

Actuality, in town or village, is a confused and evolving mixture of good and bad; and in a village actual youth premises are neither the physical possibility nor the need that they are in the city. This is by no means to say that in the perfect society the youth club would wither away, as Lenin said the State would; on the contrary, the Ecchoing $6\frac{1}{2}$ Acre of Cherry Willingham's schools are a continuing modern ideal. But a lot of the activities that demand and get trained adult leadership are in more specific fields than the rather vague one of 'youth' considered simply as such:

There was no Willoughby Tennis Club in 1965. Not only was there no organization and no play but by the end of the year the pavilion, which was not in very good repair, had gradually disappeared piece by piece, and with it the mower and remaining equipment. The football club ceased to exist (difficulty in finding officers) and there was no village cricket. The Red Cross Link is the only organization to meet the younger children's need for organized and purposeful out-of-school activity in the village. There are no Wolf Cubs or Brownies, and no Scouts or Guides. The Junior Section is now working well, and some of its members are now in secondary schools; there is a need for extending the work for over-elevens and teenagers.

(*Willoughby, Lincs.*)

It is a pity there are no Guides in Bampton for the Brownies to go to when they are eleven ...

287

Christian Education Movement Camp; *Things We Do In Camp*, written by one of the girls. At 8 a.m. it is rising time in the camp, or supposed to be. When 8.30 a.m. comes we are supposed to be washed, dressed and ready for breakfast. At breakfast prayers are said and everyone dives for the food, which thanks to Anne, our cook, is excellent. Then after breakfast there are chores to do, which is the worst part of the morning, the washing up, the cleaning, the vegetables and sandwiches. Then we come to the time for the purpose of the holiday, the walking bit, or should I say lot. We enjoy these walks a lot, but most of the time we got saturated through, thanks to the Lake District weather. Well, it wouldn't be the Lake District without, but today as I look out of the window I see we have some blue sky actually shining. In spite of this we enjoy ourselves thoroughly. Supper comes sometimes at 6 and sometimes at 7. After supper there are evening prayers and free time for all the girls who occupy themselves with all kinds of things, the energetic dancing to pop records and playing table tennis along with two of the most energetic leaders, Margaret, nicknamed Popeye by us girls, and Ima. At 9.30 p.m. it is time for evening drinks which consist of either coffee, chocolate, cocoa, hot milk, cold milk or orange. Then before 10 p.m. we must be washed and undressed and in bed. Then it is time for evening discussion in which we discuss all the problems in the world today and our attitude towards them. Then there is benediction and a prayer read by one of the girls before Lights Out. Then the lights are put out and we are told to be asleep before 11 p.m., but after Lights Out girls caterpillar across the floor to speak to friends, also biscuits are brought out for eating, torches are put on and reading is done by torchlight. Some of the books include *Lord of the Flies* and *Children of the Sun*.

(*Bampton, Westmorland*)

At the time of writing there are 5,738 'unsponsored' and 6,158 'sponsored' Scout groups; a 'sponsored' group is one affiliated to some other body, most usually a church. The number of scouts in the sixties has been fluctuating marginally round the 570,000 mark; and although words like 'spoor' and 'tracking' do not now have the currency they had in the early Baden-Powell days, one of scouting's basic appeals is that it introduces city boys to life lived in harmony with nature. Many rural-area scouts live in what might appear permanent camp-sites to their town brothers. Scouting, too, might therefore not appear so 'necessary' in the country; and in addition, as their Association points out, it may take several small villages to muster enough boys in the 11-to-15 group, with all the attendant difficulties of transport. There may be no adult volunteers, particularly younger and newer ones; or such volunteers may not be attracted to this particular, specific, one-sex, traditional form of organization (the Association are now making a special investigation into the application and relevance of the movement to the newer kinds of community). Nevertheless the rural areas more than hold their own in the maintaining of that 570,000 level.

Obviously scouting and guiding and their junior versions are not the only answer to the need for formal organization; nor perhaps is adult initiative in this quarter very likely to come from any but those whose own youth was spent in the movement. It would require a special sort of person to *start* in the scout movement at, say, thirty. Some do however; and they will probably make their choice after attending a Bessey Basic Part-time Youth Leadership Training Course. Anyone, whether from a small village, a new housing estate, or a city, who felt a vocation for part-time youth work could find himself (or herself) at one of these courses, set up and run by local education authorities following the recommendations of the Bessey Committee (named not after a hurricane but simply after its Chairman, Mr G. S. Bessey). They last six months, one night a week, with two or three residential week-ends, and give a full insight into not only scouting but all the main existing forms of youth organization, so that anyone who has done the course is qualified both to choose which and to go ahead.

The courses naturally receive the full cooperation of national bodies involved, and one of the most important of these is the National Association of Youth Clubs. It has nothing to do with finance (which is a matter of local fundraising, Carnegie United Kingdom Trust, LEA and Department of Education and Science grants) but with national coordination, programming, arranging courses (on subjects such as, say, sailing) and various special projects. I once spent a few days with one of these, in which about thirty youth club members spend their fortnight's holiday (for which they pay) with an equal number of handicapped young people. *Really* handicapped, in wheel chairs, spastic, perhaps able only to mumble unrecognizable words, having to be fed every spoonful, lolling heads held up. The great ex-country house in wonderful Hampshire parkland echoed with music and laughter, they put on plays, they played simple 'tennis', they did photography and painting courses. The healthy carried their 'patients' everywhere (although it soon ceased to feel like that, it was simply a community), bathed them, went on excursions with them, and at evening readings would often drop off to sleep after the sheer physical endeavour. For the handicapped it was the crown of the year; floods of tears on the last day, back to the hospital or the overworked, anxious mother. There are now a dozen of these projects each year; usually attended by a social worker from abroad, studying a unique English development.

The NAYC experience has been that 'in spite of modern mobility, there is a tremendous need for a youth club in any village of any size, even if it *is* one evening a week in a church hall. We often hear, unprompted, the same form of words, even: "what should I do without the Youth Club, this place would be dead without it!" Village youth clubs tend to be the most lively ones and are often the ones most interested in projects that will involve them in meeting people outside their own area.'

Quite apart from the fact that it isn't only adults who are divided into those who are naturally clubbable and those who aren't – the same applies to children – anyone growing up in a village nowadays has, if only from television, a clear picture of that huge glittering other world, with its cities and airports. It is no longer a vague Lunnon somewhere over the horizon, far beyond the woods and fields. For many, probably the majority of the young, it is what they plan to explore when they leave the nest; they are very much aware of the smallness of their community. They may not always make such an exciting break, and convey the excitement as well, as this:

From Classroom to Comet.

What a change! No Monday-morning feeling – the glorious freedom of irregular hours – exciting cities and strange lands – interesting people! This is my life as an Air Stewardess with BEA.

Each flight is new and exciting, not only because of the places I am able to see but because of the fascinating people I meet on board the aircraft – dignified Arab sheikhs with their dusky maidens; foreign nobility and royalty; politicians; big business tycoons; TV and film personalities and the inevitable pop groups!

I have stayed in some of the most luxurious hotels in Europe and been swimming in all its warm seas. I have been awestruck by the dignity of the Vatican and the glories of ancient Greece and Rome; been enchanted by the architecture of the Notre Dame and Sacré Coeur; dizzy with the delights of sunny Portugal; thrilled to the music of the bullfight and felt proud of our naval bases in Malta and Gibraltar.

I have seen the sun rising over the Alps and thunderstorms over the Pyrenees. I have ridden a camel round the Pyramids and a jeep over the Atlas Mountains to the Sahara where, along with white-robed Arabs and fierce Burka tribesmen, I was a guest at an Arab wedding.

I have seen the Acropolis by moonlight; the famous Rock apes on Gibraltar, and an Arab chieftain with his three wives!

The world of school books has come alive for me. Historical events and far-away places are mine – within easy reach of our fast jets.

(*Appley Bridge, Lancs.*)

The accompanying colour picture shows the stewardess, in her uniform, in a well-kept English garden, two red-brick semi-detached houses in the background. The whole paradox. Most air stewardesses live with these marvels (though perhaps not all could be so articulate about them), get married like anyone else, and, on a sunny summer afternoon, find themselves in just such a garden, looking at a baby in a pram who will grow up in just such a place as Appley Bridge.

When village teenagers are old enough to develop an official 'attitude' to their village, the whole modern way of life will long since have ensured that their village's real or relative isolation and uniqueness does not come as a sudden shock to them, and their notions of what should be done will very often combine a let's-liven-it-up approach with a fairly conscious preservationist, let's-clean-it-up approach:

The Congregational Girls' Guide discussed 'How I would improve Harden'. The following suggestions won. 1. Coffee bar with jukebox. 2. Paddling pool in park. 3. More shops, i.e., chemists, newsagent. 4. Village hall for dancing and concerts. 5. More public telephones. 6. Hockey and netball team. 7. More lights at top of park. 8. Park improved, more flowers. 9. Garden and seats and bowling green for OAPs. 10. All old property partly demolished to be cleaned and left tidy. 11. Branch bank to open part of week. 12. School modernized. 13. Entrance to Goit Stock improved. 14. Petrol pump and garage 15. Dustbins put out of sight. 16. Burial grounds attended to.

(Harden, Yorks.)

Sometimes the contradictory elements are recognized, sometimes not:

A Teenager: Woodmancote has been spoiled by all the new development and has lost its character. Many of the fields and open spaces we had around us as children are gone. I consider Woodmancote is still a very lovely place for children and the elderly, but for the teenager it's dead. What is needed is a social centre where clubs and hobby groups can get together. Other than this it is just a dormitory village.

(Woodmancote, Glos.)

This entry comes very shortly after one which reads

Many husbands and wives attend the classes provided by the Evening Institute at Cleeve School, in typing, foreign languages, pottery, painting, dressmaking, dog training and the ballet, amongst other subjects. Others do water colours, photography, amateur radio, wine-making and wood-carving for their own enjoyment.

*

Of course, *Woodmancote* is only five miles from Cheltenham. Behind it are hills, but they are the comfortable Cotswolds:

If one stands on the hillside it is possible to trace the line of the limestone outcrops by the position of the old farms, which were generally built where the limestone edge allowed the springs to emerge.

These are not the wild Fells which surround (say) *Dunsop Bridge*, which is isolated enough still to be a 'very lovely place for children' and for a dance to be a real event (since it is otherwise necessary to go more than five miles to one):

Leedham's Garage looks after the cars, tractors and machinery of the whole district, the school taxi service, employs two mechanics and a clerk ... for the hall building fund a Garage Fling Dance was held in Leedham's Garage, which was miraculously cleared for the night of its litter of half-dismantled cars. There was a pop group, Lee Barry and the MGs; Jeans-and-sweater Girl Competition; refreshments.

In a way it seems a pity that the profits of this noisy, successful, enjoyable evening should go towards providing less impromptu premises. Anyone can have a dance in a hall, but a Garage Fling Dance has exactly the right note of do-it-yourself social enterprise which distinguishes the best village youth activities.

*

Two sons

1. In the tidy, not-often-used front sitting room of a detached house of a new estate, expanded village in golf-course-and-common country in London ambit. Little chromium things, trolley for tea, empty time at four o'clock for women whose family has grown up. Many framed photographs of son. In good-grammar-school straw hat, with three friends, when he was head prefect. He failed the eleven-plus. 'He came home and he said, "O, mum, I could have done it if I'd had the time." ' Picture of girl with glasses. 'He was married last year. You couldn't wish for a better girl. He went to

a university, but he said, "It's no good, Mum, I can't do the languages." So he gave up his place and he went to work for Wellcome – the foot-and-mouth place, when they opened up here. He had this day off to study. Of course he's qualified now, he's got his Higher National, he's gone to open a laboratory in Switzerland. He's in charge of it. It was his wedding anniversary, he gave his wife a present – an air ticket, so she went out there. He must know what he's doing because he's trusted with buying £6,000 worth of equipment for this new laboratory. They've got a house with a mortgage – well actually it's a maisonette – and he just wasn't earning quite enough money, so they asked him at the firm how much he needed to be earning, and he told them, so they said, "Oh, we'll soon put paid to that, because at the end of the year you'll be earning that money," and on top of that they lent him £200 as well.'

2. Dusk closing in, cold Spring evening in the Fells. Felt like hotel meal and bed, as one does after several nights cooking sausages and sleeping in however well organized VW caravette. Miles from anywhere, but ah, bleak-looking high-roomed white building, *Station Hotel, Accommodation, Bed and Breakfast*. Oh well, perhaps could cook more sausages, there would be bed at least. 'Oh, we'll find you something,' said landlord. Huge electric fire switched on in empty dining-room, great gammony meal, eggs, mushrooms, and would I like some fruit salad? In snug bar afterwards, splendid old laughing couple, parents of proprietor's wife, and man from Spadeadam rocket research establishment. Talk of their son. 'Ever since he was a little lad he was very good at arranging girls' hair. He could make any girl look a raving beauty. So he went to Clarendon College, in Nottingham, and then, on his own steam, he got himself into the London College of Fashion. Then he went to Spain on holiday (oh, we've had the reporters in about him today,

you know) he came back with a fellow who's a model. He thought "I'll get in on this", so he went to a model agency and the manageress says "all right, go and get yourself a composite" – that's a photograph showing full face and both profiles – and he came back with it, and now he's earning a lot of money from this. He's not a cissy, you know, he's a good big lad, he has a passion for work. When he's here he does all the garden and his mother's garden too.' Photographs of clean-cut looking lad smoking a cigarette. 'He hates smoking. They had to shove the thing in his hand for him. But he's stuck to his work. Just before Christmas he was offered a chance of going to the Bahamas, on an advertising job for Pepsi-Cola. All he had to do was to sit under a palm tree, and a feller was to come out of the sea and offer him the drink, and it would have been 500 guineas. But he said, "No, there's another week at the college," so he didn't go. If I'd have been him I'd have said ta-ta to the college. He gets all these luscious girls, he was here at Christmas, and when we were watching the Television Toppers, he said, "Oh, that's so-and-so, and that's so-and-so." Big Fat Sue, one of them was called.'

*

Pembury Young People's Action Group offers baby-sitting at 2/– an hour, car-washing at 5/– a car, logs for burning are on sale. Money raised by these efforts will go to a mission hospital in Chabua, Assam.

(*Pembury, Kent*)

*

Jet aircraft, styled both for peaceful whispering flights to blue-and-white Mediterranean ports and for an imagined final war in which some far-off computer finally decides to make an end of us, over their ripening harvests or bare winter woods; endless, mysterious traffic through their main street, the world washing past their doors; inside those doors, the television flickering – the young who grow up in villages are no longer left in pastoral peace. They know about the world and its joys and sorrows sooner than we did. Sometimes there will be some building, in the village but separate from it, where some particular form of the sorrow is concentrated:

Longhurst Hall, now an approved school. The fact that the Hall is now no longer a stately home but a much more practical institution detracts in no way from its place in village life, for although it is no longer the centre of life it has become a practical and working partner in the village, and the benefit given to these boys by association with life in the village is most important.

(*Ulgham, Northumberland*)

Mentally Handicapped Adult Centre. Patients brought daily during term time by transport provided by the Pembrokeshire C.C. 4 in wheel-chairs. Some of those who attend are physically handicapped only. The object of the Centre is to teach these men and women to equip themselves and socialize them sufficiently so as to enable them to mix with ordinary society. A visit to the Centre brings home to one the wonderful work being done there and the happy atmosphere among those attending. Homecraft, Hygiene, Music are among the subjects taught. They are taught, among other things, how to recognize simple words such as BUS STOP. Cane-work, straw seating, rug-work are included.

(*Uzmaston, Pembs.*)

The accompanying photographs show people either smiling or working with total, frowning absorption and concentration.

On one side of *Goosnargh* (*Lancs.*), next to the church, is a most beautiful Georgian mansion, the last building before the fields with their distant view of Beacon Fell. It might be taken for a rather grand hotel or country club until one learns that it is Bushell's Hospital, founded 'for the benefit of Decayed Gentlefolks, being inhabitants of Preston, Ukeston, Goosnargh, Whittingham, and Elston, and Protestant, of the Church of England'. On the other side, in adjoining Whittingham, is

the Mental Hospital, one of the largest of its kind in Europe. Many of the patients, voluntary ones, do attend social activities in the village, so helping to dispel the feeling that mental patients should be treated as outcasts of society. Goosnargh's population is 1176; Whittingham's is 4052, this figure including approximately 2350 patients and staff at Whittingham Mental Hospital.

. . . local young people often work for a time at the Hospital. This is most often an entirely different job from the one for which they are training. This year, for instance, Susan Glover, training at Liverpool College, has been in the Physiotherapy Department, Sylvia Porter, a prefect at the Preston Park School, in the staff restaurant, Mary Smithies, a classics student at Cambridge University was a nurse on the wards, Daniel Lambert, an honours graduate from Liverpool University, in the laundry department, and Roger Tuson, a student at London University, on the male wards.

In today's uniform and interpenetrating culture, the teenage group most of all is the one most likely to be pulled from its moorings, sucked and absorbed into the general mobility, almost as it were to become a part of that mobility, to become the wind that blows rather than the leaf that is blown. This is partly, of course, the process that has gone on in all human history, the inexorable life-process of change. Jung speaks of the personality-changes after 40, the emergence of previously repressed elements (the female in men, the male in women) into a whole but more static personality, looking into and aware of itself, its essence and mortality; the old as the guardians of culture. But now we are not sure what culture we are guarding. At least that is how it might appear from inside the humming and enclosed motor car.

Across an England now not absolute but relative we drive – relative to its weather, the clouds riding up from the Atlantic, part of those conquered seas which reach to warm lands no longer mythical; a whole world, itself no longer absolute either, but relative to space (as children write on the fly-leaves of their textbooks). As well as the square church towers, the cricket under the elms, the neat copses on bare ploughland, the local architecture, snug weatherboard, solid Yorkshire Georgian – the whole unbroken visual poem of it – we see what could be seen anywhere; pylons, casting a mush on the car radio as we drive beneath them, flat functional new schools and factories, plumes of steam from huge cooling towers standing up in misty sunsets, outside county towns, motorway signs that either dispense with language altogether and show international pictures of knives and forks or, the written equivalent of I-speak-your-weight machines, say sepulchrally REDUCE SPEED NOW instead of the human SLOW DOWN; and everywhere, filling meadows, creeping over horizons, the housing estates.

We can't drive a few miles without being reminded of how it must have looked, seeing the shape of that country, with four million inhabitants, from which the enormous Elizabethan rocket burst, from which we were foremost in the process whereby Europe, in Auden's phrase, 'trousered Africa', indeed the world. The silence of those villages at night then, and the darkness, and the distance one from another! The changes of horse, the leisurely, real preparations for journeys and wars! What relevance have they today, when the trousered world tries to absorb the truth that any more large-scale 'conquest' means annihilation, when Clausewitz's dictum about war being the continuation of politics has been reversed, and politics, or at any rate economics, is the continuation of war, everyone's aim is to be Top Exporting Nation? Except for commercial preservation for the tourist *industry*, is not the village, recurring focal point of this man-made landscape, merely a dream of the past, an affectation, a pastoral fancy, in an age when to survive, let alone to win, we need a country differentiated from others not by this but by simply having more cooling towers, fractionation towers, clean modern buildings full of efficient industry, in a style mirrored by the surrounding modern houses, functional, impersonal, uncluttered by the past?

No. It is easier to create an electronics industry than a life-style with a thousand years of settled history behind it. Many examples in this book have shown how each can influence the other, how our life-style is anything but static and is perfectly capable of assimilating electronics or any other industries. But it is still there, real, ignored at our peril. It is something which, unlike an electronics industry, cannot be wholly described, viewed from outside as a finite object. It is one and one, separate, multiform, pluralist. With the first village you investigate, you feel 'the whole of Britain is here'. With the two-thousandth you would feel 'this is different *again*'.

Generations were formed in the mould. Is it now to be broken, or changed, at last? Those who are born in villages now are not likely to die in them, and they grow up knowing this. How do they feel about the mould?

He is of course only one out of all the ones, but let me

quote him. I walked across a hayfield at a village frontier post between factories and Fells. A dappled English summer day, heavy rich trees standing in the hedges. Three men with rakes and a tractor and trailer. A boy of about twenty got down from the tractor seat; a south-west, Atlantic wind blew hair across a ruddy, open-air face (the same face you see in sepia, oval vignette photographs, its owner standing stiffly by a chair, a private in a county regiment in 1915). I had been given his name in the village school, as being one of their teenagers who would be available, locally, that summer morning.

'I'm a motor mechanic, I'm just helping this morning,' he said. 'I'd like to go to Australia when I've finished my apprenticeship.' Broad, deliberate Lancashire accent.

'Why?'

'Oh, to get away from Mr Wilson's taxes. And I don't like smoke and dirt.' Yet somehow he did not say this in the standard Sunday-morning saloon bar manner. If a total stranger comes across a hayfield and starts asking you these interview-type questions you have to say *something*.

'Would you go before marrying?'

'I don't know. Got two in mind.'

I ran out of silly questions – or rather, *all* questions suddenly seemed a bit silly in this sunny field. Then he suddenly volunteered, 'Mind you, I'd come back before I were thirty. This is the best bloody country in the world.'

Hopes and Fears

Is it true that the British are *all* villagers at heart? One thing is perfectly certain; the modern village, visited by various cream or green county council vans, its district nurse just as familiar with split-levels, new bungalows and council houses as with more traditional interiors, is one for which 'classless' is becoming a better adjective than 'feudal' all the time. Never mind what the colour supplements say (and in any case *class* for them really means *income*, the modern form of class). Classless, that is, for anyone who really does have a desire to join in. The word itself appears in several of the scrapbooks.

After all, many villages have been associated with a squire family, of varying degrees of greatness. In *Charlcote* (*Warwicks.*), Stratford tourists visit the ancestral deer park of the Lucys:

They come up to the park fence to be fed. They are gentle, friendly beasts and rarely fight among themselves. The red deer are shy and suspicious. In autumn the bucks lock horns and struggle for who shall be king of the herd. Their deep roaring is an awesome sound. The winner takes three-quarters of the total number of hinds away with him, and they keep their distance, feeding on the upper slopes and across the river . . .

. . . a doll's house made for Mary Fairfax-Lucy. . . . Perfect replica of the family parsonage house at Hampton Lucy, built in 1722 by Dr William Lucy. The wallpapers are nineteenth century in date, as are the dolls. The master is drinking in the dining-room, the mistress is playing the harp in the parlour, two nurses are putting the children to bed upstairs, and one lady with her bonnet on is setting out to read the Bible to the poor.

This little world within a world reminds us that the great houses of England depended for their existence on willing, un-grudging domestic service. William came to Charlcote at the age of 21 to take charge of sixteen horses – hunters, polo ponies, carriage horses and brood mares. His patience with them was fathomless, just as he himself was tireless, rising always at five. He started exercising when it was barely light and always washed the carriages that had been out late and cleaned the harness by the light of a stable lantern before retiring to bed. He and his wife, equally beloved by two generations of Lucys, lived above the coach house in full view of the stables, and no one passed under the stable archway without his knowing it. He knew everything that went on at Charlcote but kept his own counsel and never listened to gossip.

There is no war memorial of the 1914 war at Charlcote. The three sons of the house and the menservants, William among them, went away to fight and all returned safely. He died in 1964.

Henry Montgomerie Fairfax-Lucy inherited an adventurous strain from his Scottish forebears. He did not marry, but after distinguishing himself by conspicuous gallantry in the First World War he became one of the early white settlers in Kenya and farmed there. If he had been born in the eighteenth or nineteenth century he might have been a nabob and owned plantations or joined the East India Company, as some of his ancestors did. Being a man of the crowded twentieth century he chose the wider horizons of Africa, where he lived a life of personal independence and quiet service. True to a Lucy tra-dition he left a special provision in his will for the Africans who had been his servants and companions for forty years.

Of the Lucy properties that once stretched as far as Coventry there is now, in 1965, only the south wing of the house, by courtesy of the National Trust, the mill at Hampton Lucy and a few cottages in Charlcote village. Charlcote and the Lucys have journeyed a long way through history together. It is impossible to say whether in the course of the last eight hundred years the Lucys have made Charlcote or Charlcote has made the Lucys. In this year, 1965, Charlcote House and park are part of the English scene that all foreigners want to visit, that Americans return to and that Shakespeare lovers cannot afford to miss, and the Lucys are proud that it should be so.

That was written by a Lucy. The stables at Hampton Place have been converted into flats for actors from Stratford. Residents include a steel warehouse manager, a jeweller, a research chemist, a reporter. *This* is not the village of 'the squire, the parson and the doctor'.

The old sharp distinction between the industrial north, all smoky mill towns, and the soft *rentier* south, all teashops and cathedrals, has long since been blurred; the south-east is now the main growth area. But although it isn't filled with nineteenth-century smoke, and although many of its people live in places very much more like *Fairlands* (pp. 152–6) than a real colour-calendar village like *Broad Chalke* (p. 122), where would the people live if they had a really free choice?

For years I have been asking people at parties 'suppose you had, say, £100,000, you simply didn't have to worry about money, you could live where you liked in this country; would you say "ah, I know just the plot of land, and just the architect" and get him to build your ideal house? Or would you go round till you found the perfect manor house, the perfect old mill, and do it up regardless?' Those who opt for the first alternative are very much in a minority. Of course this may simply reflect the kind of parties I go to. But I really have been asking this for years, long before this book was thought of; and I have been at parties of dermatologists, of opticians, of ironmongers, of poets, although admittedly not at parties of architects.

Some people see in this the reason why our Gross National Product isn't greater than Japan's (as if anyone's could be, with those paternalistic firms, workers' housing, factory songs), indeed the reason why we don't even think about the Gross National Product as much as they do in Japan; we are too busy thinking about the lawn we'll have when we get out of the flat into a house in a suburb, of the view of woods we'll have when we get out of the suburb into a village.

This is *sentimental*, they say. Why can't we make marvellous Le Corbusier cities and live in them and leave the country to farmers? There was a talk in the *Listener* years ago by a lady (her name unfortunately escapes me) who taught something (probably sociology) at London University, and she was very scornful about Suffolk latches. This was the first time I knew there was a special name for those things on country doors (and indeed in many town garden sheds) where you press the little tongue down with your thumb and it lifts the lever (or the bar, or the strip, or the pin, or whatever it's called) on the other side of the door. She thought it was bad enough to live in a house that had always had these, but what really enraged her was people who took out perfectly good door knobs and put these Suffolk latches in. I don't know that she actually mentioned the Japanese Gross National Product, but she made it perfectly clear that this *sentimentality* was the cause of all our, etc.

Why shouldn't people like Suffolk latches and all that they stand for? If you live in a country where centuries of living have gently moulded a domestic life-style, what is wrong (and how will it decrease your ability as, let us say, a metallurgist) with wanting to live in a house to which people have added bits, joined rooms together, made changes so that there is only one house in the world shaped like this, a house where you know people have been happy before you were born, where

> ... the leaves were full of children,
> Hidden excitedly, containing laughter.

The next lines of the poem are

> *Go, go, go, said the bird: human kind*
> *Cannot bear very much reality*

No. But it is easier to bear, with the comforting generations behind you, than in an existential nothingness.

The same word, *sentimental,* was used in a *Guardian* piece by Alastair Tod on *Strategy for the South-east,* the first report of the South-east Regional Planning Council. This was admittedly concerned more with commuter estates than with 'pure' villages, and it would be a large claim to make that all commuters would like to be villagers. Both Mr Tod and the University of Kent researchers into Greater London commuters whom he quotes seem faintly surprised that people make amenity *sacrifices* to move out where houses are cheaper, and although 'local shops are probably small and expensive. Swimming pools, libraries and other recreation facilities are few and remote ... for most the view from the picture window is limited by the houses opposite' they are nevertheless in a South-east which 'even near London, remains rural, though not as rural as it was. It is countryside in the English tradition, sometimes effectively so ... for such people work is a major preoccupation, and leisure an anticlimax in which they are exposed to isolation and frustration. The improvement and furnishing of the house becomes almost an obsession, a step-by-step operation to convert the shell they are painfully buying into a home. Almost half the commuters studied by the University of Kent said that carpets were what they most needed; many others mentioned furniture. A husband working a 70-hour week will attack his plot as if his life depended on it. It is rare to see an ill-kempt lawn or an unplanted border ...'

(Carpets! And *furniture*! I bet there's none of that bourgeois rubbish at the University of Kent, they all sit on the

bare floor.) Mr Tod says that these people are 'a phenomenon quite distinct from the affluent London countryman,
the sentimental cosmopolitan in gum-boots whom the planners already know'.

Obviously the specific problem of the Greater London
commuter is beyond the scope and competence of this book
(and, Whitehall obviously thinks deep down, of mere local
authorities and people who live out there already as well; as
the *Essex County Standard*, to name but one, points out, 'the
bodies which are going to work on the plan' are known only
as 'a small group of senior officials' and 'a full-time professional planning team', and nobody knows whether the
Regional Council, which has now rather grudgingly accepted some local authority representation, or the Royal
Commission on Local Government will have the final decisions. But one can guess.) What to do? Move a few *firms*
out as well? Step up local cultural and amenity services?
Build 200 m.p.h. suburban monorails? Whatever solutions
are posed, it is possible to sympathize with Mr Tod's sympathy for the mortgage-paying commuter with his daily 40-
or 60-mile train journey while utterly disagreeing that anything whatever differentiates him from 'the affluent London
countryman, the cosmopolitan in gumboots' (except that he
hasn't got so much money) or that what drives either of
them is sentimentality.

What drives them is a racial memory of rural England
which, however obscured, is revived by every week-end trip
to the country by the motorized millions who, a couple of
generations ago, simply accepted static urban life as their
lot. Some people have to work in the middle of a place like
London, some don't. At what point does not living within
walking distance of the office become 'sentimental'? Dul-
wich? Harrow? Sevenoaks? Hartley Wintney? Is it sentimental to live in Battersea but have a week-end cottage in

Suffolk? Is it sentimental to have as your ambition the acquisition of a perfect set of sixteenth-century Flemish weaver's cottages, set round their private quadrangle in a quiet meadow behind a noble Perpendicular church, and to live in the Master Weaver's Cottage yourself? Pretty antiquarian, eh? And here we are crying out for technologists. But the man who lives in the Master Weaver's Cottage I know is Mr Stanley Booth, Research and Development Director of B.X. Plastics, the largest purely plastics firm in the country, who says that restoring and maintaining these marvellous cottages 'kept my sanity in industry'.

This whole book has amply demonstrated two opposing truths; that there are plenty of problems, and that you can go on about problems too much (some people even *like* commuting, if they can get a seat. All that time for reading! I'd never have read *War and Peace* if I hadn't been in digs in Northwood Hills, of all places, when I was working in London. Of course, I wasn't actually buying carpet then. But it wasn't such hell as all that. A curious sense of expansion, getting off the train on summer evenings, under those spacious and leisurely trees.) This modern mobility, which so tantalizingly always seems about to destroy the very pleasures it makes available to us, poses a problem in every village (and this book, again, is a record of the successful, if modified, survival of old village structures under the new pressures). The Loneliness of the South-eastern Long-distance Commuter is merely a highly specialized version of that problem. Let us, for instance, consider the scrapbooks of the farthest-away-from-it-all village, in the Isle of Man. Naturally there is a stronger rural culture than there is in, say, Oxshott, Surrey:

Fairy Bridge, or Balla-glonny, is a small whitewashed bridge which must be very old, as it is on the boundary of the Abbey lands. At that time travellers used to raise their hats at this bridge in respect of the Abbot when entering his domain. Now in 1965 Manx people, and tourists too, salute the fairies at this bridge, coming and going. Somewhere along the line the fairies, or Li'l Folk as they prefer to be called, took possession of this bridge. Folklore says that 'fairy' is of French origin and means 'insipid, feminine character', whereas Li'l Folk both good and bad are virile, sturdy little people who scorn being called fairies, and strongly resent this bridge being called Fairy Bridge.

(*Ballasalla, IOM*)

There are farms where drinking water is fetched in pails from a stream, other farms with highly specialized beef production, all of which is sold, one reads in surprise, to 'the BBC'. But this stands for British Beef Company. And in this romantic Celtic twilight, where Hallowe'en is *Hop-to-Nua* and gossiping is *going on the houses*, there is a jam factory in the Abbey (Gold Medal 1886), another factory makes aircraft ejection seats, and

on the mink farm . . . mating took place early in March, and the kitts were born early in May; a disappointing number, only 25 instead of 60. This was due to the noise of tractors, cementmixers etc. just over the wall on a new housing estate. Mink do not like unusual noises at mating time.

The beautiful little book of *Maughold, IOM*, from which one learns '*cretchy*; irritable. *Sleechy*; sly. *Spithag*; small thing or person', is bound in the IOM tartan – like the Eisteddfod, not quite such an ancient bit of folklore as one had supposed:

At a gathering of *Ellynyn-ny-gal*, the Rt Hon. Lord Sempill, who was Chairman, urged the designing and adoption of a Manx national tartan. He told the members that as this little kingdom was a Gaelic country with its own government and the tartan was a distinctive Gaelic institution such a national tartan would be a fitting thing for the Society to sponsor. True, most registered tartans were clan affairs, but nowadays there were also distinct tartans, and at least one national tartan, that of Norway, a country also closely connected historically with Man. Patricia McQuaid took these remarks to heart and started to design a Manx Tartan, first going thoroughly into all the records of traditional designs and colours. Still taking the island scenery as her basis she included in her sett the blue of sea, green and purple and gold for the heather-clad hills, the green glens and the golden gorse that flames all over the island in Spring, and white for the white cottages and foam-tipped breakers on the shores. A design was produced which was adopted unanimously by *Ellynyn-ny-gal*. The late Governor of the island, Sir Ambrose Dundas-Flux-Dundas, KCB, KCSI, was much interested in the scheme and helped to establish the tartan on a national basis.

But here, just as anywhere else, the hopes and fears do not fall into any simple category, they can't be summarized either as all traditional and preservationist or all pro-modern-amenities.

Changes We Expect: A larger population, mostly folk of retired age, as with the disturbances in various parts of the world, many serving overseas are retiring to the Home Country, and find our island a gentle let-down after the colonial life, after the hurly-burly of England, with its traffic problems and high taxes.

Changes We Fear: The possibility of our restful little island becoming too commercialized by large industries, that we may lose our independence and our Parliament, our own Parliament which is older than that of England; too-modern architecture creeping in to spoil the olde-worlde impression of the countryside, as already two modern estates are being built in our parish of the very new design of open-planning, split-level cedarwood and flat roofs, together with the package type of house, and these contrast strongly with the, too few now, thatched cottages and odd Georgian houses to be found here, to say nothing of the general type of solid farmhouse.

Changes We Hope For: Main sewage overall, wider roads for safety, an airport to serve the north of the island, a reliable electricity supply, as overhead wiring makes it precarious with our high winds and in frequent snowstorms; better overall television reception, better housing to replace the ones in a bad state of disrepair, the abolition of customs duties on alcohol and cigarettes to encourage tourists.

Quite apart from the special kind of spoliation which tourism brings in its wake, they are perfectly aware in Maughold, without being told by Appley Bridge (pp. 116–17) that the moment you get main sewage you'll be fighting to keep off the developers with their package cedarwood houses (except of course for one or two farmers who will be fighting to get them first, with the biggest offer for the land).

I have, of course, given an extreme example there to make the point; but it is a conflict of interests which occurs to some extent in every village. But the basic truth to emerge from the generality of the scrapbooks is this; powerful as are the urbanization and standardization processes, carefully as they must be watched and sometimes definitely opposed, the notion of 'the village' is a great deal stronger, more deeply rooted in people's instinctive desires, and still capable of absorbing and transforming the new elements.

After all, what is the alternative to what the scrapbooks (and I) take to be the ideal for this country – a landscape kept as unspoilt as possible dotted with villages not allowed to be swamped by over-development, but not fossilized either (and leaving out of account the separate question of New Towns)? In a fascinating Third Programme talk reprinted in the *Listener* of March 21, 1968, Mr Lionel March speaks of the 'agropolitan patterns', based on the car and the telephone, in America; a free gridiron such as that in Bucks County, Pa. of main roads, perhaps interlaced with 'parkways', on a prosperous agricultural area of some 600 square miles. 'Smaller lanes subdivide, but no cell is smaller than 2,000 acres. The roads are freely urbanized, leaving the extensive heartland mostly in agricultural and forestry use. Almost every home has the town at the front door and the country at its back ... certain nodes expand into small centres, others remain simple road crossings.'

Mr March prints a map of this alongside a bit of our Buckinghamshire. You can see their little grey dots scattered evenly over the gridiron, our two great black clumps of villages in a wild doodle of curving roads and irrational *culs-de-sac*, covering otherwise virgin white space.

Mr March knows personally a judge, an engineer and an executive who have built houses in such an 'agropolis' with their own hands, and speaks of the powerful community sense, the active parent-teacher associations and citizens' committees, and he argues (effectively, to a layman like me) that elected boards of management that have been responsible for exurban or agropolitan developments in America are closer to the ideals of the great garden-city pioneers like Howard, to William Morris's vision of 'the country vivified by the thought and briskness of townbred folk' than our New Towns, of which the control seems more analogous to that of 'autocratic nineteenth-century company towns'.

A first layman's reaction to this is to say 'but there isn't *room* for agropolis in England' (for Mr March thinks all we have to do is release ribbon-development energies into controlled 'development routes'). He would reply that two million acres were urbanized in the 1890s when Howard was formulating his garden-city plans; since then another two million have been urbanized (but only 2% with garden cities and new towns); and planners are agreed that another two million acres will change from rural to urban use by the year 2000. (As he says 'there seems to be something magical about the figure of two million acres'). That is six million acres, out of sixty-odd. Yet '*on two million acres alone the whole population of England and Wales could be accommodated in Garden Cities of the kind Howard described, not in 1898 but in 1998*'.

At this point the layman might retire baffled, until he noticed the words 'certain nodes expand into small centres'. Garden cities and new towns must obviously be part of our population-explosion planning, the more so to make up for the time lost when, as Lewis Mumford points out in *The Culture of Cities*, 'Britain and other countries had made the mistake, after 1919, of promoting housing without using the opportunity to recentralize industry and population in complete and well-balanced garden cities.' But surely we cannot fit agropolitan grids over a country where certain nodes *have* been expanding into centres for a thousand years already.

Cities, towns, yes. Villages, yes. Agropolis, no. It just wouldn't be our country any more. The villages are facts, not to be ignored. The Suffolk village of Kersey is a church tower dominating a ridge, a steep hill down to a ford, cosy huddle of weavers' cottages, compact new estates; but you see that splendid tower from miles off in a soft solitude, nothing but lonely fields; not an inhuman wilderness but trees, hedges, crops, land shaped by gently haunting generations. And this is free for the larks, the rooks or the seagulls marvellously sitting up there on the wind, then wheeling off in delirious, random liberty – but who has said this much better? Ah yes –

313

I caught this morning morning's minion, kingdom of day-
  light's dauphin dapple-dawn-drawn Falcon, in his riding
Of the rolling level underneath him steady air, and striding
High there, how he rung upon the rein of a wimpling wing!
In his ecstasy! then off, off forth on swing.
As a skate's heel sweeps smooth on a bow-bend: the hurl and
  gliding
Rebuffed the big wind. My heart in hiding
Stirred for a bird, – the achieve of, the mastery of the thing!

The great problem is how to preserve the sense of wonder.
We were all babies once, staring in amazement at the first
magical cat or flower, delighted and curious about jampots,
the insides of handbags, things, clouds, faces, leaves, sounds,
the miracle of existence. Now, fleetingly, some of us recap-
ture it; watching our own children, or inexplicably melted
to tears by the inconsolable yearning of eight cellos in a
moulded phrase, or on the hot concrete of a strange airport,
or alone, reading familiar lines. Or in soccer crowds, or on
motor-bikes. Some of these flashes are pretty non-inter-
changeable and private; my way back is not yours. But there
is one way common to all men. Nobody is so urban as not to
be moved by nature, even if only to be grateful for bright
clouds scudding across a blue sky on the first warm day of
the year. Nobody, on such a day, does not wish he could
enjoy it more, *experience* it more, in the country, where
that mysterious wind, from the life-renewing south, instead
of blowing bits of urban grit into his eyes, still makes the
winter sound through the trees, but reminds him how that
gentle roar will soon become the summer rustle; the leaves
will come, those black venous systems will be rich trees in
their dream-dance again.

> *O chestnut tree, great rooted blossomer,*
> *Are you the leaf, the blossom, or the bole?*

O body swayed to music, O brightening glance,
How can we know the dancer from the dance?

Physically, this is a small country, we have to make room for nature. It produced the supreme dramatist; and his plays are shot through with *weather*. Sulphurous twilight in *Macbeth*, paradisal rainbowy day after *The Tempest*, the prehuman chaos-storm of *Lear*, the (I've always felt) cold Spring wind in *As You Like It*, and above all the supreme, all-healing summer magic of that enchanted wood. 'Out of this wood do not desire to go.'

But do not desire to build bungalows in it either. It is a sound instinct we have, not to try and cut the infinities of nature and weather into little domestic pieces – and yet to have clearings in the forest, inns at the crossroads, churches on the ridges, snug human settlements like anchored boats on a rolling sea, not of prairie or wilderness, but of nature treated by man with the respect it deserves.

*

There is a female side to nations, using that word in its pre-Pankhurst sense of passive, peaceful, life-producing. Historically it has been overwhelmingly the male side of a nation that has confronted other nations – the external, the formal, the territory-defending, the aggressive. One of the extraordinary things about the Cuba crisis was to hear, in that eyeball-to-eyeball situation which normally produces the same boring old male words, 'I've got more marbles/ bayonets/missiles/red corpuscles than you,' that other female side; for the first time in history, perhaps, in this kind of moment. It was conversational, *human*. 'We too know about missiles, we too know what they can do,' said Khrushchev; and one saw the world's art galleries, national costumes, concert halls, pavement cafés, millions of soft living-rooms, children called out before blackboards.

315

Is it *only* that female side represented in these scrapbooks? I don't mean purely in the literal sense of their having been written by women (not true, anyway; quite a lot in them is by men), but in the sense that this sizeable part of our internal domestic life may be irrelevant to the larger issues of the world's future? Soon after the war I read an article by the American John Dos Passos in which he alleged that one evening in Charing Cross Road he heard 'one mellow fluting Oxonian voice say to another "now there's nothing left for us but the Scandinavian *ennui*" '. Har har. (To the Oxonians, I mean. Dos Passos was quite pro-us, if I remember rightly; although of course it may have been in some professionally anti-British magazine like *Life* or *Time*.) Now we are just this country (and incidentally what scene in history could be paralleled by the sight of three men of the calibre of Gandhi, Cripps and Pethick-Lawrence – remember *him*? – sitting round a civilized table, and gravely, as in some celestial game of chess, ordering the fate of a sub-continent?) 'Leadership' of the sack of cats known as Europe has temporarily passed from its most aggressive people (while they get their breath back) to its most provincial, and everyone, just because there is more noise in other parts of the world at the moment, assumes that the capacity to breed a world crisis has at last passed away from these parts.

Is it a reaction of *ennui*, of turning inwards because there is nowhere else to turn? In *Askrigg*, where

we have relatives in Canada, America, Australia, New Zealand, Cyprus, Malaya, Zambia, Uganda, Tobruk, Transvaal and many other parts of Africa

their hopes and fear are as follows:

Many of us hope that a light industry will be set up in the

area, so that our young people may be able to stay here. Others fear that Askrigg may become a village of country cottage week-enders and retired people. It is hoped that Askrigg may continue as a working village.

I fear that ranch farming may result in the disappearance of our beautiful flowery meadows, because all the fields may be pastures, and that all walls except farm boundary walls may be removed, and that barns, already going out of use, may be demolished.

I fear afforestation in Wensleydale.

I hope that public conveniences may be built in Askrigg.

I fear that Dales hospitality and entertaining in the home may disappear, and be replaced by inviting people to drinks and then going to a hotel for a meal.

It is to be hoped that parents will do their best to influence their children to attend church and chapel services.

But they were, remember, only asked for their hopes and fears concerning their villages. Their hopes and fears for the world must be what those of people anywhere must be, or it will be the worse for us; we all have relatives in Zambia and America now. And in France and Germany and China and both parts of Vietnam.

Maybe we ought to speak to them a little more (and they to us) with their 'female' voice. Of *course* Britain is also, indeed mainly, still, her cities, her factories (happy, neutral or loveless), her male outward voice. Of course democracy is (as usual) in crisis: of course there are new problems of economics, defence, colour. But no one who has read this book will confuse its inwardness, its domestic sense of our own land, with mere passivity, with turning away from the world (in every other scrapbook, pictures of upright weather-beaten old men with medals, followed by middle-aged men with medals, followed by youngsters, walking under a leaden sky to an Armistice Day service at a village war memorial). Least of all will he sense *ennui*, Scandinavian or otherwise. There is a powerful sense of living in two times, in an old and a new Britain, with an awareness, an agility in effortlessly leaping from one to the other, that makes one realize how hopelessly wrong all those famous 'media' are about ordinary people living in villages.

They aren't bored, they are buying carpet, milking the cows, building the primary school swimming pool, bringing up their children under a real sky, under real trees. They just don't listen to the media, telling them how bored they are.

What do they listen to? Well, it's one and one, of course; they listen to different things; but let me end with what a man in Hampshire told me he listened to, and saw – a nightingale on a television aerial.

More about Penguins and Pelicans

Penguinews, which appears every month, contains details of all the new books issued by Penguins as they are published. From time to time it is supplemented by *Penguins in Print*, which is a complete list of all available books published by Penguins. (There are well over three thousand of these.)

A specimen copy of *Penguinews* will be sent to you free on request, and you can become a subscriber for the price of the postage. For a year's issues (including the complete lists) please send 30p if you live in the United Kingdom, or 60p if you live elsewhere. Just write to Dept EP, Penguin Books Ltd, Harmondsworth, Middlesex, enclosing a cheque or postal order, and your name will be added to the mailing list.

Note: *Penguinews* and *Penguins in Print* are not available in the U.S.A. or Canada

Report from a Swedish Village

Sture Källberg

A small community can often allow us to observe
in miniature all the changes and complexities of a
whole nation.

In *Report from a Swedish Village* Sture Källberg has
portrayed the lives, the thoughts, the hopes and the
failures of twelve Swedes living in a small town not
far from Stockholm. Born between 1894 and 1954,
they span three generations. Between them they
show that the prosperity and civilized style of
modern Sweden conceals the failure of Sweden's
'Middle Way' to spread power and participation
into the hands of the population. Decisions in one
of the most egalitarian nations of the West are made
by fewer people than ever.

This latest edition to the 'Village Series' available
in Penguins and Pelicans has been highly praised
by sociologists in Sweden. But it is also a sensitive
work of literature, a valuable and authoritative book in
the series that already includes Studs Terkel's *Division
Street: America,* Jose Yglesias's *In the Fist of
the Revolution,* and Ronald Blythe's *Akenfield.*

Not for sale in the U.S.A.

A Pelican Book